Smitten

A COLLECTION OF CATHOLIC
LOVE STORIES

THE RAW AND REAL TRUTH
OF FIGHTING FOR LOVE
IN A MODERN WORLD

Curated By
Sterling Jaquith

EVER CATHOLIC PUBLISHING

BOISE, IDAHO

Ever Catholic Publishing
Boise, ID
www.evercatholic.com

Ordering Information:
Quantity sales. Special discounts are available on quantity purchases. For details, fill out the contact form at www.sterlingjaquith.com.

Smitten/ Sterling Jaquith. -- 1st ed.
ISBN 978-1-946076-06-9

This book is dedicated to all the single Catholic women who are striving for sainthood and trying to discern God's will for their lives.

St. Joseph, pray for us.

St. Anthony, pray for us.

Contents

(E25/M26) means engaged at 25 and married at 26

Foreword

"Nothing is sweeter than love, nothing stronger or higher or wider, nothing is more pleasant, nothing fuller, and nothing better in heaven or on earth, for love is born of God and cannot rest except in God, Who is created above all things.

- Thomas à Kempis, The Imitation of Christ

I'm writing this foreword fresh off of that beautiful royal wedding high of Megan Markle and Prince Harry, which just so happened to be on the same weekend as my sister's bridal shower. Sisterly love, aristocratic poise, virginal or matronly affection flowed this weekend...leaving me to write this foreword until the very last second! But I think, as St. Pope John Paul II once said, "In the designs of Providence, there are no coincidences." Which is so totally applicable, both for this foreword, as well as for the stories you will find tucked in these pages from thirty-seven women from all walks of life.

When it comes to love, no story is every written twice. Sure, there's similarities and coincidences, but each story is truly unique. God is quite the author when we stop trying to write our own love story and hand over the pen. It's clear how the royal wedding stands apart from other love stories (I mean, for starters, he's a prince). Though there are echoes of Grace Kelly between the lines and glimpses of Will and Kate's pompous day, in the end, this day was its own. Similarly, my sister's love story recalls fractions of my parents' journey: first love, a small town, and deep Catholic faith. But it also bares its own plot with a much shorter time frame (they will marry one year after they met), a unique twist (building a farmhouse together for their family), and will take its own course throughout the years to come.

After this weekend of witnessing love on a global stage and tucked in the domestic and intimate corners of my home, there's no doubt that God had me write this foreword right at the deadline. And as you will soon discover, the way God's plan for these women and for your own life will unfold in a series of ways that may at first glance appear to be coincidences, will, in the end, reveal themselves to be so deeply and tenderly cultivated, planned and planted long ago. These 'coincidences' have been patiently waiting to break through the toiled and weathered soil to grow, blossom, and bear fruit in the form of love. No, there are no coincidences when it comes to Love. It's too precious to be left to chance.

Carolyn Shields
The Young Catholic Woman

Introduction

This book gives voice to the many women who find themselves clinging to the few threads of hope they have left while prayerfully awaiting their vocation. For many long years, I also agonized over my vocation and incurred so much unneeded stress over "finding" the right guy (whom I met at age 30).

The truth is that Jesus is Lord, and the real journey, as you'll hear in many of these stories, is always towards Him. As we learn over and over again throughout our walk of faith, hope comes in the form of surrender.

Smitten offers the consolation, advice, and hope of many Christian sisters who have so vulnerably shared the ways in which God has revealed Himself to each of them - through their unique vocation stories. This collaboration is a masterpiece of raw examples, displaying how God works both through human weakness as well as cooperative receptivity to His will. This book is as real as it gets – the very fingerprints of God on the rough and messy edges of the lives of imperfect people called to serve Him through a lifelong familial love with one another!

A single friend of mine used to make light of the bar in which she had set for a future spouse, and how it would slide down a notch with each passing year. We would all be in hysterics as she explained what would be lost with each birthday; e.g. by 30 hair goes, 31 teeth, 32 sense of humor, 33 personality, 34 religion, 35 sexual orientation...and of course, she would always insist that money was the very last to go! Unfortunately, however, I have watched many women settle over the years for men who broke multiple deal breakers, even where morality and ethics were concerned.

It's hard to hold onto hope and to keep any sort of standard for yourself or for the men pursuing you when you feel overlooked, unloved, or just "too picky." This book is for all of us – single women, mothers of future single women, and good Christian friends.

"It is Jesus in fact that you seek when you dream of happiness; he is waiting for you when nothing else you find satisfies you; he is the beauty to which you are so attracted; it is he who provokes you with that thirst for fullness that will not let you settle for compromise; it is he who urges you to shed the masks of a false life; it is he who reads in your hearts your most genuine choices, the choices that others try to stifle. It is Jesus who stirs in you the desire to do something great with your lives, the will to follow an ideal, the refusal to allow yourselves to be grounded down by mediocrity, the courage to commit yourselves humbly and patiently to improving yourselves and society, making the world more human and more fraternal."

~*St. John Paul II, 15th World Youth Day, 19 August 2000*

This book assures us that we are not alone in our thirst for fullness and it inspires us to take courage in pursuing that fullness. Dream of happiness, seek out beauty, and make genuine choices that reflect your authentic self as a daughter of Christ.

Kimberly Cook,
Author of My Hand in Yours, Our Hands in His

"Real love is demanding. I would fail in my mission if I did not tell you so. Love demands a personal commitment to the will of God."

--Saint John Paul II

CHAPTER 1

This Book is About Hope

THIS IS NOT A dating how-to book. There are lots of those out there - both good and bad. This is a book about hope. We are in a time of great darkness, and we need some hope right now. We don't need the false type of hope that we are fed through television and fiction books. We need hope from the Lord; hope that His plan for marriage is even possible in today's culture.

This book will give you hope that you can actually find your husband in the 21st century despite the obstacles that come with technology, the hook-up culture, and the shrinking examples of how we should even date in the first place!

We live in a world of "Netflix and chill" with fewer men being taught how to take women on dates, let alone how to form healthy relationships with women! I'm not laying the problem solely at the feet of men. We ladies do plenty to twist the dating journey too! We're confused about how to dress, when to let him kiss us, and when to let our previous deal breakers slide.

It can be easy to think it's impossible to find a nice guy and even more impossible to find a Catholic one! But the truth is, it feels impossible right up to the day it happens. Every bad date, every awkward conversation at a party, every messy break-up fades into the background when God introduces you to the man with whom you will spend the rest of your life.

If you're anything like me, you'll instantly wish you had spent so much less time worrying about, crying over, pandering to, wallowing about, and pining for the wrong guy.

I wish I had spent time working on me. I wish I had learned more about myself, cultivated healthier habits, and learned what it meant to be a wife and a mother from wise, older women, while I was waiting to meet my future husband.

I wish someone had shown me examples of strong, healthy relationships and been honest about the struggles of healthy relationships too. I didn't know the difference between toxic relationship problems that poison you and healthy relationship problems that help you grow.

This book contains two parts. First, I share what I would tell a single woman if she were in my living room, drinking tea, and asking, "What should I do?" This is the raw truth and advice that I would give any single Catholic today. Second, it includes nearly forty love stories of how women met their husbands. These stories are real, messy, surprising, funny, heartwarming, and all examples of how God brings two people together despite our current toxic culture - one seemingly determined to devalue marriage.

CHAPTER 2

Why Chastity Matters

LET'S DIVE RIGHT IN with the gritty personal stuff. I'm not going to write a long, drawn-out chapter about modesty and chastity. There are plenty of those books already. I do want to share two things though. First, I want to talk about how easy it is to have sex. Really, I'll explain how you can "accidentally" do it. Second, I want to talk about the dangers of all premarital sex and how that can affect the relationship you will have with your spouse once you do get married. Too few people are willing to talk about this topic. I hope to give you some insight that doesn't sound like religious or theoretical lecturing!

There are certainly religious reasons for not having sex before you get married. They are discussed in Catholic chastity books. I'm not going to talk about those reasons. Instead, I want to share the harsh truth of my story, and I promise, I won't say things like, "Save your special treasure box for your husband." Yes, I really did read that in a book.

Accidentally Having Sex

Some of you may be tired of being lectured to about premarital sex. I remember clearly telling my parents, "It's not like I'm going to accidentally have sex with someone just because we're alone in the same room." You too may feel confident that you're not going to have sex while you're dating but this confidence can give you a false sense of safety. If your guard isn't up, it's easy to give into physical temptation.

In truth, it's extremely easy to "accidentally" have sex. I don't mean that you trip and all your clothes come off and you lose your virginity, but it is pretty easy to sit next to someone, drink two glasses of wine, and feel a fiery heat spread through your body that will scream, "You should go one step further!"

If you give into this heat and start kissing your boyfriend, it doesn't take very long for hands to wander and then suddenly, your clothes have come off, and somehow you have sex in a haze that lasts less than five minutes.

That's right; you can start out in the morning feeling confident that you want to save yourself for marriage. Then 10 p.m. rolls around and it can take less than five minutes to have sex with someone. This five minutes can happen almost without notice when you feel like you are in love - and especially when a little alcohol is involved.

It's not that your parents, your youth pastor, or all the chastity books are questioning your values. Instead, it's easier than you think to have sex with someone, even when you don't really want to. I'm not talking about being physically forced. It's more like a force from within that's so strong, it's hard to ignore.

Your body and your passions will insist that you should have sex with this adorable, sweet, kind man in front of you. And if you do, you'll wake up the next morning wishing you hadn't, and if he turns out not to be your future husband, you'll carry the yucky feeling of the experience with you into your marriage. I speak from experience.

My Story of Premarital Sex

I didn't grow up with religion. I had your basic, "Use condoms, so you don't get pregnant or get STD's" talk in school. That was about the totality of my academic sex education. Even when I was in middle school, that seemed more like a plea for protected sex rather than abstinence. Throw in the casual education I got from my friends, television, AOL chat rooms, and the porn that I stumbled upon at ten... and by thirteen, I understood that it was common, even expected, to have sex sometime during high school.

Looking back, it's shocking to me to think of the sheer volume of toxic lies that I heard about love, sex, and relationships in my formative years. I pray every day that God helps me protect my children from being robbed not only of their innocence but of the good and true expectations of how men and women should interact.

I never thought I would save myself for marriage. That's not a common secular philosophy. Somehow though, I managed to be fairly monogamous in my relationships despite not having any religious reason to do so. When I was fifteen, my friends started having sex. And while they seemed excited about their boyfriends at first, I noticed a pattern. Once they had sex, they seemed to become sad. Things would get complicated and inevitably, they would cry more.

At the time, I didn't understand precisely what was making them cry. I doubt they even knew the real reason themselves, but the pattern was clear to me. Having sex was making my friends sad. It wasn't making them feel beautiful or loved or safe.

Because of these observations, I knew I wanted to be monogamous for a long time. This decision had nothing to do with religion. I look back and see how young and broken I was, despite thinking I had such a good head on my shoulders. My idea of a long time was one to two years. How silly it was to think I was somehow doing so much better than the other girls at school!

I lost my virginity at seventeen to a very nice boy who I had been dating for six months. Six months was an eternity back then to make a nice boy wait. We were together for almost two years. The story was about the same as the second boy I was with. I thought I was doing a pretty good job. I wasn't sleeping with a ton of people. I had rules and standards. I was with nice guys who patiently waited and who treated me well.

I will be very honest with my children when they are old enough about my dating history. I want them to know that I wish I could take back every single one of those boys I dated or slept with. Not a single one of them was dating me because they wanted to get married. Not a single one of them cherished me like a daughter of the Lord.

There is an ocean of distance between a "nice boy" and a man who wants a Catholic marriage. Your heart can tell the difference, I promise, but you have to listen to it.

When I finally met the man who would be my husband, I instantly felt the cheapness of all those other relationships. It was as if I had been playing house all those years. They did not prepare me for this man. They were just twisted fantasies played out like a campy television show. They weren't real.

I felt embarrassed that I had allowed myself to settle for an echo of a real relationship and for what? Because I was lonely? Because my friends told me I should? Because television makes it seem like if you don't have a boyfriend, you're weird somehow?

I wish I could have taken it all back; that I could have stuffed all those memories and experiences in a suitcase and shipped them to another country. I wish I didn't have to bring all that baggage with me into this new and beautiful relationship.

The man who would be my husband was very understanding. He too lived through high school and college without religion. We never really talked about our dating or sexual history. By the time we met, we knew those things were in the past, our non-Catholic past, and there was nothing to be done about them. But you can never really get rid of those memories.

Porn Culture

Gone are the days of innocence. Maybe there are a few who have been blessed to have avoided porn their entire lives but this group of people is in a small minority. Most American teens and young adults have watched porn to varying degrees, especially if they do not come from religious homes.

I saw porn for the first time when I was ten, hardly knowing what it was. I received even more sexual education from AOL chat rooms. A/S/L check anyone? It wasn't long before sexual chatting with strange boys (likely creepy old men) and porn began to form my understanding of what it meant to be sexy and desired.

It becomes very easy to think you need to dress a certain way, say certain words, and be provocative and daring in the bedroom because you think that is what men want. I became a great actress. At the time, it didn't feel disingenuous. Like I said, I thought I was in good relationships with nice guys and this was just how I showed them how much I loved them. It all felt rather normal to me back then.

My husband went to college where porn parties were a regular thing. Boys would get together and watch porn in someone's dorm room. With access to high-speed internet, porn addictions grew quickly and my husband was no exception. After all, if you're not religious, it's practically expected of you. I'm thankful he had gone through the hard work of kicking that habit before we met but the temptation still lingers. To this day, we do not watch any television or movies with nudity or sex scenes in them.

To say our view of sex was twisted would be an understatement. And I don't mean that we were into kinky behavior, we just really didn't know what healthy, loving sex rooted in the Lord was supposed to look like. In truth, we're still trying to figure that out.

Shortly after we started dating, we knew we were going to get married. Once you've become a sexual person, it's so hard not to have sex with someone especially once you've decided you're going to marry them. We had sex a month after our first date. We both regretted this deeply. We had sex a few more times in those first few months before drawing a hard line in the sand. Our entire dating/engagement period was only eight months but I am glad that we spent the last five of them chastely, even for those weeks we lived together, but that caused a whole separate problem.

The Dangers of Living Together

After living in sin for much of my twenties, I hoped that after becoming Catholic and trying to pursue chastity until we got married, that God would bless us with abundant grace in our marriage and I would finally experience what a great sex life was! That's not at all how it happened for me.

You see, the devil knows exactly how to tempt you at every stage of your life. He's been doing it for thousands of years. We often hear that the devil will try his hardest to get you to have sex before you're married. Here's something most of the books don't mention. The devil will also try his hardest to get you NOT to have sex once you are married. Why? Because sex is crucial to marriage and he knows that if he can make you bitter, angry, or hurt so you won't have sex with your husband, your marriage will be hurt.

There's often talk of a honeymoon period in marriage. Through books and television, I had this idea that sex was fun and plentiful in the first year of marriage even if it did drop off after that initial time. My husband and I didn't experience that sort of honeymoon time at all. I believe this was due to our previous sexual relationships, failures in our early dating period, and because we lived together, albeit chastely, for six weeks before we got married.

We had both been living in apartments, and our lease was up six weeks before we got married. We decided that we would buy a house, live in separate bedrooms and treat each other like brother and sister for six weeks until we got married. And you know what? We did an awesome job! We didn't exchange anything except short kisses hello, goodbye, and goodnight. We kept our distance so we wouldn't be tempted to have sex and we didn't!

Unfortunately, and neither of us understood this at the time, there was a price we would pay for this six weeks that we didn't anticipate. After walking around the house in our sweats and keeping each other at a safe and friendship-like distance for six weeks, we had stamped out a lot of the passion in our relationship. It was almost as if we had fast forwarded to having been married for years having gotten too comfortable with each other.

Instead of creating extra passion on our honeymoon, we didn't know what to do with each other! It was awkward and passionless. We had been living together for six weeks, so none of the daily stuff felt that exciting. Our sex life was mediocre to begin with and sadly, we both knew it. Worse, we internally compared it to previous relationships.

Comparison is one of the poisons of previous sexual relationships, and it lingers a long time. Furthermore, loss of passion is a danger of living together before getting married even if you don't have sex.

I imagine everyone has a unique story when it comes to their intimate life in their marriage. It's also something few people are willing to talk about at all or at least with complete transparency. To be fair, marital intimacy is and should be private. It's not supposed to be broadcast, but I do wish more people were willing to discuss the real reasons behind not having sex and not living together other than "because Jesus said so." It really is so much more complicated than that. Chastity is necessary to help start your marriage off on the right foot.

Don't Be Discouraged

If you've already been with other men or if you're already living with your fiancé, I don't want you to feel like it's "over" for you. God can heal anything, and His mercy is endless. I don't want you to think you're tainted or broken. We are all stained because of original sin. The beauty and grace of confession is that it washes you clean.

Many of the stories in this book feature women who were not living Christian lives before they got married, some who were pregnant before getting married, and many who have suffered abuse in some form. Let these stories give you hope that God can heal anything.

Having had previous sexual experiences doesn't mean that you can't find a wonderful man or have a great marriage. It means you're going to have to try harder to wash out those memories and see your husband with fresh eyes.

Marriage is poisoned by comparisons. Try to erase those other relationships and experiences from your mind. Look at the amazing man that God has put in front of you and try to act as if he is your first everything. Don't hold him up to the standard of your past relationships, your relationship fantasies, or the relationships you've seen on television.

Read your Bible, study what God's plan for marriage is, and try to live up to that standard yourself. While it's easy to try and measure your spouse to determine if he's good enough, marriage is really about asking yourself, "How can I better serve my spouse and get him to heaven?" No matter where you're at, you can be a good wife by asking yourself this question every single day.

This leads me to a few pieces of advice that I'd like to share. Learn more about yourself and relationships. Find out what it takes to be a good wife because there are some concrete things that you can learn to help your marriage run more smoothly.

"Grant me, O Lord my God, a mind to know you, a heart to seek you, wisdom to find you, conduct pleasing to you, faithful perseverance in waiting for you, and a hope of finally embracing you."

St. Thomas Aquinas

CHAPTER THREE

What To Do While You Wait

WAITING CAN BE ONE of the most frustrating aspects of life. When I am unsure of the future and when I feel powerless to exert some control in my life, it can drive me bonkers. I'm the queen of distracting myself from my own pain by setting goals, reworking my budget in an Excel spreadsheet, looking for new places to live, and dreaming up new businesses to start. Waiting is so painful.

I wasted a lot of the time I spent waiting to meet my husband distracting myself with activities that were empty or wallowing in sadness in my room. I wish I would have put that time to better use! On the following pages are some ideas of what I think Catholic women can do to better use this time as they try to discern God's will for your life.

Study Relationships

Why do we spend so much time in our society talking about college and so very little time talking about marriage? Most people only go to college for four years and yet they hope to be married for more than fifty! Think of how much time we spend preparing for the SAT's, researching colleges, and thinking about majors. Shouldn't we give relationships and marriage at least the same level of study?

If you want a good marriage, study what good marriages look like. I certainly wish I had prepared myself for what was to come -- both for the incredible joy and satisfaction of being married but also for the fire, pain, and reshaping that marriage forces you to endure as you shed your selfish tendencies and strive to become more like Christ.

Read books about marriage, not just about dating. I've listed some fantastic books on my website at www.sterlingjaquith.com/bookrecommendations. Some of the tips won't fully make sense, or you might not understand their importance without having lived through some of the issues, but you will be better armed going into marriage than if you hadn't read them at all. Even just knowing which book to reference later will give you a huge leg up.

Talk to people who are happily married in their 30's, 40's, and 50's. Pay attention to the common themes that these couples share with you. They know what it takes to make marriage work day in and day out. No marriage is easy, despite what it might look like. Wouldn't it be great to know some of those secrets before getting married?

If you don't know any happily married couples personally, it's great that you live in the time of the internet! Find a Catholic Facebook group and ask people to tell you about what makes a successful marriage. People love talking about this topic! Get curious about relationships and what makes them work.

In addition to getting to know other married people, spend some time getting to know yourself!

Personality Matters

Understanding your personality and understanding the personality of others is important when it comes to forming healthy relationships. This can make a huge difference in your dating strategy as well as how you relate to your future spouse. It removes so many barriers when you understand the unique personality types that God has given each of us.

I've always enjoyed personality tests. I took the Myers-Briggs test when I was in high school, but I didn't do anything with the result. I certainly didn't dig into my personality type or learn how it relates to the other ones. I didn't learn how to spot other personality types so I could better communicate with them. How helpful that would have been while navigating new friendships and relationships!

My husband and I began taking personality tests after we got married. We have continued to discover new ones in the seven years we've been married. Each one impacted how we communicated with each other, some in big ways, and some in small ways.

Communication in any relationship is crucial and yet, it's so easy to get it wrong even when we have pure intentions. When you love someone deeply and you want so badly to show them how much you love them, if you're speaking a language they don't understand, your message will likely get lost and feelings will get hurt.

Here are just some of the personality types you can explore:

- DISC (My personal favorite)
- Myers-Briggs
- *The Five Love Languages* by Gary Chapman
- *The Temperament God Gave You* by Art and Loraine Bennett
- *Love and Respect* by Emerson Eggerichs (not a personality test but helpful in understanding the different ways that men and women want to be loved.)

Knowing your personality and that of the people you are interested in will help you navigate relationships so much more smoothly. It will also give you insight into the likely communication problems you will encounter and how to manage those better. All marriages have problems because devoting your life to a person with a different personality and gender is hard!

Having problems, disagreements, and even painful fights doesn't mean you have a bad relationship or marriage. Refusing to learn about your spouse or to adjust your communication style to help your spouse better understand you can be a big obstacle in overcoming the issues you will face.

You don't need to wait until you're married to learn more about your personality and communication style. Start off on the right foot by arming yourself with the knowledge of how to better serve the person you love and field the challenges that are likely to come your way more gracefully by studying your personality as well as the other personality types out there.

We tend to marry our opposites so spend some time paying attention to the personality types that are very different from yours. Learning about personality will not only impact your future marriage, but it will likely transform your work relationships and your family relationships as well!

Reading truth about healthy relationships is absolutely crucial in the 21st century because our culture feeds us lies daily about what relationships look like. It is necessary for us to counteract those toxic messages with truth. If your parents have an unhealthy relationship or if your only examples of relationships are found on television, it's likely you have no idea what a healthy, day-to-day relationship even looks like. Don't let that be an excuse not to do your homework.

Television Love is a Lie

Most of us begin paying attention to relationships on television when we're in our teens. We watch shows about people in high school, in college, or out in the working world. We are dazzled by their outfits, their hilarious life situations, and the swell of romance that we watch build between two characters. We are drawn in. We begin to map out a formula for happiness in our minds whether we realize that we're doing this or not.

Honestly, I think we'd all be better off not watching 90% of what's on television. If I was really strong, I'd stop watching television altogether. I'm not sure it's helped me in any meaningful way. I realize that's unreasonable for most of us though. Having been raised watching television, it would take a significant amount of self-discipline for me to give it up entirely.

I imagine I will give up almost all television in the next five years but in the meantime, while I'm not strong enough to pull that off just yet, I think it's important that we start a conversation about the lies that we see on television. We need to teach each other how to spot the lies in the shows we're watching. Spotting lies will help us to avoid embedding these messages in our mind as truth. Read through these common lies that are found in most television shows and see if you can spot them the next time you sit down to binge-watch something on Netflix.

LIE #1 - ACTORS ARE RARELY THE AGE THEY PLAY

I think back to the shows I watched when I was in high school and college. Now I clearly see that the actors were much older than the characters they were playing. Teenagers are played by twenty-three-year-olds. Of course, the poor kids watching these actors, nearly all of whom are extremely attractive, are going to feel bad about themselves!

From the get-go, we internalize that we're not pretty enough, we're not rich enough, and we're not as smooth sounding as the people on television. You're not supposed to look twenty-three when you're sixteen!

Interestingly, as the age of the characters gets older, the reverse happens. Actors who are in their thirties start playing actors who are in their mid-to-late forties. This is a lie that older women have to guard themselves against. The message is the same though. You are not enough. This is a lie.

LIE #2 - ALL HOMES ARE THIS BEAUTIFUL

The next time you watch a show or a movie, take a moment to appreciate the background. Most of the houses you will see are perfectly staged with just the right furniture to make the home feel warm and inviting. The items in the house will all appear new as if no one has used them... because no one has!

I didn't begin noticing this as much until I was in my thirties. Then I suddenly began to see that most characters lived in million dollar city lofts or perfectly remodeled craftsman homes. This can be a dangerous trap for women who can quickly become unsatisfied with their own apartments or houses for not having white baseboards and perfectly curated decorations.

When you begin to feel the need to perfect your room or your apartment with decorations from Target or Ikea, ask yourself why. While creating a warm and inviting home is not bad, in itself, it has to fit the budget. If it is not in your budget to buy lots of furniture or if it is causing you stress not to have an HGTV style space, these are not yearnings that come from Christ. These are lies the world has sold you. If your home isn't beautiful, you are not enough. This is a lie.

LIE #3 - EVERYONE'S WARDROBE IS LIKE THIS

Americans have a clothing problem, and in my opinion, the main source of this problem is television. The outfits have been meticulously put together by a fashion designer who is given nearly endless options by advertisers. Yes, the clothes you see on television shows are meant to get you to buy what the characters are wearing.

What does this have to do with dating? It's rooted in self-esteem. If your clothes don't look like a window display, you might fall into the trap of feeling worthless, not cool enough, and thinking that maybe, just maybe, if you had better clothes, you'd get a better guy.

Take a look at your closet right now. How many pieces of clothing do you have? How much did you spend on these clothes? And just what percentage of those clothes do you wear regularly? I talk a lot about the clothing problem of our culture in my book *Not of This World: A Catholic Guide to Minimalism.*[1] If you wear the same thing too often and if your clothes aren't expensive or perfectly matched, you are not enough. This is a lie.

LIE #4 - DRAMA IS GOOD

This sentiment is perfectly captured by Taylor Swift's song The Romantics.

Please take my hand and
Please take me dancing and
Please leave me stranded,
*it's so romantic (it's so romantic)*2

When I was younger, I thought dancing was a much larger part of dating than it really was. I would get dressed up with my friends, stay up late, pay an expensive fee to get into a club and hope to have a magical night with a nice guy. Not once did that ever play out.

I appreciate how Swift also says, "Please leave me stranded, it's so romantic." Not only do we want the swell of love, we kind of like the swell of heartache too. The more dramatic, the better. Television has programmed us to think we should be fighting and kissing in the rain, that it's okay to send ultimatum text messages and the worse the fight, the more dreamy the make-up later. I really had to rewire my brain about drama when I started to date a real-life Catholic man who wasn't a buffoon or a character on a show. It's not real love if there isn't drama. This is a lie.

LIE #5 - REAL MEN SPEAK IN ELEGANT MONOLOGUES

I know this one sounds obvious but trust me, we're falling hard for this lie even though we think we're above it. How often have you gotten a text or a phone call from a guy and thought, "Wow, he really bumbled his way through that."

We are disappointed when men don't profess their deepest feelings to us in award-winning speeches. There are many different personality types, and each presents a little differently with men and women, but by and large, men do not typically process their feelings verbally and are not often proactive about discussing the feelings they have.

Since we've been trained by rom-coms and novels, it's easy for us to feel like "he doesn't really love me" if he isn't good at communicating his feelings. Now don't get me wrong, communicating is an important part of a relationship. Finding someone I could have a reasonable conversation with was a big priority for me. But even men who are great communicators often need time to think about what they want, and even great men won't use elegant speeches to tell you how they feel. If he isn't wearing his heart on his sleeve or wooing you with poetry, he isn't into you. This is a lie.

LIE #6 - GOOD RELATIONSHIPS DON'T HAVE BIG PROBLEMS

When I see married people on television, I notice how they only have cute problems. Things like he leaves his socks on the floor or she doesn't know how to cook. The other thing I see is people who are unhappily married and turn to affairs to make them feel better or divorce. Rarely do I see solid marriages that show deep darkness and how you can weather it.

You can have a good marriage and still go through dark times. You will wonder if you made a mistake. You can sneer at your spouse in a moment of profound weakness and say "I hate you" or maybe "I never loved you." I have thought those things, and they were lies. That didn't mean I had a bad marriage.

Marriage is supposed to burn away your selfishness and help you become more like Christ and guess what? That's extremely painful. Sometimes we react to this pain by lashing out at our spouse. It's only through prayer and reflection, and sometimes reading marriage books or going to counseling, that we see our role in the problems of our marriage.

I wish I had been more prepared to expect big and deep problems in my marriage and that these problems didn't mean I made a mistake or, worse, that I shouldn't stay married now. If you have big problems, you don't have a good marriage. This is a lie.

How Important Are Shared Hobbies?

I remember a few super cute boys in my high school who were in a band. They wore perfectly trendy "I don't care" clothes and had shiny instruments. They played okay music, but to a girl of sixteen, it looked like stardom. I remember thinking how great it would be to date a boy in a band!

A few years after I got married, I went with a friend to a Christian concert. There was a cute guy, super talented musician, playing the guitar. He talked about his wife and kids which made him all the more attractive. That's what's attractive in your thirties. But as I was watching this man, who had been given a gift from God, all I kept thinking was, "Wow, I'm so glad I didn't marry a man who travels most weekends of the year."

What I once thought was so cool, I saw more clearly now as a career that would likely be at odds with wanting a family and being a stay-at-home mom. Musicians don't make much money either.

Fight the urge to find someone based solely on sharing your interests. Do not seek people *just* because of the things they like and do not discount people *simply* because they do not share your interests. You will be tempted to think that if he likes the same bands and the same television shows as you that it must be love! That is not necessarily true.

Hobbies change. Interests change. Preferences change. You will like different music later; you won't have lots of time after you have kids to pursue the same hobbies you did in your early twenties, and that's okay. You may end up with a man who does like all those same silly things but you may not. The important thing is that he has the same core values as you. Does he loves Jesus? Is he a hard worker? Does he have a kind heart? Does he wants to be a good husband and father?

Those things exist at the core and will be the same throughout time even if your hobbies change. Don't overlook people who don't instantly fit into your transitional social life.

My husband and I don't like the same music, we prefer different food, there is a small crossover in movies that we enjoy, and the way we would naturally spend a free Saturday is completely different. When I met my husband, he had a terrible wardrobe and the most bachelor style apartment you can imagine.

Even though I knew we didn't have a lot of social similarities, I knew we were both new Christians, deeply into our faith, and very committed to staying married no matter what. We wanted a big family, and we both wanted to give homeschooling a try. He did love dogs, and that was genuinely important to me because I couldn't imagine living without a dog, so that was (and still is) a deal breaker for me!

Talk to someone in their thirties or forties and find out what they do for fun, both now and when they were younger. I'm a big fan of moms having something to do other than just take care of their kids, but the truth is, I spend so much time taking care of my home and my kids that there isn't a ton of time for me to cultivate many hobbies.

Imagine how much you will change by the time you are that age. What things might you be into? You might want to consider learning some skills or cultivating hobbies now that will be helpful in your married or parenting life down the line. No matter what you choose to work on, choose to grow in some way.

Be The Woman The Man You Want is Looking For

If you don't want a husband who ignores you on Sundays to watch football for four hours, don't be a girl who chooses to binge watch Netflix every weekend. Television isn't intrinsically wrong, but when we make an idol out of our favorite shows or when we waste several hours a day watching tv, we miss out on other opportunities. Furthermore, hours of TV is not a good basis for a relationship.

Make a list of the character traits that you want in a husband and then ask yourself what kind of character traits that type of man will want in a woman. You will likely have very different personality types but if you want to marry someone who works hard, ask yourself, in what ways are you a hard worker?

Spend some time and think hard about the qualities you're looking for in your future husband and then start right now improving those qualities in yourself. If you want a man who is passionate about his faith, then spend time growing in your own faith. If you want a man who is virtuous, then develop virtue in yourself first. We attract what we value. Identify what you want in a husband, and start living those values and ideals now.

The Three Things

There are three disciplines that every person has to develop no matter what their vocation or current life situation: suffering, discernment, and hope. In all walks of life, we will each experience suffering. We will all wonder if we're doing what God wants us to be doing. We will all struggle to have hope at times. These are not merely three feelings that we experience, they are actual skills we can cultivate and get better at.

It is important that we first acknowledge struggling with these disciplines is completely normal. You are not alone in your suffering, your confusion over what you should be doing with your life, or your bouts of hopelessness. It will only make matters worse to add guilt on top of these challenges thinking that they're not normal.

Second, we have to learn how to cultivate these three skills and they are, in fact, skills that we can get better at. I will not attempt to tell you how to do that here since I could easily take an entire book to tackle each of those three topics. Instead, I just want to put it on your radar that you should be using this time, right now, to learn more about how to discern the will of God, how to suffer well, and how to have hope when it seems like there are no reasons to hope.

I have listed some books about these topics on my website but you're smart, you know how to use Google and YouTube to learn more about these topics. Schedule some time in your week specifically for personal development and learn how to grow in these three areas.

CHAPTER FOUR

Why God?

WHETHER YOU HAVE BEEN single for a year or a few decades, no doubt the question that is often found on your lips is, "Why God?"

Why haven't I met my husband yet?
Why do I keep meeting terrible guys?
Why do all the good guys seem to be taken?
Why am I still alone?

There is a deep yearning inside of us to feel connected to others. We intuitively believe that this can be fulfilled through a marriage relationship. Most women grow up with the desire to get married. The longer this goes unfulfilled, the more we wonder... why?

As we lay in bed at night, it's easy for us to send up this familiar cry to the Lord: Why?

Don't fall for this trap.

"Why" is Satan's Question.

Why is a dangerous question because it feeds into Satan's plans. The devil wants us to doubt the Lord. The devil wants us to doubt God's goodness and His plan. As soon as we find ourselves crying out "why" we are expressing doubt. We want what we want right now instead of in God's timing. Or, worse still, we want our plan instead of His plan. When we cry out "Why?" we are expressing our frustration with the Lord.

I cry out "why" all the time. I'm still new in my faith, and when I hurt deeply, I want to know why the Lord has done this to me. It's a natural reaction, given our stain of original sin, to feel a sense of injustice when we are in pain. These feelings are a lie. The truth is that there is no injustice in God's plan, no matter how wronged we feel.

Should you feel guilty asking "why?" No, it's a natural question. God wants your truth. When I'm feeling pouty about something, I tell God. He wants all of me, including my bad attitude. It's not as if I can hide those feelings from Him. He knows all. Instead of beating yourself up about crying out "why," begin to see it as a red flag. Let it help you to ask yourself, "What am I scared of? What am I not willing to surrender to God?"

God is keeping you single on purpose right now. Instead of asking Him "why," let us use Mary as an example and ask Him "how?"

How can this lead to my sanctification? How can you use me, Lord? How can this pain be used for others? How can I show others your glory Lord through my story?

"How" is Mary's Question.

Mary went through a great deal of suffering in her life. From the beginning of her story, she finds out that she is going to be the mother of God. This was not particularly joyful news. When Gabriel first appeared, she was troubled and perplexed. This is likely because she knew the scriptures, and knew that every time God summoned someone for a specific task, it was going to be difficult. Without knowing the details, she knew that suffering was her fate. This premonition was later confirmed by Simeon.

And yet with strength and humility, she says, "Be it done to me according to your will." She wants nothing more than to follows God's plan and to honor Him with her life.

How can I serve you, Lord? How can I use this to bring you glory? She shows us what our hearts should long for.

In no way am I trying to make you feel bad for all the why's you've tossed up to the Lord. I asked this question for the first thirty-three years of my life until I heard this teaching from a priest. Even now it is still a knee-jerk reaction for me to stomp my foot and cry out "why Lord?" But ever so slowly I am changing my heart. I am bowing my head and opening my hands and asking, "How" instead.

Lord, how can you use me to save souls and bring you glory?

This shift immediately gets the focus off of myself and my pain and back to Him. It also implies trust. I know that God is all goodness and He wants what's best for me. More than anything else, He wants me to spend eternity with Him in Heaven. That is what I want most of all so I surrender my ideas about what should be happening in my life and I open myself up to His plan whether I understand it or not.

Making this shift will require some training and discipline, but it's a shift we need to make. The more practice you have asking God how he can use your hardships for good now, the more naturally this will come to you when you experience the hardships of marriage.

Wait For Your Own Love Story. It's The Best.

I never get tired of hearing someone tell me how they met their spouse. Their eyes light up. The look at the ground and smile as if remembering a sweet moment that's just for them. It's special every time because I'm hearing someone's real-life fairy tale romance.

God has a plan that is just right... for you. It's not going to be the same as a book you read or a movie you watched. It's not going to be your best friend's story or your sister's story.

It may not even be sensational, but I have yet to hear someone's story about falling in love and thought, "I don't know, that seemed kind of boring to me." It's never boring because it's always a miraculous gift from God.

I consider every story a miracle, especially in this day and age, when a man and a woman cut through the noise to find each other. And against all odds, they decide to commit their lives to each other in a world where... they don't really have to. It's amazing to me that humans have that deep capacity to love and that we willingly bestow that special love on another person. Perhaps I shouldn't be amazed because we are made in God's likeness, and He is love.

Your story will be perfect. Your story will make you smile every time you tell it. Even on the darkest, most challenging days of my marriage, if someone were to ask me how I met my husband, I would smile as I shared the story. I consider it a miracle that God brought the two of us together. We don't make sense on paper. We should never have given each other a chance. And yet through all the mismatched hobbies, the two different religions, and the significant personality differences, we stuck it out and chose each other.

One of the reasons I could never leave my husband is because I believe our marriage is a gift from God. It was as if the Holy Spirit came down and shoved us together, so we had no choice but to fall in love. Who am I to challenge such a divine present?

I won't lie to you. There are certainly some women who never get married. I can't promise that you'll find your prince charming. I also can't promise that if you do, things will be smooth sailing. In fact, I can guarantee that things won't be easy. Marriage is hard. One of my favorite books says, "Nothing prepares you for marriage except marriage."

Hold out for the man God has picked for you. Open your heart and pray about vocations in case Jesus is the man God has chosen for you. The world certainly needs more nuns. And in the meantime, while you're waiting, go out and serve the Lord. Love the people around you. Deepen your relationship with the Lord.

Work on detaching yourself from the idols that you have. I promise you have them. It will be much easier to let them go now than to let marriage and motherhood rip them out of your hands later.

The subject of identifying idols and giving them up could fill an entire book! Take this seriously. If I were to tell you that you'd have to give up Netflix, playing soccer, wearing nice clothes, hosting major holiday events, etc. after you got married, how would you feel? Those things aren't bad and you probably won't have to give them up but you will find that your vocation of marriage and motherhood will reveal the things you have unhealthy attachments to.

We should love nothing more than Jesus. Our peace should come from the Lord. If you're soothing yourself on a bad day with something else, it's a good place to start when considering what idols there are in your life. I don't mean to make this sound like something you can accomplish while you are single. Detaching ourselves from the comforts of the world is a lifelong process but one that is certainly worth the effort. The more we cling to Jesus, the more peace we will have.

For Catholic Singles in their 30's, 40's and 50's.

Being single can be deeply painful. Though you may think you have experienced the depth of this pain in your early twenties, those who find themselves single in later decades know that it can be a harrowing pain that pulls us deeper down into despair and seems to touch every aspect of life. Of course, one can experience moments of consolation from the Lord but there will be those times when it's easy to think, "Where are you, God? Why have you left me in this lonely place? Just tell me what you want me to do! What are your plans for me?"

Many of the following stories are about women who met their husbands in their twenties. These stories are meant to give hope to those who can't possibly imagine how one can meet a nice Catholic guy in today's twisted culture. There are a few stories of women who met their husbands in their thirties and one who met her husband in her forties.

While I'm sure there are many stories of women who found their spouse later in life, this book is not meant to promise you marriage. God does not promise us marriage. He promises us love. He promises us a life of peace and joy when we walk closely with him. It takes years to learn how to experience peace and joy amidst suffering but it is absolutely possible and in fact, a lesson we are all called to learn while we live on Earth.

We have a deep longing to be loved and to be truly known but this longing is not for a husband, it is for God. The world says that you need a romantic relationship to fill this hole but as married women will attest, a husband does not actually fill this hole at all.

We all must learn that nothing can fully satisfy us except the love of Jesus. Husbands, children, work accomplishments, missionary trips, and serving those around us may feed our soul but not to satisfaction. We will all spend a lifetime longing for the Lord until we are with him in eternity. That sucks to hear, I know.

As I write this, my own freedom has been taken from me in the form of back-to-back pregnancies and a body that's failing to keep up. I am in bed most days longing for the day when I can be free to live out my vocation of marriage and motherhood. In the meantime, I have been sidelined and am learning that those things do not define me. I am not worthless when I cannot be a wife or a mother. My worth comes from the God who created me. I am defined as a daughter of Christ. I am His and He loves me.

I imagine it will take the rest of my life to learn how to really sit in that love and to desire that love above everything else. I'm capable of that in short bursts now but it's easy to be pulled away by the world, by my own selfishness, and my desire for a pain-free life.

I wrote this book to give you hope that God is love. His desire for you is to be overwhelmed by love for all eternity. He knows precisely what life you need to live to make that possible. And you are completely capable of discerning this plan. Saint Ignatius of Loyola says, "God gives each one of us sufficient grace ever to know His holy will, and to do it fully."

Spend time with the Lord in prayer, by attending Daily Mass when you can, by making a holy hour in Adoration, and by reading about the lives of the saints. The closer to you draw to him, the more clearly you can hear His voice.

Catholic Love Stories

Continue reading this book to discover nearly forty real stories of true love. See how God can use ordinary people and ordinary situations to bring about the extraordinary gift of the sacrament of marriage. Keep these stories in your mind as examples of everyday people finding deep love. These are much better stories to hold onto than the lies we see on television.

God is love. He is all goodness. He never changes. We can see glimpses of this love in all of these stories. Whether marriage is in your future or not, read these stories and let them stir in you a deep desire for God's love. No other love satisfies. I will be praying for you. I often pray for single Catholics that they may discern the will of God and pursue His plan. Though our paths will all look different, we all have one goal in common: sanctification. This is no small feat, but it's the only adventure worth pursuing.

For this is the will of God, your sanctification.

- 1 Thessalonians 4:3

Love Stories

Begin on the

Next Page....

The Pride Before The Fall

Sterling Jaquith (E25/M25)
Podcast: Coffee & Pearls
www.sterlingjaquith.com
Instagram @sterlingjaquith

This story is about pride. I struggle a great deal with this sin. I think too highly of myself, and I'm often too judgmental of others. Don't get me wrong, I also struggle with deep, wallowing, self-loathing too. Inflated pride and self-loathing are merely different sides of the same coin – both are focused on oneself. I'm working on curtailing these tendencies, and I'm a lot better than I used to be (through no power of my own). Having children has greatly humbled me. I also spend a great deal of time praying to Jesus, Mary, and the saints. Goodness knows I need all the help I can get!

My husband helps me battle my pride, too. I need his help every day. God gives us marriage so we can help each other get to Heaven. Most days, I am grateful for my husband's gentle nudging toward sainthood. If ever I squirm a little when he gently reminds me to let the air out of my own balloon a bit, all he has to do is give me a small smile, and we both know why. I instantly stop resisting and start praying!

I met my husband on eHarmony. I was certain that I was too cool for him, and that we'd never get along. He was N-E-R-D-Y, and I don't mean the cute, hipster kind with black rimmed glasses and skinny jeans. He studied analytical chemistry, which is considered nerdy even by the other chemists. I deigned to give him a chance because he was the only guy I had been matched with who said Jesus multiple times in his profile.

I had been searching for a strong Christian man, but I was meeting a lot of "I go to church sometimes and I listen to Christian music" type guys, who didn't seem to have a real relationship with Christ. I decided to give this goofy chemist a chance. God soothed my doubts along the way by revealing that this man was a huge dog lover. We found common ground in that and started corresponding a little. Then it turned into a lot.

Suddenly, I found myself getting quite attached to these words on a screen and the person they represented. I started to wonder,

"What if I'm wasting all this time writing to this chemist, and it turns out we have no chemistry together?" I reached out to my nerdy chemist and said, "Let's meet."

On our first date, he wore light blue denim shorts with white puffy tennis shoes. It was a nod to the 80's... not because he sported vintage fashion, but because he'd literally been wearing the same style of clothes since the 80's. His phone was in the front pocket of his white polo shirt like a sad Dilbert joke. I smiled and fought the urge to run away.

I had struggled to find any young man who loved Jesus (both online and in the person), so I couldn't simply throw this guy over because of some unfashionable clothes. I'm glad I stuck it out though because we had a great first date. It was full of laughs. It also had plenty of heated debates. I was a die-hard Protestant and he was an uber-conservative Catholic, so we had a lot to spar about. It turns out we liked our debates because we had four dates in four days.

We were quite smitten with each other despite my constant claims that it would never work out because of our differing religious beliefs. He had enough hope for the both of us, and we continued to date. On the fifth date, he graciously, and most impressively, made me a delicious salmon and asparagus dinner at his apartment. He opened up a bottle of wine and offered me some.

PAUSE.

I always pause for a moment before drinking alcohol. I'm a very lightweight drinker. In fact, I can handle just about two drinks. Sometimes not even that if the glasses are too big. I don't drink often, but whenever I do, I always make a plan in my head to only have two drinks followed by two glasses of water. I know this about myself, and I respect my boundaries.

There we were. I was sitting on his awful, green, puffy microfiber couch in his poorly decorated apartment. I still thought I was way cooler than him. He took out these tiny wine glasses. They are the kind of wine glasses you would get in a wine tasting room. He told me he used to enjoy wine tasting when he lived in upstate New York. I thought this was adorable and I gladly accepted my tiny wine glass. That was my problem right there.

I just assumed the glass was so tiny that I could probably have three glasses of wine and be just fine. I'm not even sure that this was a conscious thought, but there we were, cozy on his couch, watching a movie, and sipping wine. I was super nervous, and I wasn't paying attention to how many glasses I had.

Another thing you should know about me: I have a great game face when I'm drinking. I appear to be absolutely sober until two minutes before I jump down the rabbit hole and appear totally sloshed. There's almost no warning. Now don't get the wrong idea about me. I rarely get drunk. Really, I'm a nice girl, and I hate feeling sick. But that night, while sitting on the couch, watching a movie with this man I didn't know would become my husband, it hit me.

I realized I was about to throw up. If you can't read stories about throwing up, bail right now. If you can handle it, the story gets pretty funny. I stood up, headed quickly, but not running so as to create alarm, to the bathroom. I walked through the door and I realized I wasn't going to make it to the toilet. It was an absurdly long bathroom with the toilet at the end. So I did the only thing I can think of...I put my hands up to catch my throw-up.

For future reference, your hands aren't really capable of holding liquid. It basically hit my hands and then splattered back on my own face and shirt. I stumbled to the toilet by the second heave and threw up all over it. I'm not sure how I got so little actually inside the bowl. I sat back with wide eyes. I just stared for a few minutes at the scene before me.

Feeling much more sober and void of anything in my stomach, panic and adrenaline set in. What else was there to do? I started cleaning. I grabbed toilet paper and started sopping up the mess. I wiped down the floor and the seat. I couldn't tell if two minutes or twelve minutes had passed by, but everything looked clean except the wad of toilet paper I'd put in the toilet. Without thinking, I went to flush the toilet and it started filling up... and it didn't stop.

It was going to overflow. I think my heart stopped in that moment and with no time to come up with a better plan, I reached in, grabbed all the toilet paper, which was now covered in yuck, and held it up above the toilet so the water flushed. I was kneeling on the floor, holding a wet mess and I didn't know what to do. I looked over and noticed a small waste bin. I had no choice. I tossed the wet wad of toilet paper into the garbage.

At that point, I was just going through the motions. I'd stopped asking myself how awful this situation was. The floor and the toilet looked clean and the puke-soaked paper had been contained. I looked down at myself and saw that there was throw up all over me and in my hair so I did what any reasonable girl would do in this situation. I decided to take a shower.

I hopped in the shower, thinking I'll never get another date with this man. I mean, this poor guy must think I'm a crazy person. I'd spent so much time thinking I was better than him and suddenly there I was, cleaning throw up out of my hair.

Turns out, he did think I was crazy. I love my husband's version of this story. When you ask him, he'll tell you that when he heard me turn the shower on, he definitely thought I could be a psycho. He was actually worried that an insane person was in his apartment. He didn't have much time to dwell on this, though, because he remembered that he had done laundry that day and had taken all the towels out of his bathroom.

I cleaned up, turned the shower off and reached for a towel but of course, there wasn't one. I heard a very gentle knock on the door. "Are you alright?" He asked. I didn't say anything because really, what could I possibly say at that point? He quietly asked, "Do you need a towel?"

"Yes," I squeaked out in the most embarrassed, mousy voice adding, "And a t-shirt."

He opened the door just a crack and handed me a towel and one of his t-shirts. I came out of the bathroom, and my eyes were on the floor. I didn't know what to say. I was mortified. I had no words to explain that I really am a nice girl. Previously a crazy night to me would be drinking a Coke with caffeine after 7 p.m.!

"I'm so sorry. I'm so sorry." That's all I managed to say. And with no more words, he just let me lay down on the ugly couch, which now mocked me with its cozy puffy pillows. This man, who would one day become my husband, didn't say anything about my wet hair soaking through the microfiber. Instead, he gave me a blanket and said, "It's okay. Goodnight."

The next morning we talked for four hours. Amazingly, our relationship survived and grew even stronger. I think God allowed this embarrassing event to happen in order to knock me down a few pegs. I immediately stopped looking down my nose at my nerdy chemist and began pleading for him to give me another chance. I stopped thinking of him as this nice, funny guy who I could never really be with. I started to see him for the strong, forgiving man who was able to see through my façade. He gave me a chance when I certainly didn't deserve one.

We often joke about that night. We say that God had to knock me down a few rungs so I could see what a good thing I had right in front of me. Ultimately, I would love and trust this man so much that he would lead me to Catholicism.

I was confirmed in the Catholic Church at Easter Vigil in 2010 and we were married two months later. We have four, soon-to-be five, children which is quite incredible for a previously agnostic girl who thought she'd never tie herself down with marriage or kids. We still struggle with the scars of our sexual past and our lack of healthy marital examples to look up to. We have put Jesus in the center and we place our hope in Him even when we have no idea what the future holds!

Love in the Age of Social Media

Justine Rauch (E23/M24)

It was Thanksgiving. I was taking a break from writing some papers for one of my last college classes to share a recent blog post on Twitter. I had just recently started blogging and had no idea what I was into yet, but I was having fun settling into my little place on the internet. I hardly had any readers, and the ones that I did have were pretty much just my family members. I had recently gotten out of a relationship and I was starting to get a little frustrated with God. I remember asking to meet my future spouse that year, and hoping that when I did, I would recognize him. Or something.

Sometimes I would wonder if I had already met him. I'd go through most of the single guys I knew and rule them out one by one... you know, like in the chick flicks where she likes the popular guy who ends up being not right for her and then she ends up with the one who was her best friend all along... Actually, that's not too far off from what happened. But we'll get to that.

Anyways, one of my friends gave me a shout out on Twitter for a particular post I had written at the time. Her cousin (a guy) happened to find it and actually read it! He sent me a direct message on Twitter. The message is gone now, but it was something along the lines of "Hey, I'm Jackie's cousin and I just wanted to say I read your blog and I think it's really good. Keep up the good work!" Then he started following my feed.

Oh, a fan! Someone I had never met before read my blog and liked it. I must be dreaming. Who is this pioneer of fandom? His Twitter name had Joel in it... so I figured it was a safe assumption that was his name. He's kinda cute, but the picture is super tiny. *clicks link* Dayton, OH - I go to school in Ohio. How far is that from me? Oh, too far. We'd never meet. I'm going to follow him back. I made sure whenever I wrote another post, I linked it in my Twitter account, just in case he was still paying attention. A few weeks later I got the impression from his feed that he had a girlfriend, so I dropped it.

Two Years Later

I had graduated a couple months before and I was ready to pursue my passions and start a career. I wanted to travel around the country and teach people about healthy relationships, maybe even write a book. I was a hopeless romantic though I had somehow managed to graduate without the "ring by spring." I wanted to someday end up living in Denver or Colorado Springs. I had visited friends there a few times and it was the only place I had ever visited that made me think "Yeah, I could definitely see myself living here." However, an opportunity presented itself in Pennsylvania, so I followed the job there.

It was thrilling to venture off on my own and start my career as a chastity speaker, but I was six hours from the closest family member, which was a big change for me. I was starting to panic a little, especially after trying unsuccessfully to make friends with people in my neighborhood close to my age. I frequently visited my friends who were still in school, only about an hour and a half from where I had moved. I ached to feel connected and part of a community.

I started to go back through my list of good guy friends and look for the love of my life... because, well, maybe I had overlooked him like in the movies... maybe he had been there all along! I ended up in a relationship with a nice guy, but it wasn't a good fit. I kept trying to make it work, but I just had this feeling that it wasn't supposed to be.

I stuck it out anyway because I was scared. Scared that maybe this is just what relationships were like, that they needed a lot of work to mesh, and that it's okay that you have less and less in common, or you disagree on a lot of things, etc. Scared that maybe this was my last chance to find someone because I had so much trouble meeting anyone in my area, let alone anyone dateable.

I kept a giant framed poster of Pikes Peak in my kitchen. I used it to remind me of where I wanted to go, to remind me of the awesome beauty I found in the Colorado landscape, and to remind me that life was bigger than my little lonely apartment. I remember sitting on my kitchen counter, drinking coffee, looking at that poster, and posting this on Twitter, "I'm in the mood for Paris... or Colorado... I'm always in the mood for Colorado."

And then I remember jumping off the counter to tackle my pile of work when I received a response from Joel. I had completely forgotten that we were still following each other. He had recently moved to Denver himself and was curious if I was still around.

Who is this? Oh my! IT'S MY FAN! I forgot about him. Does he live in Colorado? Figures. I want to go there. I should probably respond.

We tweeted back and forth on occasion, but we were only friends on Twitter. Looking back, I used Twitter more that spring and summer than I had ever used it before or ever would since. Our interaction was predominantly quoting movies, but it was becoming more and more frequent. I started to refer to him as "my Twitter friend." And that's all it was... for the spring at least.

As the months passed, I started to feel more homesick and restless about where I was (figuratively and literally). As much as I tried to connect in my physical community, it became more and more of a struggle. With summer beginning, the school year was ending, and the local university Newman Center was cleared out and the last of my close friends had finally graduated and moved on. I was giving fewer presentations to youth groups and instead, working more behind the scenes, which was hard on my little extrovert heart.

I ended up spending more time watching television, Skyping my family, and browsing social media on my computer. And with that came more conversations with Joel. We added each other on Google Plus, Facebook, and Skype, joking that we were reaching higher levels of a "social media friendship." Tweets graduated to Facebook chat. The more we went back and forth, the easier it was to talk to him. It was hard to find something we didn't have in common. I started to catch myself leaving my computer open so I'd be able to see if he was online and wanted to chat, just in case I'd miss it. It wasn't a romantic interest, he was just slowly becoming a dear friend. He made me laugh (a lot) and I looked forward to hearing about his day. Our conversations came with ease and never seemed to end.

However, I was still trying to make it work in the relationship I was already a part of. We had different ways of communicating, and I remember thinking that it shouldn't be that hard. Although it took a couple of months to finally call it, I think there was a part of me that knew it wasn't supposed to be. We officially parted ways. In a very roundabout way, I think it was because of Joel. I told one of my girlfriends, "Even if nothing ever happened with my Twitter friend, or if we never even met in person, I feel like he just has some role to play in my life. Maybe it's just to show me how easy communication can be. I'd want to end up with someone I shared that with."

After a visit back home, it really hit me how much we had been talking. We were Facebook chatting for hours every night. My family was concerned that we hadn't met in person, and I don't blame them. I've heard plenty of stories (ok so mostly on the news) about people getting tricked or catfished or whatever the kids are calling it nowadays. I called Jackie because as the only person we knew in common (and who knew and cared about both of us), I trusted her input. Once I reassured my family with her approval, they were a little more at ease.

Eventually, I mustered the courage to ask if he wanted to talk on the phone. Putting myself out there like that was terrifying. I imagined myself as a turtle throwing a love note out of its shell and then quickly retreating back inside while waiting to be rejected. Waiting for his response felt like for-flipping-ever. I could see the little bubble showing that he typed something, then deleted it, typed something, then deleted it.

On August 25th, at 12:06 a.m., Joel called me. We talked for 4 1/2 hours that night. My face hurt from smiling and my stomach hurt from laughing. We talked again the next night for six hours, despite the two hour time difference. And it still seemed like we'd never run out of things to talk about.

Within a few days, we were officially dating. And I had never been happier! That September was one of the longest months of my life.

Joel and I had a blast chatting as much as we could on and off throughout the day. We'd break for driving home and dinner, then jump on the phone and talk for another few hours. I was completely smitten. I wanted to know anything and everything about this dear friend who was rapidly making himself a permanent placeholder in my heart. But it was still a tad embarrassing that we'd still never seen each other's faces outside of pictures posted online.

Within a week of becoming official, we scheduled our first Skype call. It was all I could think about all day. I did my hair, kept my makeup minimal, and wore a loose pink pinstripe button up. About an hour before Joel was scheduled to call, my nerves began to get the best of me. What are we doing? What am I doing? What if he is nothing like his picture? What if his voice doesn't match his face? What if he doesn't like me anymore? I started sweating and up went the curled hair. I needed to relax. I poured myself a glass of wine and tried to act casual.

Here's the thing: when I'm nervous, I mess with whatever is in my hands, in this case, the wine glass. It was a giant wine glass... that I overfilled. All of a sudden there was only a sip left and we're about a minute and a half out from the call. I'm all loosey goosey and blushing... from the wine and the nerves. I answered the call and we talked for a good 3 1/2 ish minutes without a hitch.

I looked away from the screen for a few seconds and heard a noise come from the other end and all of a sudden, Joel was gone. I heard movement, I could still see his apartment, but no Joel. Then his head popped up from behind the desk. The folding chair he was using spontaneously fell to pieces. He only had a desktop computer and no backup chairs in his little studio apartment. So, this is it, I thought. That was fun while it lasted. But Joel, just as excited about this opportunity as me, made the chivalrous sacrifice and offered to kneel in front of his computer long enough for us to finish the conversation. I couldn't believe he would offer to do that for me, instead of just ending the call and using the phone.

We talked for four more hours before I remembered he was KNEELING. He made no complaint, was still fully invested in our talk, told stories, asked questions, and was the same incredible man I was falling for over the phone.

Skype calls became our new regular. It wasn't long before he bought a ticket to visit me. We still had a couple of weeks to wait, so I spent my free time planning our itinerary and freaking out. It was a risk, inviting this man to come for the weekend, especially if it didn't go well. But how could it not go well? I still couldn't shake the feeling that he had a big role to play in my life, whether it be for this season or for the long term.

I'll never forget the night we first exchanged "I love you's", but I'll save just that little bit for just the two of us.

I'm not sure at what point exactly we knew, but it was definitely before Joel arrived. We hadn't talked at length about the long term, but I had an unmistakable peace in my prayer and in my heart that this was the man I was made to spend the rest of my life with. It was almost too good to be true... but not quite. ;)

On September 21st, I packed up my mixed tape and some Kung Pao beef for Joel's dinner and drove an hour to the airport to meet Joel, officially, in person, for the very first time.

I was going to wait in the parking lot, but I was too excited and looked for him at the outside pick up. He called and said he was looking for me. I panicked. How do I greet him? Do I hug him? Reach out for a handshake? A handshake? Why would I do that? To be funny maybe? Not funny. Don't do that. What if he's far away? Do I run to him? Walk? Wait for him to come to me? I'd better play it safe. Thinking on my feet, I played the super cool move of staying on the phone with him, at the same time ducking behind a pillar at the end of the pickup line to wait for him.

Just before I could hear his voice in person, I stepped out from behind the pillar and there he was, only a few yards away, walking towards me. Joel dropped his bags, enveloped me in a hug, and all I could think was, "This is the first time I am hugging the man who will be my husband."

I never wanted that weekend to end. We toured my work, sipped pumpkin spice lattes, strolled around my neighborhood, built a blanket fort, watched HGTV, and ate at my favorite Mexican restaurant. On his last day with me, we stopped at the mall (90's style) and took photo booth pictures. That was the first of what would unintentionally become one of our date traditions.

Before Joel made it back home I bought a ticket to go out and visit him... and the rest is history. That's the story of how we met on Twitter. Joel and I have been together almost six years, married for almost five, and have three kids and I could not be happier!

Be Bold - God Will Give You Courage

Courtney Tanis (E22/M23)

Today I often hear the term "relationship goals" being used among people, whether they are young or older in age. I really had no relationship goals when I was entering the dating stage of my life. While I was close with my mother in some areas, I never felt comfortable with the idea of discussing relationships with her. I had convinced myself that I would more than likely experiment with dating in my high school and college years without any concern for the future. In fact, most of my family, including myself, believed I would lead a single life in a large city somewhere working insane business hours once I "grew up." Little did I know, God had different plans for me.

It was the start of summer session and I was returning to campus from a quick visit home to see my parents. The drive was roughly six hours and I had time to listen to music or be alone with my thoughts. I had the window down, wind blowing through my hair, and I was quietly having a conversation with the Lord. I was reflecting on the last year. I had watched many of my friends actively date good guys. I had maybe gone on a few dates, however, nothing seemed to stick or become serious.

I remember telling God that if He wanted me to remain single and spend the rest of my days worshipping Him, that I was willing to accept that life. As I look back now, I am sure He was grinning knowing what moments were ahead for me.

The drive was exhausting, however, I wanted to stop by my friend Brian's off-campus apartment to say hi. As I drove up, I saw a man moving into the apartment complex. I can see him now, rolling the rear window down to his white Ford Bronco wearing a white tank undershirt and khaki shorts. I decided to be polite and friendly so I introduced myself. Nick was moving in and after our brief hello, we went up the same stairs and then off to our respective apartments.

Brian, being the social extrovert that he was, encouraged Nick to come over and hang with us. As the three of us sat around the living room, our conversations bounced from topic to topic, which included music. I was interested in the Dave Matthews Band and envious that Nick had been to several of their concerts, which unfortunately I had not done yet. Our time together soon came to an end and I was on my way back to my own place on campus.

I am not sure what it was, but I could not get Nick out of my head. There was something I enjoyed about him and the time we spent talking. I made it a point to mention to our mutual friend Brian that I found Nick to be interesting with hopes that it would lead to Nick approaching me. What I did not know at the time was that Nick is a social introvert.

A short time passed by and I was out with friends when I happened to see Nick with his fraternity brothers at a local favorite restaurant. While we shared similar friends, our lives really had not crossed until our recent introduction at the apartment complex. Again, I had hopes that Nick would make the first move and come talk to me. We made eye contact and came within close distance of each other several times. Nothing.

I could have just walked away feeling defeated that evening but instead, I decided to take a leap of faith. I approached Nick. I had no formal plan of how to start our conversation and felt a mixture of emotions at the idea of being rejected. However, something deep inside gave me that extra push to accept the outcome whether it was in my favor or not. Before I knew it, I boldly skipped the hello and told Nick that he was taking me out on a date!

I suggested he take me to see the Dave Matthews Band in August. Sure it was only late May but I wanted to spend more time with this guy and this is what I came up with. Amazingly, he said yes to my request!

If you ask Nick today to recall the moment, he says in jest that I bullied him into taking me out on a date. He will also acknowledge that he was surprised by my bold request. Later I found out that his mother had to ask his father out on their first date as well!

We dated for five years before getting married. We met at a young age and both wanted to finish college before making any further decisions. Following college, we decided to live together for at least a year. Based on the history of my parents, I felt living with a person was very different from loving a person. I knew I was in love with him, however, I still had fears about our relationship lasting.

It was during our time living together that we both started attending weekly Mass. Nick was raised Catholic, while I was raised

Baptist. We started having serious conversations about our future. I never felt completely myself in the Baptist church and was comfortable with the idea of converting, especially if we were to get married.

When Nick did propose, we both agreed to get married in the Catholic Church. We made adjustments to our living situation to prepare ourselves better for the sacrament of marriage. During our engagement, I participated in the RCIA program. I was fully welcomed into the Catholic Church Easter of 2003 and we were married a few months later in the month of June.

Twenty years later, I am grateful that I did not hold myself back. Not only did I gain a husband, I became a better version of myself as well. I started attending church, converted to Catholicism and learned how to pursue a life for God.

As we near our fifteenth wedding anniversary, I feel blessed each day to have him by my side whether it is a bad or good day. Our time together has not been perfect, we have had struggles. However, I see these challenges as just what God felt was necessary for us to grow as individuals and as husband and wife.

Best advice to Catholic singles, be bold. God has great plans for us and if it is His will then it will be done.

Some Enchanted Evening

Elizabeth Otte (E30/M30)

"Take delight in the Lord, and He will give you the desires
of your heart." - Psalm 37:4

These words from Psalm 37:4 were my guiding light when I worried if God would ever grant me the desire of my heart to find a holy Catholic man to share my life with in marriage. Many tears were shed while I waited and many more prayers were said in hopes for an answer. While I had to wait on God's timing, not mine; God prepared me to be happy with myself as single Elizabeth before I was ready to meet Kurt.

About three months before meeting Kurt, I was in my early twenties having never really had a steady boyfriend and I finally just reached the peace, confidence, and joy of being a daughter of God and my worries about meeting someone. When I least expected to meet someone, that's when life became interesting!

Kurt and I met at a New Year young adult retreat in 2005 called "Living Your Life with Purpose and Passion." The retreat was held at a seminary in Denver. The opening night was a social night; we were supposed to mix and mingle with other young adults that would be on the retreat. I wasn't at the social night for very long when BOOM, it happened!

You know that song "Some Enchanted Evening"[3] where the lyrics run something along the lines of "when you see a stranger across a crowded room," that was us! From across the room, we instantly recognized each other. Coming together, we smiled and said hello! There was an immediate familiarity and warmth felt between us but we truly didn't know each other's names! We couldn't remember where we had seen each other before.

After we introduced ourselves, we quickly started running through the young adult activities in our diocese that we might have run into each other. We realized we were on the same young adult retreat six months earlier held up in the mountains. We talked for a little while at the social night and then left for the evening.

The next day was the actual retreat. We just happened to sit near each other for the day. At the time, Kurt worked for a cell phone company. I happened to have a phone from a competing company. He said, "I really shouldn't consort with the enemy," but he asked for my number anyway! Though I felt giddy inside, I managed to gracefully stay calm and gave him my number.

Later Kurt would tell me that he did try to talk to me at that first retreat we went to but I had snubbed him. I vaguely remember going to lunch with him and about ten other adults and that I had been interested in getting the attention of another guy. I honestly don't remember him trying to talk to me but we think God gave us a second chance to meet six months later.

Kurt called me about a week after getting my phone number; we set up our first date for January 23rd. Our first date was amazing and nerve-racking all at the same time! He invited me to his house for dinner. I was super impressed with the steak dinner, salad, and brownies that he prepared. Oh, and I'll never forget his fully stocked spice cabinet. It wasn't a spice rack like mine; it was a whole cabinet full of spices! I figured this meant he knew how to cook more than ramen noodles, which was my level of cooking expertise. I remember thinking, if he knows how to cook, he knows how to take care of himself, which is one of the qualities I was looking for in a man.

After dinner, we drove down to the Cathedral for the young adult Sunday night Mass which was always said by Archbishop Chaput. What a gift it was to have our first date include the celebration of the Mass! After Mass came the most nerve-racking part of the date....dancing. I was very intimidated because Kurt competed in Ballroom Dancing during college.

The dancing was not like it is in the movies. It was not romantic at all because I was so horrible at it and he wasn't smiling. Years later he would tell me that guys have to concentrate so hard on leading... the timing of the music... not bumping into other partners... that sometimes you forget to smile! After dancing, we ended our first date. I didn't expect a call back because that was how most of my dates went. Sometimes, I wasn't interested in going out on a second date with some of the guys I met, but sometimes the ones I really wanted to see again, they never called either. With Kurt, I was hoping he would call me again.

As I am sure you have figured out, Kurt did call! We had a second date and a third date and the dates kept coming. Around six months after dating Kurt, I started to think if Kurt could be "The One."

I very much wanted to do the Lord's will in regards to my vocation so I called upon my favorite saint, St. Therese of the Child Jesus, for her help. I prayed a nine-day novena asking for St. Therese's intervention in asking God for a pink rose to be sent as a sign if Kurt was to be the one I would marry. St. Therese's prayer was powerful! Like many novenas that I had prayed with St. Therese, I would finish them and then just kind of forget about the novena.

On June 1, 2005, I was reading the newspaper before going to work. Down in the bottom corner of the page was a picture of a beautiful light pink rose and I was immediately reminded of the sign that I asked God to send me should Kurt be the one to marry. I had a deep sense of peace and joy on that day.

In October, Kurt proposed though not without some flexibility, seminarians in the background, and a little stumbling in the dark. Our date night started out with dinner at a local restaurant. At the restaurant, Kurt told me kind of last minute that he wanted to take me to the seminary chapel to show me some things he discovered on his recent tour with one of his classes. After dinner, we originally had plans to go to Theology on Tap which started at 7 p.m. I didn't quite understand why we would stop at the seminary when it would delay us getting to Theology on Tap but I went along with Kurt's plan.

We got to the seminary and the guard at the front desk said the seminary chapel was closed to the public. Kurt, unbeknownst to me at the time, started to panic a little. However, Kurt, being the great persuasive speaker that he is, managed to convince the guard to let us go to the chapel. We walked into the chapel and it was completely dark except for a few lit candles. There were a few seminarians praying around different areas of the church. We walked up to the front of the church and then to a side chapel, but as we kept walking around I noticed Kurt's hands getting clammier and sweatier.

We ended up at the back of the church in one of the side chapels where he finally found a light switch to turn some lights on. This particular side chapel had a beautiful statue of Jesus kneeling in the Garden of Gethsemane. At the statue, there is an angel ministering to Jesus and one of Jesus' hands is raised so that you can hold Jesus' hand while you pray. This is where Kurt got down on one knee and asked me to marry him! I cried tears of joy as I said "Yes!"

We shared a very small kiss at that time because of the seminarians praying in the church and then we quickly walked, what seemed like an eternity, through the building to get outside and hug and scream and be loud and joyful about what just happened in the chapel.

While his proposal was wonderful, it was all the more special because I had always dreamed of being proposed to in a place that had the presence of Jesus. I had never shared this with Kurt. It felt like God's providential hand had been with us through dating and in a special way with the proposal.

We got married in July of 2006 in my home parish with three priests present to say Mass. We were surrounded by family and friends. Kurt planned an amazing honeymoon trip to Hawaii to start our married life and eleven years later life is still really good!

We have been blessed with three wonderful children; two boys and a girl. One of the desires of Kurt's heart in finding a wife was finding someone who wanted to stay home and take care of the children. I love staying home and being there not only for our children but, also being there for Kurt. Kurt is proud of being a wonderful provider for his bride and his children.

I worried a lot that I would never meet someone but I never stopped praying. I prayed and asked family and friends to pray for me, as well. I wanted to find a strong Catholic man because I knew that would be a path to happiness, but most importantly, it would be a path for us toward heaven. I thought many times it would be better to be alone than to be with someone who would pull me down in my faith and/or my relationship with Jesus.

I held out for a Catholic man that loves God more than me and that has made all the difference. Kurt is such a Godly man that he truly makes marriage magnificent. Hold on for what God has stirred in your heart for your vocation to marriage; God is faithful! To close, I would like to share with you a favorite scripture verse that Kurt and I both love.

" 'For I know the plans I have for you,' declares the Lord, 'plans to prosper you and not to harm you, plans to give you hope and a future.' " Jeremiah 29:11

Head Over Heels for a Man in Uniform

Amy Thomas (E21/M22)
www.catholicpilgrim.net
Facebook: /amythomaspp
Instagram: @catholic_pilgrim79

The first time I met my husband was my first day of Air Force ROTC my junior year of college. I walked into a classroom and he was sitting at a desk. I instantly knew that he was the one for me. I know that sounds crazy, but seeing him was like the feeling of coming home. At that time, I was engaged to another man, Gary, but as soon as I saw Dustin sitting in that classroom, I knew my present relationship had to end. I had to break it off.

In many ways, I felt extremely guilty for breaking off my engagement with Gary. We had been together for three years and I felt obligated to stay with him. In bad form, I sent him a "Dear John" letter just as he was entering the Navy. It crushed him. He couldn't understand why I didn't want to be with him anymore. I tried explaining that we were just two very different people, but it was hard for him to understand. He is married now with three girls and I'm happy that he found someone more suited for him.

Dustin and I were friends first. We both secretly liked each other but were unable to say it out loud. It was good that we were friends first because we both were getting out of long-term relationships.

On the night of my 21st birthday, I went out with a couple of girlfriends and Dustin. With the help of a few margaritas, I professed my affection for him. It was such a relief to finally tell him that I liked him. After that night, we became a couple. We didn't have a first date or anything; we just *were*. Being in a relationship with Dustin was the most natural thing in the world to me.

During my teenage years, I had suffered at the hands of two abusive boyfriends. With those two guys, all I ever knew was pain, suffering, and the feeling of never being good enough. My self-esteem tanked and I struggled to believe that I was lovable and valuable. The guy I was engaged to before I met Dustin was a decent guy, but we were unequally yoked. Our trajectories in life were just too different. He was good to me, but we fought a lot and I knew deep down that a marriage to him would have been a constant struggle.

When I started dating Dustin, though, I experienced romantic love like I never knew existed. He was kind, patient, interesting, intelligent, and motivated to do good things with his life. He complimented me all the time. I struggled to hear his words of affirmation because of the damage inflicted by my two previous boyfriends. Thankfully, he has never stopped lifting me up by his words.

He was patient with me while I worked through the pain of the abusive boyfriends. I finally felt free to unpack all that hurt and I wanted to be emotionally healthy for Dustin. I knew that I wanted to marry him, but I was fearful of dragging all my baggage into a marriage. Dustin assured me that he would be there with me while I worked through it all. He really did heal a lot of hurts caused by other men.

Our senior year, we foolishly decided to move in together. We spent so much time together that we felt justified in living together before marriage. Our parents were less than pleased and my baby sister even tried to talk me out of it. I tried to explain my behavior away, telling her she'd feel the same way as me someday and blah, blah, blah. I gave a poor witness to my sister, which is something that I regret to this day. I see now that God was using my sister to prick my conscience, but I was unwilling to listen.

I thought my love for Dustin made it okay to go against God's plan for marriage. Consequently, I got pregnant out of wedlock my senior year of college, which was difficult. I had terrible morning sickness, which caused me to miss a lot of morning classes. I was scared because neither of us had any money. Also, being the pregnant lady on a college campus is like being a leper in some respects. You lose friends. Nobody wants to hang out with you because your big belly is kind of a reminder of what can happen to them if they don't behave. And, nobody wants a pregnant lady at a college party.

Dustin was extremely supportive, though, and always assured me of his love and commitment. Dustin and I now see the beauty in waiting to live together until marriage and I would encourage any couple to do this. We are an anomaly in that we stayed together because most couples that live together before marriage do not make it. It isn't a path I would recommend.

When Dustin and I started dating, he was Catholic and I was Protestant. Neither one of us were practicing our faith and I'd say it was stagnant, at best. It wasn't until we had our daughter that we really had to face the fact that we came from different faith backgrounds. It was probably what we fought about the most. Dustin wanted to baptize our daughter and I was adamantly against it. Baptism for Catholics and Protestants means very different things, but I didn't understand the Catholic understanding of it and, honestly, I didn't really want to hear it.

I had grown up believing that Catholics were some kind of weird cult. I had never done any research into Catholicism and mostly disliked it because of the beliefs of others around me. I'm also a pretty prideful person, so I didn't want to hear that I was wrong about anything. But God has a sense of humor, and I fell in love with a Catholic man.

In June of 2001, we welcomed our beautiful daughter, Rhianna, and two months after her birth we were married. We have two other earthly children--a daughter and a son. We also have ten saints in heaven that we look forward to meeting someday.

Over time, I finally started listening to Dustin when he defended the Catholic Faith and I found out that I was wrong about everything I believed about Catholicism. It was a very humbling experience. For the first time, I opened my ears and listened to him and very slowly I came to the truth of Catholicism. Dustin never once pressured me or asked me to convert. I came to it all on my own and in 2009, I converted to the Catholic Faith.

It is seriously one of the greatest joys of my life. I absolutely love being Catholic. I think my conversion helped Dustin, a cradle Catholic, to rediscover his faith, too. It's been a beautiful journey. Dustin and I have been married for sixteen years and our love for each other has only grown more beautiful and deep. We have had our share of trials to power through, but married life is that way. You won't make it through marriage without having to weather a few storms.

Praying For Metanoia

Elizabeth Watson (E29/M29)

My love story starts with prayer. Prayer has been a huge part of my life for as long as I can remember. I am so grateful to my parents for teaching me to pray. As I matured in my faith, I also matured in my prayer life. God always came through. I learned that God spoke to me in the silence. He spoke to me in nature. He spoke to me through people. God showed up: He never failed.

Then, as I watched my family and friends get married and start families, I started to get upset with God for taking His sweet time to give me these same gifts. Upset is putting it mildly. Jealousy boiled inside of me. I picked fights with family members and friends. Every wedding I attended required great strength. I felt happy for those getting married, but self-pity, anger, and sadness pierced my heart.

The summer before my 28th birthday, I realized my life needed an attitude adjustment. I needed what my college theology professor called metanoia: a change of heart. As I started seeking out ways to change my heart, I discovered Focus on the Family's Boundless podcast and Matthew Kelly's books and audiotapes. I posted this quote from Matthew Kelly in my apartment: "Our lives change when our habits change." I needed to be reminded constantly that I had to make a choice to change my anger and change my heart.

That summer I took a risk in being vulnerable: I asked some dear people in my life to pray specifically about my singleness and God's will for me. I welcomed my sister Erica into my struggle with anger about being single. We both were in a season of singleness and leaned on one another often in our struggles in life. I shared my heart with some of my closest friends. They started praying for me. During his Holy Hour, my great-uncle Adam started to pray for my sister and me to find husbands. I talked to my parish priest, Fr. Ken, about my anger and working out areas of my life that needed healing and forgiveness.

I realized I was carrying around some baggage that needed to be sorted out. My folks divorced while I was in college. Bitterness at how their relationship ended became a heavy burden to carry. I was especially angry with my dad, who had left the Catholic Church when I was in high school. Counsel from Fr. Ken helped me to realize I needed to let go. "It can either make you bitter or better," he told me. I decided it was time to choose better.

My aunt encouraged me to attend an Enneagram workshop that she taught. It opened my eyes to my personality and my anger. I started taking steps to be aware of my anger, process it, and grow from this powerful emotion. I started taking adult education classes at my church about spirituality and faith. This major interior housekeeping really helped me learn more about myself and made me more aware of God's presence in my life.

Then on my 28th birthday, I received an email from my uncle, a Catholic priest, wishing me a happy birthday. He wrote:

Elizabeth,

Happy 11th anniversary of your 17th birthday--the day that left an indelible scar on the national consciousness.

The good news is that now 28 years before today something tremendous happened. You were born. And that has made a big difference for the world today. To do a little modification of the responsorial psalm refrain for today: "The Lord takes delight in you." Never forget that.

Celebrate wisely. Remember: you have to give a good example, etc., blah, blah, etc. ... Further note: 28 is a crucial number; it usually means some big changes are in the offing. So, watch out this coming year--and don't be surprised that I didn't warn you!

The best to you all year,
Valerian

My heart smiled as I embraced the "warning." I wanted this to be the year that my life and my heart would change. A scripture verse that found me in my daily reading was Psalm 37:4: "Delight yourself in the Lord and He will give you the desires of your heart." I wanted to be free from the cloud of unhappiness that I kept clinging to. I kept seeing my singleness as a curse rather than a blessing. I kept defining myself by what I saw as lacking in my life, rather than what I possessed. Homilies at church brought me to tears as Fr. Ken preached that God's will for our lives was to be a light for Him in our little part of the world.

Encouraged by the messages I was getting from the people around me, what I was listening to and reading, and my daily prayer, I started using my singleness as a way to bless others by giving the gift of time and talent. I began working toward my Masters in Education. I worked on changing my teaching style to be more student-centered. I tried different approaches to coaching extracurricular activities and celebrated my students in those activities. I went camping with friends on weekends. I offered to babysit for my married-with-kids friends. I found ways to be more involved in my church through classes and volunteering.

I changed my prayer from "God, please give me a husband and family," to "God, I surrender my desire for a husband and family to You. Please help me find my happiness in You." This prayer took strength every day to turn over what I wanted most in my life to God. I struggled. I found my way to the confessional. The sacrament of reconciliation helped me be honest in my failings and struggles. I learned that a good confession has nothing to do with making excuses for my sins. It has everything to do with owning up to my shortcomings and accepting God's grace and forgiveness as a gift.

One day while praying, this thought came to me. I felt an unusual, but very real tap on the shoulder of my heart: you would make a good wife to a man who wears a uniform. It scared me because I had friends who had dads and husbands in the military, and I saw the sacrifices that they made as a family. I shared this new insight with Erica, my sister. We laughed a little about my revelation, but I added it to my prayer life.

I started to pray for a man in uniform--where ever he might be. I prayed for his safety, his daily activities, his faith life, whatever needs he might have. I was praying for a man I did not know. That took faith. I offered this prayer over to God to do whatever He wanted and continued to work at my relationship with trusting Him. It was not easy. I wanted to give up. I still struggled with anger. Jealousy would bite me as I watched families play at the park and couples hold hands in the shopping mall. I don't have words to adequately describe the deep ache I felt inside of me. I realized I was battling with the Devil in my journey toward God. And the thing was, they both wanted me: God and the Devil. But what I read in Matthew Kelly's books repeatedly is that "Every journey toward something is a journey away from something."⁴ I needed to be focused and firm in my journey toward God.

However, even with my awareness of its tendency to become an idol in my life, I still wanted to hold onto that desire for a husband and family. I wanted to be angry that I wasn't living the life that I saw my friends having. I struggled, prayed, cried, prayed some more, and argued with God. But my arguments went from "God, I'm so mad at You for keeping me single," to "God, please take my anger, take my hurt, and help me to know what Your will is for me, right here, right now in all of this."

As Christmas approached, I felt happier and more content than I had been in a long time. I was choosing God, even when it wasn't easy. I had been on a couple of dates with different guys, but nothing that became serious. I had discerned religious life when I was in college and that thought came back to me during this time too.

After school one day, I went to visit with a colleague of mine about a student. When I walked into her office, Colleen asked me to close the door because she had something personal to ask me. I was a bit rattled because I wondered what the guidance counselor would have to talk to me about that was personal.

"Are you dating anyone?" she asked as I sat down. I can't remember if I laughed or sighed.

"No, I'm not, why?" Shocked that this was her personal question, I couldn't really imagine where this was going.

"Well, there is this guy and I told him about you, and he's been asking about you..."

My mind couldn't believe that a single guy outside my school might know that I existed.

"...he's a big teddy bear...wants to settle down...police officer..."

My mind picked up on details and my heart pounded. I had still been praying for a mysterious man in a uniform, for his well-being, his safety, his joys, his challenges.

"He's free tomorrow. Would you be up for meeting him?" she asked. I could see the excitement in her eyes as she waited for my answer. Being set up in the past never went well for me, but I felt compelled to take this risk.

"Well," I paused gathering my courage. "Sure, why not?" I replied, catching a bit of her excitement. I told myself not to put too much pressure on this arranged meeting. It was hard. As a single person, meeting someone often preoccupied my time. Everywhere I went, I could potentially meet someone from the gym, to the grocery store.

I left our conversation a bit foggy. I had been planning on attending the reconciliation service at our parish that night. Since Uncle Adam had started praying for my sister Erica and me, she had met a wonderful man. After one conversation, she felt confident she was going to marry him. I rejoiced for her but fought that familiar feeling of jealousy continually. It didn't seem fair that my younger sister was dating a wonderful man and I was still single. I headed to church to admit to God where I was failing: that my anger and jealousy were out of control again and I needed His help. Reconciliation continued to offer a sense of peace to me and helped me to see that I am not strong enough to do this life thing on my own. I knew that before I met this guy, I needed my heart to be reconciled with God.

As I prepared to meet the mystery guy the next day, I offered God all my fears and insecurities. I felt excited, but I had no idea if this meeting would go anywhere beyond that. Near 3:45 in the afternoon, a tall, handsome, smiley man knocked on the door, walked into my classroom, and introduced himself.

"My name's Travis," he said. We fell into conversation easily about how his day off was going, his family, my family, his plans for Christmas, working out, hobbies and what we were reading. I was a teacher after all, and this was an important detail! I invited him to join my friends and me for game night. He gave me his card, and I gave him my phone number. Our conversation was pleasant, and I could hardly believe we talked for nearly an hour. He walked me to my car. As I drove home, thoughts about him raced through my mind. Travis was really nice. I knew I wanted to see him again and I hoped he felt the same way. I sent him a text, thanking him for stopping by my classroom. He texted back! Over the Christmas break, we visited some more and realized that we had more to talk about. My excitement over meeting someone continued to grow. I spent a lot of time asking God to help me know what to do with this guy.

As December turned into January, we went on walks, watched football, and shared meals together. Our conversations turned into a friendship. I spent afternoons thinking about our conversations and looking forward to when we would get to spend time together. We started talking about our faith lives. Initially, Travis shared that his faith was a private matter, but his priorities in life were God, family, then friends. I had never met a man who was so easy to talk to and made me feel so comfortable. His sense of humor, honesty, and sense of service attracted me to him. His genuine interest in me as a person felt foreign. I had several female friends, but now this man noticed me and pursued me. One night when Travis came over to my apartment to visit, he noticed that the cupboard doors were squeaky. "Would you like me to fix the squeak in those doors?" he offered. I hadn't even noticed they were squeaky. He took out the trash in the apartment before he left to go home. Having someone who noticed areas of my life that needed attention made me feel secure and cared for.

Our friendship and time that we defined as "hanging out" officially became a dating relationship. We were both happy about this arrangement and so many people around us were enthusiastic about it too. His boss talked to me about doing ride-alongs with Travis so I would know what sort of work he had to do as a police officer. It was very eye-opening. I started to wonder if this was the man I had been praying for.

Two months after we met, we just finished a ride-along and Travis was dropping me off for the night. I felt I needed to share my heart with Travis about what I needed in a relationship. So there in the police vehicle, I told Travis I was looking for a relationship that would lead to marriage. I wanted to know what direction he thought our relationship was going. Were we just dating to date? If that was the case, I wanted to be respectful of one another and our time and break up now. I didn't want us to be placeholders in one another's lives. But if he wanted to explore if our relationship could be headed toward marriage, then we could be more intentional about getting to know each other. I didn't really know what to expect after telling him all this. He told me he didn't want to lose me. We chose the latter. We chose prayer. In my prayer, I asked God what He wanted me to do with this relationship. In the quiet of my heart, the response I got was, "Love Travis." To be very honest, that was a very scary response after only two months. I also felt this wasn't just a romantic love. It was also God's love through me.

We got our churches involved in our relationship. Travis attended a Baptist church and came from an ELCA Lutheran background. I went to the Catholic Church and had been Catholic all my life. I knew that this could be one of the biggest obstacles in our relationship. We both knew that we needed to understand our faith traditions as part of digging deeper. Our pastors, Pastor Aron and Fr. Ken, agreed to meet with us on a weekly basis to help us discern marriage and explore each other's churches. One of the most memorable conversations had to do with service. Pastor Aron told us that the goal of marriage is to be falling over one another to serve each other. Acts of service is Travis' primary love language and my secondary. It totally clicked for us at that moment. If marriage was what we were called to, service would be a huge part of our lives.

In our meetings with Fr. Ken, we were learning more about the Catholic Church. We knew if we married we wanted to be united in what church we were going to go to. Travis felt that it was important for kids to see parents going to church together. Later we learned that about the time we were having this conversation, Fr. Ken expressed to the parish secretary after we left one of our meetings, "Those two should just get married already!"

We got to know our families. We talked about our pasts; we talked about our goals and dreams, our fears and failures Thank you, Matthew Kelly, for your book *The Seven Levels of Intimacy*[5] and Dr. Gary Chapman for your book *The Five Love Languages*.[6] These provided such good material for us go through. We took road trips. Being in a car together gave us time to play games, to listen to music, to tell stories, to talk about life experiences and to be silly.

We chose each other and marriage. Our conversation that fall went something like this:

Travis stated, " I'm going to marry you, Elizabeth."

I responded, "Really?! When you ask me, I will say yes."

Loving Travis proved to be an incredible test. When the Boston Marathon bombing happened, I shared with him how scared his job made me feel when crazy things like this happen in the world. Trusting in God that it would be okay and learning how to be supportive of his job made me grow and remember my prayer that God gave me about the man in uniform.

On February 1, a little over a year after we met, Travis planned a date night of dancing. He's not incredibly fond of dancing, but we were practicing for my sister's wedding. We practiced two-step, polka, waltzing, more two-step, and then Travis put on one of our favorite slow songs, "When You Say Nothing At All" by Allison Kraus.[7] While we were dancing, he asked me to close my eyes.

I figured he was up to something silly because Travis is the king of doing something silly to make me laugh. But when he asked me to open my eyes, he was down on one knee and asked me to marry him. He jokes that then I did the chicken dance, flapping my arms as I said yes. I was going to spend the rest of my life with an incredible man! That night my heart was filled was so much love for Travis and gratitude to God for bringing us together.

As we moved forward into being an engaged couple, Travis ultimately chose to join the Catholic Church. His choice to become Catholic blessed me so much as I watched him grow in his faith and tackle questions. I also grew with him as we learned more about the Catholic faith together and how we wanted to live out our faith in our home as a married couple.

We wanted our wedding planning to be simple. We knew it would be easy to be distracted by the wedding industry, so we were intentional about prayer. We planned a wedding for six months away in August. We read a book called *Before You Plan You Wedding... Plan Your Marriage* by Dr. Greg and Erin Smalley.[8] This really helped us keep the focus on God's gift of marriage to us and the gift of ourselves to one another and not all the million and one details the wedding industry sells. We planned our wedding Mass to reflect our gratitude for God's faithfulness in bringing us together. At our wedding, my sister Erica shared in her toast about my prayer for a man in uniform. It gave us all a good laugh. Sharing this part of our story was a testament to God's faithfulness and His beautiful way of crafting our lives together.

As I talked with Travis about submitting our story for this book, I asked what he thought I should share. One of the things we discussed was faith. He said while he was actively going to church, he was at a point in his life of searching and our relationship helped him to deepen his relationship with God. He said I challenged him.

Our relationship isn't perfect. We have worked through a lot of areas from discovering personality qualities (we highly recommend the Enneagram) to learning to be honest, to areas of temptation. Our different faith traditions gave us many topics to talk about when it came to faith, spirituality, and religion. We involved our pastors as we navigated the waters of marriage with different faith tradition backgrounds, as well as coming from families of divorce. Both pastors were excellent in helping us better understand each other.

We also talked about the idea of "the one" and "soulmate." We both believe that while these ideas are perpetuated by our culture and Hollywood, they aren't real. We ultimately choose to love a person and become "the one" for each other through God's grace. And in marriage, the gift of sanctifying grace given to us in the sacrament of marriage helps to strengthen us in our vocation to love.

Travis' decision to join the Catholic Church challenges me to grow in my faith. He does a terrific job being the faith leader in our family. As we reflected on our journey to becoming a married couple, we realized that details and events seemed to come together rather seamlessly. We didn't have to manipulate, plan, or jump through a bunch of obstacles. Things fell into place and we felt a sincere sense of peace. This is not to say that what we had to experience was always easy, but generally speaking, the process of going through the experience had a sense of ease. We continue some of the practices we started when we were dating. We are always reading a spiritual book, whether together or separate. We read the Sunday Gospel together during the week to prepare for Sunday Mass. We do a weekly devotional together. We take time to pray together every day. These habits help us to keep dating one another. Most of the time it's a lot of fun. Other times we experience growing pains. But it keeps us in constant communication and puts God in the center of our lives.

My encouragement to you, dear reader, is to remember God is faithful. God is in control. God has a sense of humor. God loves you. God desires you. God desires for you to desire Him above all else. God wants you to know yourself and for what purpose He created you. God doesn't want you to be miserable in the wrong relationship or a relationship that is hurtful. I can't promise you that God has marriage in your story. I can promise that God has His unfailing love in your story since the beginning of time. Seek Him in all things. I promise that He will guide you every step of the way through a sense of peace in the quiet of your heart and in prayer.

Mozart in The Dating Fast Jungle

Christine (Maher) Clancy (E29/M29)

Discernment and vocation. Two words that can incite a wide variety of emotions in the heart of a practicing Catholic. Growing up attending Catholic school we were taught to discern our vocation. Where might God be calling us?

"Marriage is not a universal calling," one priest would frequently announce from the pulpit. "Many are called to the married life, but some are called to the priesthood or religious life." Those kinds of comments always left me with a knot in the pit of my stomach. We are called to follow God down whatever path He has chosen for us, but what if I didn't like where He was leading?

In the latter half of my twenties, as an unmarried practicing Catholic, I began to spend a lot of time reflecting on my vocation. Did God want me to remain single? Enter a religious order? Get married? These questions left me paralyzed by fear and confusion. I joined several online dating sites, rationalizing that if I could find the right man, I could forget about those questions of joining a religious order. In my limited view of discernment, meeting a man would be a sure sign I was called to marriage.

Online dating can be wonderful because at least on the surface, the intentions are very clear. In theory, men and women join these sites because they are looking for romance. Online dating helps to lessen the ambiguity of male and female relationships. There is likely to be less confusion or getting stuck in the "friend zone." Many of these websites use complex formulas to try and match clients with someone compatible.

The downside of online dating is that it is almost too personal. It offers a window into someone else's life, their interests, values, and career. Whenever I would start messaging a potential match, I started to feel like I really knew the person, often without having met him in real life or even getting his phone number. Every man I dated could be "the one" based on my self-imposed checklist.

- Did he seem interested in me?
- Was he about my age?
- Church-going?
- College educated?

It must be a sign! He is the man I am *supposed* to marry. I often jumped to these conclusions too early in a relationship. I would give too much of myself, too quickly. Ultimately the relationship would crash and burn.

After a few rounds of failed relationships, my fears heightened, and I continued to wonder if maybe I should discern a religious order. I felt such a profound pressure to figure out my life.

The devil had his way with me, through recurring thoughts: "There aren't enough good men out there. No one will want me. I am too tall/overweight/loud etc. to find a man. Clearly, since I am *still* single, and a teacher, I am *supposed* to consider religious life. After all, many sisters are teachers. Numbers are down in religious communities. They could use more people. It's the *"right,"* thing to do."

Here's the thing. The Lord doesn't work that way. God doesn't call us down a path that feels out of sync because of a forced sense of obligation. Yes, we have a duty to discern but, His call should ultimately bring us peace. I'm not talking about some sort of blissful, follow your passions type of peace that is void of challenge and suffering. I'm talking about contentment, a subtle confidence of being on the right path despite imperfections, brokenness, and fear.

After years of anxious thoughts and misguided relationships, I slowly started to let God work His way into my heart. Prayer helped me to reconcile my feelings of inadequacy and anxiety. I told God I would resign myself to His will, whatever that may be, even though I was so terrified that I wouldn't like the answer. I started going to Adoration more regularly, stopping by a chapel on my way home from work. I began attending young adult Catholic events and even signed up for a weekend discernment retreat.

This particular discernment retreat was not a "Come and See" weekend for a specific religious order. Rather, it was a co-ed retreat meant for young adults to reflect on the discernment of all vocations. During the retreat, I started to think about the pull in my heart to seek a spiritual director. It had been on my mind for many years to find someone, ideally a priest or religious person, to offer guidance about my vocation but fear had always gotten in the way. I'm embarrassed to admit that I was afraid a priest or sister would put pressure on me to discern a religious order, even though deep down that didn't feel right. At that retreat, I met a priest named Fr. Zaleski who agreed to see me for spiritual direction.

During our first spiritual direction session, Fr. Zaleski asked me many questions about my life, my family, career, spiritual life, outside interests. I began to tell him all about my frustrations with dating and with wanting to figure out my life's purpose. I expressed the fear that I was somehow offending God by not seriously discerning religious life – that maybe there were more concrete steps I should be taking. This is another way the devil can weasel his way into our hearts and make us feel inadequate by making us feel we aren't *"doing enough."*

I asked father if he thought I should discern religious life. "Hm. I don't think so." In fact, Fr. Zaleski wisely felt I should take a break from any form of discernment. Rather than asking me to discern *more*, he was asking me to discern *less*. He even recommended a dating fast. This means I would make a commitment to avoid pursuing any romantic relationships with men for the time being. His advice filled me with profound relief. I had a chance to not obsess about my future and just accept this stage in my life.

I left our first meeting content with putting discernment aside, but I still had some questions. How exactly does a dating fast work? How long should the dating fast last? Doing some research online, I bought a book called *The Dating Fast: 40 Days to Reclaim Your Heart, Body, and Soul*,[9] by Katherine Becker. It was a simple yet beautiful book full of daily reflections, journal prompts, and actionable steps to take to embrace single life in the present while preparing for the future. I highly recommend it to anyone who senses they need a break from dating.

While I was working through the daily exercises in *The Dating Fast*,[10] I ignored my online dating account, refusing to log in. It wasn't too hard since it was the Christmas season which provided distractions in the form of decorating, baking and buying presents. I had already decided not to renew my account when my subscription was set to expire in early January. However, while an account sits idle if another person is really interested they can send a message that goes straight to your email inbox.

On New Year's Eve 2016 I received an email titled, "Pat wants to meet you." The email stopped me in my tracks. His profile was intriguing, and we seemed compatible. Could I be looking at my future husband?

After the New Year, Pat and I traded messages back and forth about our shared career in teaching, our love of traveling, and family for about a week. Then, I sent Pat my cell phone number – my account was going to expire in three days, and I wanted to keep the conversation alive. The whole time we were text messaging, I thought about my dating fast. Was it okay to talk to a man during this time? Was I getting myself carried away as I had done in the past? The dating fast had only lasted a little over a month. Concerns and fears lingered, but I chose to get to know Pat. I could sense he was a good man.

Eventually, Pat asked me out on a date choosing a location he had been curious about, but never wanted to visit alone: the Philadelphia Orchestra. While reading my dating profile, Pat saw that I played the clarinet in my spare time and enjoyed the Amazon series *Mozart In the Jungle*. It seemed like a natural first date choice. Prior to the concert, we enjoyed a drink in the lobby, and within the first thirty minutes, we broke almost every rule of first date conversations. Politics, religion, and money issues came up. I even admitted to him that I had been on a break from dating and that I had broken my fast for his invitation. We felt very comfortable with each other.

In the next few weeks, I met with Fr. Zaleski for spiritual direction and admitted that my dating fast had only lasted for a little over a month and I was seeing someone. "Is it ok to break my fast?" I asked.

"Christine. You're an adult. You have the ability to make your own decisions. You know what is best." He was encouraging of my new relationship. Father wasn't telling me what to do, nor was he making my decisions for me. He provided a much-needed source of wisdom and guidance, which is the essence of spiritual direction. He affirmed my decisions and encouraged me to *trust myself.*

The brief dating fast caused me to recalibrate my expectations and my approach to dating. With Pat, I was completely upfront about my values and my identity as a practicing Catholic. In the past, I tried to minimize the role of God in my life, not wanting to sound like a holy roller. My expectations were also more realistic. If this relationship was meant to last, great! If not, I still had a great career as a teacher, a loving family, and a circle of supportive friends. I didn't fall too hard and too fast. My identity didn't ride on the relationship; rather my identity was rooted in Christ.

As our relationship unfolded, I wish I could say that I was 100% confident and ready to embrace love, but that would be a lie. The experiences of past failed relationships weighed on my heart. I didn't want to fall in love too fast and get my heart broken or worse, break his heart. My spiritual director was a wonderful guide through this time. Additionally, I sought the assistance of a counselor who didn't share my faith but who was supportive of my views.

The combination of spiritual direction, prayer, and counseling was extremely transformative. Whatever stage in life you find yourself, consider seeking a spiritual director and/or counseling. It can be difficult to find someone, but with prayer you will connect with the right person. Receiving the sacraments and spending time in Adoration is also very powerful.

Eventually, I was able to get out of my own head, set my anxieties aside and fully embrace my relationship with Pat. In July 2017 after seven months of dating, Pat proposed on the Falls bridge in Philadelphia, a favorite spot of mine since childhood. The next day we surprised our family and friends with the news of our engagement at my 30th birthday party. We chose to get married Memorial Day weekend. It is still hard to believe how dramatically my life has changed from that discernment retreat in November 2016 to now.

If you feel called to date, don't be afraid to put yourself out there online. Choose one of the more reputable sites. While I know a couple of people who have met on the free apps, the paid sites are worth the investment. You are more likely to meet people who are looking for a relationship and not a casual hook-up. I liked the Catholic dating site I tried but didn't meet anyone. The pool of available men in my area was relatively small.

eHarmony.com proved to be the best choice for me. It was a significant financial commitment, but I found many men who seemed serious about dating. The questionnaire is also extremely in-depth and asks faith-based questions to connect you with like-minded individuals. It is 100% possible to find someone who shares your Catholic faith on a secular dating site.

I think about the title of the show, Mozart in the Jungle and my experiences that led up to meeting Pat. Being a single person can be challenging. I have never traveled to a jungle, but I can imagine dense humidity, insect bites, and hiking through overgrown trails. It is probably pretty difficult to navigate, just like discernment. I can also picture lush greenery, scenic waterfalls, blue skies, and rafting down a river. Spiritual direction, counseling, and prayer, like peaceful experiences in nature, can feel like a welcome respite to the unpredictability of the single life.

I recently heard a piece of music by Mozart called "Dona Nobis Pacem,"[11] which means "Grant us Peace." My prayer for anyone who is single and discerning a vocation is to recognize that God indeed grants peace in these times even when it is challenging. If you are single and still searching, take heart.

Trust yourself and trust God. He will guide you in the right direction.

Love on the Nun Run

Jenny Bales (E22/M23)

The summer just after graduation, I was working at my father's company, sitting in a miserable cubicle all day, biding my time until student teaching that fall. Since I hadn't found my future husband during my college years, it made sense to start discerning religious life. I'm a logical person, after all. I read through all of the post-cards and pamphlets from religious communities that kept coming through the mail and figured after my student teaching stint, I would visit a few convents and sort through those options just like I had sorted through college options five years before.

The highlight of my summer was going to be speaking at my college campus ministry's summer retreat for students in late July. All of the speakers attended a speaker retreat a few weeks before the main retreat to give us a chance to compare notes, get feedback on our talks, and attempt to present a cohesive message to the retreatants.

The first event of that speaker retreat was daily Mass, and after Mass, several of the speakers gathered on the porch of the church to chat. I told a friend that I was really looking forward to his talk on discernment, as I was actively discerning religious life. The guy giving the closing talk asked me if I had heard about the Nun Run. I had not.

He took me to the student center and explained that he was helping our campus minister plan a discernment trip for young women to visit various convents at the end of the summer. He was handling the logistics of travel and lodging for the women and encouraged me to consider going. I took the handout he gave me and wondered how I could pitch this to my parents without freaking them out.

Before that chat on the porch, I had never been in a conversation with this guy. I honestly had avoided getting to know him previously, because he seemed like an overly zealous convert, a little conceited, and a silly flirt. Over the weekend, though, I learned that he, too, was discerning religious life. He had spent a week at a monastery working on his talk for the main retreat, and I was intrigued.

When I went back to my cubicle job, we began emailing about our discernment.

In prayer a few days before the student retreat, I had this crazy thought that I was pretty certain came from God: "You are supposed to be friends with this guy; keep him in your life." Okay then.

At the retreat, we didn't talk that much, because we had a small group and speaker roles. At one point, we were spreading out blankets on the floor to claim space for our small group, and I saw him lying on the floor. I walked over and sat on him, saying something about it being a lumpy blanket, when he declared, "What is this feather that has alighted upon me?!" In retrospect, we were flirting, but I still thought nothing of it.

For the rest of the summer, we emailed constantly. Those emails are full of silly stories and back-and-forth banter. I saved every one. We had fun sharing about our mundane days, and I was so grateful that he brightened up my cubicle with his messages. I signed up for the Nun Run, and he made the arrangements for the group to visit nine convents in seven days.

Because of the Nun Run trip, I had to move back into my apartment almost two weeks before most of the students would be returning. He agreed to help me unload my things two days before the trip since very few of my other friends were around yet. We met at my apartment and went to an evening Sunday Mass before unloading. Again in retrospect, I guess that was our first sort-of date?

The next evening a group of students from the Catholic center was meeting for miniature golf, and we both went along. Everyone went for ice cream afterward and then went home. But, we were having so much fun that we decided to go for coffee next. Our discussions ranged all over the place that night.

After a while, a group of ladies going on the Nun Run along with our campus minister happened to come into the coffee shop. They came over to say hi, and we invited them to join us. I remember that we really had to talk them into sitting with us, because they thought we were on a date, which we weren't, of course! Eventually, they left, and we closed down the shop and moved to the deck outside. I remember when we both decided we would stop checking our watches (no cell phones back then) and then when we finally felt too tired to talk, it was four or five in the morning.

He had planned to cook a farewell dinner for me the next evening, before I went on the Nun Run, but he got called into work and had to cancel. I didn't see him again before the trip, but he left me a note.

When I arrived the morning of the departure, the girls who were already there delivered his note to me. I thanked them and didn't really notice their giggles because I thought he had written every one of us a note. But when I got to the van, they were reading aloud the one note he had written to the whole group and left with the gigantic paper chain rosary he put across the hood of the van. He promised prayers for all of us on our journey, but I was apparently the only one who got an individual note.

Thus, inevitably, that first morning of our drive while most of the van was asleep, and I was navigating for the driver, she turned to me and asked, "So, are you and [that guy] dating?" "NO!" I responded vehemently, shocked she would think such a thing! And her next question was the best gift I have ever received. She said, "Are you open to dating him?" At that moment, I didn't know and told her so, but I pondered that question for the rest of the day.

The next day we were staying with some Franciscan sisters, and several of them were sharing their vocation stories. I can still remember where I sat taking notes in my journal. One sister talked about how her parents had such a strong and holy marriage that it made her want a strong vocation too, and my mind wandered back to that question...

Are you open to dating? Right now, no, not really. Why not? Well, logically, I want to be holy, and it seems it would be a faster road to holiness to have designated times for prayer and service while living in a religious community. Why not dating and marriage? Well, marriage is hard. Men are super confusing. And there's another person's faults to deal with and no one telling you when and how to pray and work for the Lord.

Just then, another sister was talking about the challenges of living in community with several dozen other women and comparing those relationship challenges to married life. My mind took off, and I began writing furiously. I remember friends around me giving me strange looks like they wanted to ask what I heard that warranted writing that much that quickly.

Married life can be holy, too? Right! That's the point. And it's hard work because you have to do it without anyone telling you how. Well, I love a challenge. In fact, isn't doing the harder thing often the better thing? Maybe I need to be open to both marriage and being a sister then and not be closed to either. Oh. OH! Yikes!

When I spoke to my campus minister that evening, in confidence, I shared these thoughts. As the days went on, I felt like I didn't really belong with these women discerning religious life. More and more I heard nudges to consider marriage as a holy possibility, and I was asking God to make it obvious.

Near the end of our trip, we were visiting the Nashville Dominicans and had one more stop to visit some of Mother Angelica's sisters. We learned then that we were going to appear on EWTN; our campus minister had kept it a secret so that it wouldn't distract from the rest of our trip. One of my friends (who had been at that coffee shop a week prior) suggested someone call that guy who arranged for the trip and share our exciting news; he didn't even know!

Back then, we had to plug the cell phone into the van to make a call, and since I knew his phone number, the two of us went out to the van. He didn't answer, and we left a giddy message. But that friend delivered another nudge. She reminded me of the time earlier in the year when she complimented me on my organization skills, and I responded how difficult it was going to be for me to find a guy to marry that appreciated orderliness as much as me. She picked up the binder we had been using all week that was full of printed maps, schedules, timed rest stops, and a minute-by-minute itinerary for our seven-day trip that this guy had prepared for us. And she smiled. And I knew. I was supposed to marry him.

I came home from the Nun Run and told him I felt called to marriage. He finally cooked me dinner. We dated a bit. Nobody was surprised except for us. We went on a road trip together to the wedding of the young man who had given the very discernment talk that started our first conversation. On the long drive, inevitably, we both started talking about how we wanted our weddings to be. At one point, one of us said, "We are really talking about *our* wedding, aren't we?" We still banter about which of us said that.

At that point, we decided we needed to talk to our pastor. We weren't officially engaged, but we knew we wanted (and that we were supposed) to be married. We were thinking about a wedding within a few months. Our beloved and wise priest, now a bishop, told us he wanted us to wait a year. He explained that we had only been dating two months and needed to go through the seasons of a whole year together before he would agree to marry us. We conceded, were engaged a month later, and were married nineteen years ago this fall.

I am thankful that we were both so open to religious vocations because it helped us feel more certain when we finally felt the call to married life. We didn't choose each other out of desperation, and even though it was challenging, I'm glad we waited a full year before we got married!

Love In High Heels

Lise G. Goertz (E22/M22)
www.tamingtheworld.wordpress.com

Before I met my husband, I had been engaged to another man for two years. He called himself Catholic, although unlike his parents, he didn't always go to Mass. We spent a lot of weekends up at his family's cabin, often with other friends, so I know we both weren't going to Mass on those weekends. After we unexpectedly broke up, I was ready to have some fun in dating and not be so serious!

I went on a string of dates for a couple of months meeting new people and enjoying the fact that if I didn't feel a connection, I wasn't required to see them again. However, there were two things that were missing that I really wanted in the men I was dating: I wanted to date someone taller than me and someone who was at least Christian, if not Catholic.

My last two boyfriends were both shorter than me by a few inches, and it was a problem....for them. I wanted to go dancing with someone where I could wear high heels (I had some crazy shoes back in the day!) and still feel beautiful instead of being shamed. I was never one of those girls that hunched over to hide my height. I was used to towering over everyone! At 5'11", this often caused conflict with shorter guys. The average man's height is 5'10" so with my fancy shoes on, 6'3" was out of the question!

The other big problem was that none of the men I dated were Christians. Despite being a cradle Catholic myself, I wanted someone on the same religious wavelength as me, and if that was with another denomination, I could live with that. Dating agnostics and flat-out atheists cut out a huge portion of my life. My faith was really important to me, so I didn't like boxing that part of me up and leaving it on a shelf. It felt like my faith was off limits to talk about. It wasn't working, and I knew I had to find someone who believed in Jesus. If he was already attending church, all the better!

My best friend knew what I was looking for, so I asked her to set me up with someone. Her husband introduced me to the tallest guy he knew from work, Mike. Incidentally, he was also a Christian though he wasn't a church member at the time since he had moved to town fairly recently.

We went on a blind date, doubling with my friend and her husband, to a pool hall, where the only thing that started off well was that I impressed him by crushing him game after game. I hated his shirt. He hated my hair. He was SO quiet. I had dated quiet guys before, and it never went well. I wanted the conversation to feel natural, not like I'm pulling teeth just to get someone to talk to me!

When the pool hall closed down, he asked me to meet some of his friends at a club nearby. I was excited thinking I had finally met a guy who would dance with me. Ha! No. He wanted to see if I could beat his friends at pool. Later he would tell me that he wanted them to be impressed by me so they would like me, which is actually kind of sweet, but also rubbed me the wrong way since I didn't care if they approved of me or not! When the club closed for the night, we were starving so we went to a 24-hour restaurant and ordered breakfast.

Finally, he opened up a little. We had some light conversation, but it was so much work! I was tired and ready to go home. He drove me back to my car at the pool hall, and I remember thinking, "Please don't kiss me!" He didn't, but he did ask me for a second date, which totally surprised me. Even though I was a little nervous and reluctant, I agreed. I had a policy that if a guy asked for a second date, I would go because first dates are usually so awkward and weird. Maybe I would get to know him a little better, and we would hit it off.

A few days later, I got into a car accident on the very day of our second date. I was rear-ended while delivering flowers for my job. I had to go to the hospital and get X-rays, and they put a neck brace on me. How unattractive! He volunteered to go with me, which I thought was a sweet gesture. It was the first moment that I thought maybe I was wrong about this guy. Not many guys would willingly go to a hospital, especially with someone they just met and didn't even really like that much on their first date!

Afterward, we went back to his house, and he made me dinner.... from a box. Still, it was dinner. I guess you could say we did hit it off because one thing led to another and four months later in my grandma's backyard we agreed to get married! We were officially engaged four months after that and were married two months later. It was a whirlwind courtship! One that I was not prepared for.

I repeatedly told God I was not ready to jump into another serious relationship, let alone get married so quickly, but I felt like God kept telling me this was what He wanted, so for once, I obeyed.

While we were dating, Mike went to Mass with me, but coming from "a borderline Pentecostal church," the structure was too rigid for him, and so we ended up going to non-denominational churches for a while. When our last one broke up, we went without any church at all for a few years.

Then one day my mom asked me if I could help out the choir at her church because one of their members was going on a work trip for a few months and they were really shorthanded. I agreed. When he came back, they asked me to stay and keep singing with them. I talked it over with my husband, and he agreed, so I started going to Mass regularly again. Shortly after that, he started attending too, although more sporadically. Often he was late or slept in rather than attending. This caused some conflict between us until I just decided to let God have His way with him, and I prayed.

I prayed a rosary for him every day for over three years that he would convert to Catholicism, hoping I wouldn't have to be like St. Monica and pray for fourteen more years! Don't get me wrong, I would have if I needed to. That's how important it was to me for us to be on the same page before we started our family. I didn't just want to be a three-strand cord, I wanted our children to be able to ask either of us identical spiritual questions and receive identical faith-based answers, showing that we were a united front and doubling down the authority on their catechesis. Miraculously, one day his work schedule changed and he was open on Tuesday nights to attend RCIA. Several months later he was confirmed, and our infant son was baptized by immersion at the Easter Vigil celebration!

I've always thought I could have saved myself a lot of trouble if I had just been more specific and prayed for a strong Catholic to date instead of thinking any sort of Christian would be a good enough fit. I guess I was hoping that by leaving it more open to a bigger pool of fish in the sea that it would be easier to catch one that worked for me, rather than trusting God to give me exactly what I wanted. However, this is our journey, and as always, God knew exactly what we both needed after all to serve Him best: each other.

Sea Turtles and Rainbows

Leslie Clay (E21/M23)
https://gardensandcrowns.wixsite.com/gardensandcrowns

"Ben called me! He asked me if I want to go to the beach with him!" I called my brother with my heart pounding. It was the first time a guy I liked had called me to go with him somewhere. Alone. I was trying not to put too much into it. I didn't want to get too excited and have my dreams dashed again... but... he called me! Apparently, he wasn't repulsed.

As a high schooler, I watched as any boy I liked stared at my two best friends. My besties were gorgeous. I was cute. I was the one the boys would open up to, tell their secrets to, but never the one that would get asked anywhere. I wish I knew then what I know now about God's creation of me. However, public school has a way of sucking you into societal norms and pushing God's awesomeness to the wayside thus, leaving a girl thinking she isn't worth all the tea in China.

College came, and I thought maybe, well just maybe, there would be someone who would notice me. After all, there are men in college, right? They are more mature. They aren't just looking for a girl that looks like a pin-up when they know she can't hold a deep conversation. Now, I do know there are women out there who look like pin-ups and can hold a deep conversation, but at this time in my life, I was tired of being overlooked. Well... I managed to make it through the first four years of college without one single how do you do.

There was one time I mustered the courage to give my phone number to a guy. Let me tell you, that was one of the scariest things I had done. Turns out, however, in his words, he wasn't "really into girls, at the moment." I had no clue. He did turn out to be one of my dearest friends. Aside from that exciting adventure, so far, college left me feeling even more wanting.

I had one and a half years of college left after switching majors. I began hanging out with a guy I knew from high school and started thinking that perhaps he was the one that a relationship would come from. A long story made extremely short, he looked at me as someTHING, not someONE. I had never been more heartbroken even by all the guys I never had a chance with in high school or previously in college. However, God had me exactly where He needed me to be.

I decided to stop looking. I was going to focus on my own growth, finish out my final school year well, and not worry about the fact that I had the possibility of ending up as one of those old cat ladies. However, I prefer dogs, so old dog lady.

Summer began and one of my girlfriends, Tearah, invited me and another girl to a Fourth of July party at the house of her friend Seth who she knew from high school. To say this was an out of the blue invite, would be an understatement, but, I figured why not. Tearah's nice. We enjoyed each other's company in nursing school. Might as well go.

We knocked on the door and Seth's roommate, Ben, answered it. The guy's smile and crystal blue eyes nearly blew me away, but I was pretending not to look because I had told myself that I wasn't paying attention to boys anymore! My girlfriends and I had a good time that night, and I thought that was where it was going to end. But, we went over again the following week and watched a movie with Ben and Seth. Ben was still just as fine, but I was still trying not to look. Okay, well, maybe a little in my peripherals. The four of us hung out quite a few times after that, and my interest in Ben couldn't help but grow. I was trying so hard not to fall for him because I was tired of being let down. Ben was attractive, kind, funny, smart, and laid-back. I found that not looking for a relationship was very difficult with this guy standing in front of me.

Not long after, I was at home finishing up a paper for one of my courses, and I knew that Ben had the day off. I wishfully thought it would be fun if he called me to hang out but I knew from history that was never going to happen. To my surprise, my phone rang, and it was Ben! He asked if I wanted to go to the beach with him. I tried my best to casually get out a "Sure. But, I need to shave my legs first." Yep. I actually said that.

Ben chuckled and said, "Ok. I'll see you in a bit."

Ben was a surfer so as soon as we got to the beach, he headed out to the water. It was oddly nice that there was no need for me to perform. We stayed at the beach for a bit and came home. Now, you may think that doesn't sound very thrilling, but Ben took us to a beach that was an hour away. Two hours in the car together! The silent moments felt just as natural as the conversational moments. We both found out that day that we were very comfortable with each other. However, at this point, neither of us knew if the other one liked the other or if it was just a friendship.

A few days later, I got a phone call from Tearah who excitedly whispered, "I'm over at their house, Leslie! He likes you! He asked me how I thought you felt about him. What do you want me to tell him?"

I loudly said, "Tell him I like him!" He liked me and I liked him - I was so excited I could have jumped up and down. I'm pretty sure I actually did.

Now, I just had to wait until Ben called me to tell me himself! As it turned out, he was about as excited as I was because it didn't take him long to call. He asked me to go out with him the following Tuesday. My first official date at the age of twenty-one! And so, my adventure with Ben began.

He took me to a seafood restaurant on the river. As we were driving there, we saw a rainbow in the sky. That may not seem like much, but we had both noticed this rainbow and later discovered it would continue to be part of a theme that was unfolding in our relationship. Throughout the entire date, the fact that I didn't have nervous tummy cramps made it all the more lovely. He was relaxed and so was I. After dinner was over, he asked if there was anything specific I would like to do. At the same time, we both suggested... the beach.

If you have never been to the beach at dusk or nighttime, I highly recommend you do. It's peaceful, the stars and moon are so much brighter when they aren't fuzzed over by city lights, different creatures begin popping out, and the sound of the waves continually crashing is refreshing. We sat on the beach and right away began noticing all of the ghost crabs coming out to run amok. We were getting a kick out of their defensive claw positions once they caught us watching them. They were everywhere and out of the corner of my eye, I saw another one moving, or so I thought. It was small and dark, so I assumed it was a different type of crab. But, behind the first dark spot were hundreds more dark spots moving toward us.

As they came closer, we saw that they were baby sea turtles making their way to the ocean! We didn't move, and the cute little sweet peas continued to go about their business right around us! I can't tell you how badly I wanted to pick one up, but I didn't want to mess with any natural instincts, so I kept my hands to myself. It was, by far, one of the neatest things I have experienced, and I experienced it with Ben on our first date.

As the night went on, our conversation went more in-depth about our likes and dislikes. It moved onto church, and I told Ben about the parish I went to and being raised Catholic. I asked him, "Do you believe in God?" He looked out at the ocean and said, "I'm not sure... Is that a problem for you?"

I asked, "Are you open to Him?"

He told me, "Yes." Plain and simple... just yes. And, that is where we allowed God to begin his real work in both of us. It would be great if I could say I was a crazy Jesus girl my entire life, but alas, the world is overwhelming at times. God knew I needed Ben just as much as he needed me. Thank goodness He pays attention to everything even when it seems like He isn't.

After that first date, Ben and I saw each other a couple of times a week, and went on a "date" once a week. On each date we had for the rest of the year, there was always something that made us stop. There was always a rainbow in the sky. Now, there may be some people who say that it was just a coincidence, but I have never seen that many rainbows in my life. What I know of my Father in Heaven now, I believe He was reminding us of the importance of a covenant, and they were beautiful reminders.

We had been together less than a month when Tearah and I were over at the house again. Tearah blurted out, "So Ben, when are you going to church with Leslie?" Funny thing about that was that Tearah wasn't a very religious person but Ben, just as quickly as Tearah asked said, "I'll go Sunday if you want me to." And, he did!

He went the Sunday after that, too. After his third time of going to Mass, he asked me in the car, "What do you have to do to become Catholic?" I looked at him slightly stunned and asked if he was serious.

"Yeah. It's the first church I have ever been to where everything has a reason, an answer, and a purpose. I want to know more." I proceeded to tell him about RCIA, and so it began.

I went to the RCIA classes with Ben and was amazed when he would tell me about his "AHA" moments. Here I was this cradle

Catholic, and my almost agnostic boyfriend was helping me to discover a new found relationship with each of the persons of the Blessed Trinity and the Church that Jesus Christ began. The following Easter Vigil, Ben came into the Church with the full party- Baptism, First Communion, and Confirmation!

Later that month, Ben proposed to me. We hadn't even dated a year, and we both knew that forever was right where we wanted to be. A year after that, I graduated college, and a month after that we were married in the Church. It was and still is the best wedding I have ever been to.

Now, this isn't where the story ends. On the contrary, this is where true love began. Love should be free, total, faithful, and fruitful. This is what Ben and I promised to each other, and that is what we still give to and receive from one another thirteen years and four children later. Aside from our love, our faith, too, has grown into a faith I never would have imagined. This has all been possible because we were and are working and growing together with God. I think Jesus was on to something when He said, "For where two or three are gathered together in my name, there am I in the midst of them." Matthew 18:20

You may think I'm lying when I say marriage is all sea turtles and rainbows, but I can tell you from experience it is true. Baby sea turtles dig their way through a foot and a half of sand packed on their heads. Once they reach the top of the climb, they begin the long trek to the ocean waves. They are preyed upon by raccoons, seagulls, foxes, crabs, fish, sharks, and plenty of other animals. They aren't safe until they have reached something they can hide in. Marriage itself is a dig and a trek. A couple's goal in matrimonial bliss is to get each other to Heaven. During the trek, there are predators lurking.

Our society is one rooted in selfishness and taking pleasure at all costs. Marriage can only flourish with selflessness and true joy. A couple must continue to dig and crawl together to make it through the predators. It is possible, I suppose, that the two of them can do this on their own, but in my experience, it comes in a whole lot handier when you have a hundred other sea turtles behind you. God needs to be invited into a relationship. And with God, comes a whole communion of saints and angels. The journey seems much more achievable, and they won't let the couple stop until they've reached their place to hide in Jesus' Sacred Heart.

After Ben and I had our first child, I was hit with the undeniable fact that women and men are two very different creations of God (both very good, but very different). I honestly don't know why I was annoyed with him this particular night but annoyed I was. It was midnight, and I huffed and went out to the living room to grump. Ben came out shortly after. "Apparently, we need to talk about this," were his words.

"Obviously," was my retort. We hashed it out for what seemed like hours - our expectations, our disappointments, what we hoped for, and what needed to change. At the time, it didn't seem like that heart to heart was going to be pivotal in our marriage, but it was the turning point of how we came to realize the responsibilities of our covenant. A covenant is an agreement between two people. Beyond an agreement, the two people are literally giving themselves to the other. I am yours, and you are mine.

The rainbow was the sign of God's covenant with Noah, His covenant with one holy family. When it comes to a covenant, it's not a simple matter of signing on the dotted line. The two parties are to give and receive, to create a bond, and to nurture its growth. God placed those rainbows in the sky for us as a reminder that a true covenant is more beautiful than words can describe.

Love is not a feeling. It is a choice. God has the best plan and the best person for you to begin a relationship with to continually make the choice to love. It is through that love that you will make the journey to Heaven and experience the awesomeness of sea turtles and rainbows.

Loving Quillan

Maria Bourassa (E20/M21)

I was born the 7th of eight children. At the age of four, my dad walked away and began a nine-year separation from my mom. I experienced nine years of my parents working on their marriage while they were separated. In those same years, I came to learn what I wanted, and what I would never receive from my father. My father was a figure in my life that I saw the first and third Sunday of every month. He took us to a fast food joint of our choice for dinner and then off to see a movie or a quick activity, usually a maximum of four hours with him. To say my developmental years were in need of a father figure would be an understatement.

Due to a lack of father's influence in my life, mixed with a strong mother who raised all of us, I later realized I had those "daddy issues" that young women tend to have when they didn't get positive fatherly affection as children. I was needy and always hyperfocused on boys wondering why none of them were attracted to me. It was simply by the grace of God and his protection that no young men showed me any interest before I was old enough to date and prepare for marriage. Looking back at how desperate I was for any attention, I can say now, without a doubt, I would have given away my most precious gifts in a hurry simply because I was craving any kind of attention.

Fast-forward to my high school life. I was homeschooled as a freshman and began at a local high school for my sophomore year and beyond. I was a constant flirt with the boys in the dramatic arts hall and had nothing more than friendship with all of them because none of them were attracted to me. Finally, by my senior year, I had had enough of my silly antics and realized that I needed to focus on my life and being successful as a student to really be happy. I realized that vying for male attention was not making me happy, and only one thing would! I denounced boys and the thought of any possible relationships for my senior year and by golly was I going to stick to my resolution!

One day, I was having lunch with a kid at school named Alfredo. He was blind and had mentioned that he was able to attain the help of a band student to assist him with a problem he was having with his flute. I was curious as to which band kid because I basically knew all of them as I was a choir student and the two types of students in these classes tended to mesh together well as friends. He told me about a band student named Quillan.

Quillan was the kind of student the whole school knew the name of. Everyone had heard of him. He was a junior, he was the resident "smart kid," and he always wore different and funky hats. He was "that kid." I had never actually spoken to Quillan myself, but I knew him, and we were friends on Facebook. That night, after getting home from school I was browsing Facebook, and my messenger application told me that Quillan was online. I decided to just go for it and talk to him about what a kind person he was for helping Alfredo with his flute. We ended up talking on Facebook every night after that as good friends.

Quillan had just gone through a 'rough' break-up and wasn't looking for any relationship, and this was perfect for me as I wasn't either! We went through life as high school students in a high tech world. Early on, we never spoke in person even though we saw each other at school often and spoke online each night.

As normal high school life went on, I went to school dances and just did my thing. I invited my best friend's older brother to winter formal as he was a homeschooled student and had never been to a dance. He seemed to enjoy it. When March rolled around, I was still talking to Quillan online. I could say without a doubt that he had become one of my best friends. We spent hours talking online and had even begun talking for upwards of several hours on the phone when parents permitted.

In March, I started wondering who I would bring to my senior prom, and I would celebrate my eighteenth birthday. I only mention my birthday because that was the age my mom would allow us to begin dating. She had made us very aware that dating was for marriage and therefore not something one does with reckless abandon. I knew at eighteen or beyond I would be ready for marriage, but I also knew that the boys around me were just not mature enough to consider for marriage or dating.

I asked my best friend's older brother to prom since he had seemed to enjoy winter formal and prom would be so much more amazing. He told me no, he did not want to go and that he had really seen enough at the formal. I moved on. I needed to find another person to ask to prom because I wanted to go to my biggest high school dance with a date. I decided Quillan was a worthy person to ask to this dance. He was a junior, and as a senior, I could bring any age of a date.

After asking him to prom, I realized that I really liked this kid who was a year younger than me, but I had many concerns about dating him. He was not religious, and I was a cradle Catholic. If we dated, I would do so with the intent to marry him and that he would likely not share this mindset. He wanted to go to college about an hour away after graduating in a year, and I was staying local and didn't like the idea of any kind of distance relationship.

We had started to hang out between my zero period early class and second period when I had my next class. He had late start and lived close to the school, so I would walk to his house and walk back to school with him so we could talk. It was a love blossoming from a friendship that neither of us really had with anyone else. Quillan was everything I wanted in a person. He was respectful and kind. He was only sixteen and seemed more mature than most 25 year-olds and he understood me.

On March 7, 2011, I walked to his house so we could walk to school together. In a previous conversation, Quillan had mentioned that if I had anything important to say I should just tell him because he wanted me to speak my heart and hear what I had to say. I, on the other hand, wanted him to say it first because I knew he felt it but wouldn't say it. So, on our walk to school, I was shaking from being nervous, and I just spit it out. "I kind of like you. Like...like like you." And he looked at me and smiled and said, "I kind of like like you too." So we linked arms and skipped the rest of the way to school. What a morning!

That afternoon at lunch, we sat together to decide what this meant for us. We decided that we could be boyfriend and girlfriend and I guess that meant we could hold hands as well. When we walked back to the school from the yard after lunch, we were holding hands so people could see our new relationship.

Through our dating lives, we experienced so many ups and downs. The low points were the physical temptations we faced. Quillan was steadfast when I faltered, and I was steadfast when he faltered. We were fighting a battle against the devil on a constant basis. Yet, through it all, I was going to confession and still adding my intentions during my family's daily rosary for Quillan's conversion. I wholeheartedly believed that he was the one for me and that God's will would either be his conversion or our separation as a couple.

As Quillan's graduation in 2012 came closer, he decided that he wanted to break up when he left for college so he could have the full college experience. I begrudgingly agreed to this but decided that I wanted to do a "breakup" photo session with one of my classmates who excelled in photography. This way, while Quillan was separate from me, he would have fond memories and photos of us as a couple to look back on, and secretly, I was hoping these photos would make him want to come back to me!

As the summer progressed, we were both having difficulty with the idea of leaving each other. We kept on making future plans even though we were "planning" to break up. We even drew up a contract that stated that in the summer of 2014 we would take a road trip that would span many states, no matter either of our relationship statuses. Needless to say, I was having a hard time letting go of someone I was sure I was in love with. I continued to pray for him because any soul brought to God is a miracle, even if I wasn't meant to be with that person.

Through our whole relationship, I was straightforward and told Quillan that I dated him with the intention of dating toward marriage. He never acted like it was a weird idea. Eventually, he came with me to Mass when I invited him, and he would say every part of the Mass except for one sentence in the apostle's creed: "I confess one baptism for the forgiveness of sins." He told me he wasn't sure that he could say that yet since he wasn't baptized.

Quillan has always been a deep person. Before he dated me, he had been reading about several different religions, trying to understand them and trying to understand what he believed. He was introspective and wanted to find his own meaning in his life. As he left for college, he told me that he didn't want to be separate from me and that he would still like to date me.

In his first year, conversations turned toward more serious matters. How many kids do you want to have? I asked him many questions and told him about the Catholic faith and how that lined up with my life. I also told him that I would marry him if he ever asked me, but I would expect that all of my kids be raised Catholic and that their father, Catholic or not, would attend Mass with them to give a good example. He completely agreed with me, and I fell even more in love than I had been.

I told him I would not marry him if he converted to Catholicism simply because my family wanted me to marry a Catholic or because he did it for me. I wanted him to want to convert because of his love for God and Jesus Christ and the Catholic faith.

In August of 2013, Quillan and I were saying goodnight in my car after a date. He said to me, "I think I want to be baptized Catholic." I could not believe my prayers were being answered! It was just such a joyful moment. I told him the process of classes first starting in September, and if he decided he believed what was being taught, baptism followed at the Easter vigil after all the different rites preceding it during the first part of the year.

Quillan proposed to me on December 21, 2013, with my mother's ring, which told me that she approved. He was baptized in April and we were married on June 21, 2014.

We still got our summer 2014 road trip. I got to take that road trip with the love of my life and the man I'd been waiting for my whole life. We went through nine different states and saw many large beautiful monuments and parks. After moving all of my possessions into his house the week before our wedding, I found a prayer I'd written as a little girl, eight or nine years old.

Lord, I pray to you he's chaste,
And time with him won't be a waste.
Make him holy for your keeping,
So my faith will not start seeping
Lord, I pray to you he's chaste and
time with him will come post haste!

Little did I realize that God truly hears the prayers of the young.

Everything Beautiful in His Time

Teresa Hitchcock (E26/M27)

I sat on the edge of the couch watching the clock nervously. He said to meet at 9 p.m., and the minutes ticked by slowly. There was some delay with the rental car. Why did he pick such a late flight anyway?

I was 26 years old, and it had been four years since my last date. Four years since anybody had shown any interest in me. Unless you count creepy old men. I worked in a male-dominated industry, but I wasn't the type of girl modern guys wanted.

I had spent my late teen and adult life waiting to be noticed, thinking if it were meant to be, my future spouse would show up one day in my circle. I'm not social by nature, but I forced myself to go to a few young adult functions at church. They were mostly populated by recent high school graduates who didn't know the Catholic faith and 40 year-olds still clinging to the "young adult" moniker. When men my age did enter my circle, there wasn't a spark of interest.

I began to feel unlovable. What was wrong with me that there was zero interest in me?

There was one brief interaction with a guy I knew through work, during which we went on a few dates and he casually flirted with me. I wanted so much just to be in a relationship, but I couldn't ignore that he had no use for religion. He was "spiritual." He also once expressed his desire to be the father of Rachael Ray's children (...ew). That brief hiatus from feeling unlovable ended in even more despair that I could ever fulfill the calling I felt to marriage and motherhood.

Week after week in the Adoration chapel, I poured out my complaints to God. Why did I have to be this way? Why did guys have to be the way they were? Did God want me to be an old spinster cat lady? Then why put the desire for marriage in my heart at all? I began to pray that He would take the desire away if it were born only out of wishful, Hollywood-inspired ideologies. Instead, my desire only grew.

Finally, when I paused my complaints long enough to listen, God placed quite clearly in my mind a simple question: "How can you love a man with your whole life if you do not first love me?" This was a loving rebuke that I spent more time complaining to Him than listening, a reminder that I had grown complacent in my faith.

I can't say I stopped complaining, but I at least indulged it less. I tried to put my obsession with being wanted out of my mind and to focus instead on becoming a better woman. I read books about marriage, about traits desirable in a wife, and about the nature of man and woman. I highly recommend Dr. Edward Sri's *Men, Women and the Mystery of Love*[12] for his treatment of St. John Paul II's philosophies on the theology of the body.

Finally, shortly after my 26th birthday, I decided if God meant me for marriage, I needed to more actively seek it and take the risk of facing rejection. Local opportunities having fallen short, I decided to sign up at CatholicMatch.com. I was an introvert, afraid of change, and had felt implicitly rejected all my life, none of which lent itself to writing a profile meant to attract the kind of man I was seeking. But I gave it my best effort.

When you set up your profile, Catholic Match asks you if you prefer to stay in your location or if you are willing to relocate for the right person. My fear wanted to check the first box, but I had recently read an article by Anthony Buono, the founder of Ave Maria Singles, that opined that we limit what God can do if we refuse to consider potential spouses outside our immediate area. I took a leap and checked the box that I was willing to relocate, and sent my hopes out over the Internet, fully expecting them to be dashed repeatedly.

Within a day, I received a message from John. Although I had to squint to make out his distant and low-resolution profile picture and I was less than enthused seeing that he was from the San Francisco Bay area, his profile detailed a man who was serious about his faith. He attended daily Mass, worked at a Catholic school, was homeschooled through middle school and had gone to a Norbertine high school where his appreciation of the Church developed and flourished. I didn't expect anything to come of it, but I didn't want to limit God, so I replied.

The first thing that drew me to John was that he was genuinely Catholic. The second thing that drew me to him was his humor. Although corny at times, he always had a joke or observation that made me laugh. I always had a smile after reading a message from him, which works out well because he said it was my smile that first attracted him and made him click on my profile. We began to share about our history, our family, and our... frankly... pathetic dating lives.

John was 27 and had been searching for his future wife for years. In his words, he had been rejected for every reason and sometimes for no reason at all. He also had to do his share of calling things off when it became clear that things would not work out. He had traveled from Washington State to Chicago to meet dates from Catholic Match. He did have some promising relationships, but they fell apart. He is ever the optimist though and continued searching for a woman to share his life with.

I remember quite clearly the day he suggested we meet in person. I had no idea what was normal in a long-distance situation like this. I thought it would take months of promising correspondence to warrant a plane ticket to see me. About three weeks after we began talking, imagine my surprise when in the middle of a casual instant message chat one day on my lunch break, he said, "If I could get the time off and I knew you wanted me to come, I'd be there tomorrow."

I read that over again, feeling the butterflies rush all the way up to my heart. I didn't know whether to be nervous, happy, frightened, thrilled, or to freak out. I spent the rest of my lunch break in the Adoration chapel, thanking God for this dawning of hope and praying for wisdom so that I wouldn't let wishful thinking cloud my judgment.

As we made plans for his visit the next month, I laid some ground rules. He wanted to plan our activities, which was fine, but for my own peace of mind, I asked that my brother accompany us in case he turned out to be "some weirdo from the internet." I also asked if he would be willing to meet my parents. Talk about testing him right off the bat!

At last the day came. I sat and watched the clock, waiting to hear that he was on the way from the airport. He had a five-hour drive from where he worked in northern California to the nearest airport, and he wanted to spend some time with his parents that afternoon, so he took the latest flight. Finally, he sent a text that he was on the way and I headed to the restaurant to meet him. I saw him walk into the building just as I pulled in, but on my way in he came back outside.

And the first words from this man who had come a thousand miles to meet me were, "Are you ready for some bad news?"

It turned out to be not terribly devastating. They had shut down the grill at the restaurant, so we had to relocate our date to somewhere open later, but to this day I still give him a bad time that "Are you ready for some bad news?" was how he chose to kick off our in-person relationship.

Once we ordered and started talking, I noticed that all of my nervousness was gone. Normally I am a worrier who feels awkward in social situations and has trouble coming up with conversation, but from the very beginning with John, I felt none of that. It was like we had always known each other and we didn't have to stand on formality or try to be more interesting than we really were. Everything came naturally.

The next day we met for Mass with my parents, and then we all went out to breakfast where he talked about his family and upbringing. He seemed to make a positive impression with my parents. Then John had a whole day of activities planned. We walked around Old Town and bought a mysterious amoeba-shaped cookie cutter in the Christmas shop, then we visited the zoo. My brother came along and trailed behind us. John found out later (at our wedding reception, actually) that my brother had been carrying a knife the whole time, "just in case." Fortunately, I was also unaware of this, or it might have made things awkward, to say the least.

The rest of the visit went quickly. Bowling, ice cream, an unexpected introduction to my parish priest in the coffee shop, miniature golf, and suddenly the two days were over, and I was seeing him off at the airport. When he had gone, I felt a strange combination of happiness that it had gone so well, sadness that he was headed a thousand miles away and something I hadn't felt in years: hope.

For the next few months, we took turns visiting each other. The fun and excitement of dates that lasted for days began to wear off, however, as we started to fall in love and realized that no matter how much we talked, texted or Skyped in between visits, it was getting harder to be apart four or five weeks at a time. That was when God providentially opened a door that would change our future.

Summer was approaching, and since John worked at a school, he had a few months off of work. He was trying to devise a way to spend that time with me but living out of a hotel would have been too expensive. Then, one day at my church's choir practice, I was talking to my friend Cindy about the situation, and she said, "He's welcome to stay at my house. I have an extra room." She had never met John and only knew that I thought the world of him, and that was enough. John came out for two months, and we got to experience what a traditional dating relationship was like.

If I had any uncertainty, it was gone after those weeks. I loved this man. I loved his goodness, his generosity, his faithfulness, his goofiness, his ability to quote random movies he'd only seen once eight years ago. He made me feel wanted, something I never thought I would feel. One day we sat in a favorite spot at a nearby park. I leaned against his chest, and he wrapped his arms around me and told me that I was the most important thing in the world to him. To his dismay, I began to cry. I couldn't help it. I had waited so long for someone to tell me that. I finally felt loved. I finally felt at peace.

The day before he had to go home, he took me ring shopping. It's an odd thing, going ring shopping because you know that he intends to propose, but you still don't know when. I knew that it wouldn't be until he came again to see me in October, however, because he hadn't asked for my dad's permission, something I knew he would do in person, and he wouldn't see my dad again until then. So we went back to seeing each other once a month, and I started to wonder what our life would look like. I had put on my profile that I was willing to relocate, after all. I did begin to worry then, but I was determined to trust God. He had placed this wonderful man in my life; He would give us a way to be together.

We saw each other next in August. I flew to California and stayed with John's parents. He wanted to take me hiking at a lake where he had spent many happy summers with his family as a kid. He bought me a pair of hiking boots, and we set off on the two-hour drive early in the morning before dawn. I had never been much of an outdoors person — the desert climate I lived in made it unappealing — but I enjoyed the hikes that John and I had been working into our weekends together over the five months we had been dating.

We started out on the four-mile loop around the sparkling blue lake, taking in the fresh air of the late summer morning. As the path got steeper and rockier, the sounds of children shouting on the beach and splashing in the water faded and the air became still. We came to the top of a natural stairway where the lake suddenly came into full view and paused to take in the sight while a few groups of hikers behind us passed. John seemed in no hurry to continue and kept saying, "Let's wait for these guys to pass" as each group appeared around the bend behind us.

Finally, there was a gap, and I asked if he was ready to go. Instead, he took my hand and said, "I love you. There is not a cross or a burden, a joy or any significant moment of your life that I don't want to be there to help you through." I smiled at him. He was prone to sudden and seemingly random expressions of affection. He stood up, I thought to continue our hike. Instead, he knelt down, right in a crevice in the rock, pulled out a black velvet box, forgot to open it, and asked me to be his wife. Eventually, he did let me see the ring!

He caught me completely off guard. I was sure he wouldn't propose without asking my dad's permission first. As it turns out, the morning he was going to drive back to California, he stopped at my parents' house at 4:45 a.m. before my dad left for work and asked both my parents for their blessing, which they happily gave. And so, unaware of all this, I had the benefit of a surprise proposal after all.

One of the amazing things about being with John is that his love has a way of overcoming my greatest weaknesses. All my life I have worried. I feared an unknown future and needed to know what was going to happen so I could make a plan. I would second guess every decision. Not with John. When I said yes to him, I never once questioned if I did the right thing. All the way up to our wedding day, and beyond, I had no doubt: this was the best decision I would ever make.

Another amazing thing about being with John is that he loves me with the most selfless, unconditional love I have ever experienced apart from Christ's love. He really does live out the message of Ephesians 5:25, "Husbands, love your wives, as Christ loved the church and gave himself up for her." So much so that when he realized what a struggle it was for me to face leaving my family and relocating to California, although I was determined from the beginning to do it in order to be with him, and when logistically it started to make more sense for him to move, he didn't hesitate to offer. When the months of being engaged but separated by so much distance took their toll on me, he once again didn't hesitate to leave his job and move, even without a new job lined up yet. He was able to stay with my parents and find work, and we got to spend the last five months of our engagement together every day. We got married just over a year after our first date.

We've now been married four years and have been blessed with two beautiful children, Emily and Patrick. Some people find it's hard to get married, especially at an older age, and merge two established lives together, but I haven't found that with John. I think because we spent so long looking for the right person to share a life with, any of those little things that crop up as annoyances or misunderstandings in the early years didn't seem like anything to worry about.

We always say, there's nothing about our relationship that we would go back and change, except maybe meeting each other earlier. We wish we could have spared each other the pain of those years of loneliness. And yet, it was in part the struggles of being alone for so long that formed us into people so wonderfully meant for each other. God truly has caused all things to work for good in our lives.

Time Well Spent

Janna Nelson (E25/M26)

I grew up knowing I wanted to be married and have a family. For some reason, I thought that I would emerge from college with the perfect man on my way to the white picket fence and happily ever after. Surprise! That's not how it happened.

A few years after graduating, I became involved in my local young adult group at a nearby church. I really enjoyed going and became good friends with many of the people there. During this time, I was still hoping to find a good Catholic man, but I had arrived at a place spiritually where I was open to what God had for me. I told Him that I would be open to religious life, or open to a year of mission work, but it needed to be clear to me. I was looking into ways that I could take a year off and go on mission, and even asked a childhood friend, who at the time was a Benedictine Brother, to pray that I might find some clarity. At that same time, I had been praying to our Blessed Mother to help me choose the right partner and to bless our courtship.

In April of 2012, I was attending the wedding of two church-group friends. During the reception, I was enjoying the party, and at one point, my friend Laura said something to the effect of "I know somebody I think you'd like. He was my childhood neighbor. He's a good guy, moved back from Boston a few years ago. His name is Brendan," although I couldn't remember at the time if she said Ben or Brendan or some other "B" name. I told Laura that I'd be up for anything! I'd love to meet someone, and to let me know when.

The next day, there was a playoff hockey game on television, and my brother invited me over to watch. He lived with some friends at the time, so there were a few people hanging out - most of whom I had previously met. We were sitting and watching the game, and a new guy just walked in and sat down. He puts his six-pack on the ground by his feet, and settled in.

I sort of nudged my brother and asked him if he was going to introduce me. He goes, "Oh, I thought you guys knew each other, that's Brendan - Brendan, this is my sister, Janna." We exchanged hellos and went back to watching the game. At this point, I felt like I knew this guy already - he seemed so familiar to me. I quickly texted Laura and said "What was the name of your friend you wanted to introduce me to? Something with a B?" Laura replies "Yeah, Brendan." I texted her back and said "I just met him..." I left not long after that, and on my way out I said, "It was nice to meet you!" and he replied the same.

Brendan would later tell me that he didn't want to ask my brother for my phone number. I can't really blame him. He did reach out to me through social media though. We sent a few messages back and forth, mostly asking about how we might know each other, because we felt so familiar to each other. We finally had the opportunity to meet up in person, and there was a sense of comfort and ease from that first date. Over the next few weeks, we saw each other often.

Brendan went to a concert with a couple of my friends and me, and even agreed to be my date for a wedding that I was in! He never shied away from meeting people and being with me, even though I considered it brave to do those things. We would go to the young adult group together, and afterwards would spend hours just sitting in the car talking. The conversation just flowed so easily, and I obviously never wanted to leave when it was time to go home.

While I feel it's crazy to say that I knew he was the one...I never doubted our relationship. When we met, I had been talking with another guy, but after my first date with Brendan, I really never went back. I no longer had interest in any other guy, because what I had with Brendan was definitely something different.

I continued to pray, and thanked God for bringing Brendan into my life. I also prayed to ask for blessings, because I was sure I could screw something up. Throughout our time dating, we spoke about what family life we wanted and what values were important to us. I don't recall ever discussing whether we would or would not be married, it just seemed more a matter of when. The following spring, Brendan proposed. Eight months later, we wed in my church. I cried the whole way down the aisle, because when God's grace fills you up, you can't help but overflow!

I had been on many dates before meeting Brendan, and some of those relationships would last a few weeks, or a few months, but they never seemed right. I would end up finding flaws, or not finding anything, and I was always the one to end it. Looking back, I realize that it was important that I find myself, and learn to love myself and be open to God's will. He knew I needed that first. I had to stop looking, and simply be open. I had to trust His timing – God's timing is always perfect.

Remember, O most blessed Mother, that never was it known that anyone who fled to thy protection, implored thy help, or sought thy intercession, was left unaided. Inspired with this confidence, unworthy as I am of thy protection, in the presence of God the Father, the Author of Life, of God the Son, Who gave marriage the dignity of a sacrament, of God the Holy Ghost, Who sanctified marital love, I entrust my courtship to thy motherly protection. Guide me in the choice of a partner. Keep my courtship pure and chaste. Bless our union with a holy love. Watch over us from Heaven. Send us grace to live in the favor of God and to share in the eternal love in which we shall be united forever in heaven. Amen.

Fighting Dragons Together

Anne Schmit (E22/M22)

At twelve years old, there was nothing in the world I liked better than winning an argument. So naturally, when the opportunity to join a debate club came around, I was one of the first to sign up. The team lasted about a year, and we weren't very good, but I enjoyed the experience nonetheless.

There was a cute boy there, Alan, who always wore a four-way medal. I liked him okay but I mostly liked him because I would always win the arguments when he was on the opposing team. He, on the other hand, was mercilessly teased by his little sister for having a crush on the loud-mouthed girl who thought she knew everything.

After debate club ended, I didn't give Alan another thought. I started dating at seventeen. I didn't choose great guys and my taste kept getting worse and worse. Technically, I was always dating "Catholics," but with one short-lived exception, they were not anything like the brave knights I had always wanted to be with. Most of them pushed me outside my comfort zone and had no interest in protecting my heart or my soul. Mercifully, each ended before getting too out of control.

Seven years after debate club, I was at the tail end of a train-wreck of a relationship that had been dragging on for six months. A friend of mine told me, "You know, you just need to meet my friend Alan, he's totally your type."

Like any self-respecting Millenial, I Facebook stalked this guy who was supposedly a perfect match and recognized the boy from debate club.

"Oh, I'm not interested in him! He's a nerd!"

Despite my protests that I wasn't really interested, my friend invited this guy to a youth group event. As soon as I saw him, I was a goner. He'd grown about a foot and a half, had a classic country boy look, and was still wearing that same four-way medal. It didn't take more than a month before we were inseparable and totally in love.

He really was a "Good Catholic Guy." He went to our local Newman Center with me every week, he went to Mass and Confession regularly, he even would pray the Rosary with my family via Skype! Despite our strong faith, we still found ourselves in the confessional every few weeks, having letting our physical relationship go a little too far. We weren't having sex, but we both knew that "not having sex" was an extremely low bar. We knew we were falling short of what we were called to be, and that didn't bode well for our future.

Soon after our six-month anniversary, there was a particularly bad incident, and I told him I needed a few days alone to think about our relationship. We both wanted to be good Catholics, but something kept dragging us down again and again into impurity.

After 24 hours, Alan sent me a message:

"We need to talk. Not like "the talk" that we've had before, about boundaries and what we can and can't do. This one is me talking to you. It's about what I think happened, and what I know I can do. It's gonna be hard, both the talk and what I'm going to have to do, but if you back me up, I know I can do it.

I love you, so much. I know I didn't act like it. Some knight I turned out to be. More like the dragon. I hope that side of me never, ever rears its ugly head again. If it does, the knight in me will have to slay it."

He asked me if I would meet him at one of the local parishes for confession and to talk. I don't know exactly what I expected to hear, but I knew something had to change. After we both confessed and said our penance, he spilled it:

"I watch porn."

Sure, I was nineteen, going to a public university, but in my mind, pornography was still something that only creepy, gross, and perverted guys watched. Good Catholic Guys didn't do that! My boyfriend wasn't creepy, gross, or perverted! He was a Good Catholic Guy... right?

We both cried about it. I was hurt but I decided almost immediately that this man was one that I wanted to fight for.

We made some changes fairly quickly. I asked him if he would talk to someone. He agreed to have a long talk with one of the youth directors we trusted who gave Alan some tools to fight what really was an addiction to pornography. He put accountability software on his laptop, so any time he visited a flagged site, I would get an email. I started to realize my behavior could be a trigger and we tried our best to put a stop to our bad behavior. We kept going to confession regularly, and going to Mass, and started to pray together a little more.

There were a few slip-ups. Each time hurt just as badly as if he had gone to a strip club, or if he had had a one night stand. For a while, he even gave me his iPod, and had a heavy password protected filter on his laptop. He began talking to some of his male Catholic friends about the issue, and many of them had the same struggle. Some of them began to be accountability partners and prayer warriors for each other as well.

As I worked through my own trauma and betrayal, I noticed that people tended to fall into one or two categories about pornography. Either it wasn't a big deal because all guys do it, or it was an absolute deal breaker.

As I began to actually research pornography addiction, I found a middle ground. It is an alarmingly common problem. 70% of Christian men admit to struggling with pornography. Morally speaking, it has the same effect as infidelity. It can be a serious addiction, and it is a factor in over half of divorce cases. Nevertheless, it is possible to break free from pornography, and to heal from the damage that it causes. While it most certainly is a major red flag, it doesn't automatically mean a death sentence to a relationship.

The one thing that made me stay and decide to fight for my relationship with Alan was his honesty. If I had to be sneaky, to snoop through his internet history to get the truth, or if he had told me, "It's no big deal, all guys do it," it would have been a different story. I would have left. But through our entire relationship, he's never lied to me or tried to sugarcoat his faults.

Since that fateful confession, not a day has gone by without me being incredibly proud of the man who is now my husband and the father of my children. While he will likely always struggle with this particularly vicious dragon, he has the humility to accept help, the strength to persevere, and the wisdom to know that victory is impossible without God.

I've wanted to share our story for quite a while. I've met so many women who have been wounded by their boyfriend or husband's pornography use, and so many men who feel trapped in their addictions. Alan and I agree that we want our story to be one of hope. Pornography use doesn't have to be a deal breaker. We are proof that with honesty and the grace of God you can break free from a pornography addiction, and you can heal from the great damage it causes.

Dear Future Husband

Erinn Folts (E23/M24)

It was 1999 and I was eighteen. I had survived the first semester of my freshman year of college at a huge state school in my hometown of Corpus Christi, TX. I say survived because it was a huge culture shock coming from a Catholic, college prep school. While my small high school was coed, I was still sheltered more than public school kids. When I graduated from high school, I felt that my sole purpose was to pursue my vocation, which I felt was to be a wife and a mother.

My college environment certainly didn't make this easy! How would I even pursue this if I was constantly surrounded by young men who had little in common with me but also who didn't share my morals! It seemed like there was no hope. This was a dark time in my life full of hopelessness, despair, and the constant feeling of loneliness. Thankfully, I was given some wonderful friends that were going through something similar! We all felt rather alone in our principles compared to the huge school we were at but at least we had each other.

Little did I know, God was working in the background! Unbeknownst to me, the man God chose for me was living in the very same town! This man was not from Texas but God planted him there and he was quietly growing in his faith while waiting for his own vocation to begin.

I kept reflecting on the vocation I felt I was being called to. In the meantime, I would attend Mass as often as I could with my busy college schedule. I liked the 6:30 a.m. Mass on Tuesdays and Thursdays. I would often go with my parents and then would go for my usual four-mile run that I did six days a week. I would see the sunrise and marvel at God's tapestry.

Despite the beauty around me, I was desperately seeking direction. I felt off balance whenever I set foot on my college campus, amongst my peers. I began to go to confession twice a month with the same priest, Fr. Tony. He was not only my confessor but he became my spiritual director as well. He was positioned at a small, Catholic college in Corpus Christi that had opened that fall. I had chosen not to attend this school because I was pursuing a nursing degree and they didn't offer that track.

It was about this time that I remember reading how it was a good idea to write a letter to your future spouse. By doing so, you would not only be making him real to you; but you could pledge your purity and fidelity to this person. Getting it down on paper makes it feel like a legitimate promise. I jumped on this idea and wrote not one, but three letters in a six month span.

Writing these letters truly helped me spell out just what I was looking for and hoping for in my future husband. These words would eventually become my prayer to God.

God, please bring me a true man of faith. Let him be so rock solid in his faith that he will not waiver. Lead me to a man who will bring me even closer to you, Lord.

Sometimes, we go through deep spiritual exercises and then we think the Lord will show up the very next week. That's not what happened for me. Fast forward two years. I found myself resolute in my vocation of marriage but still no man had surfaced. I continued on my path of frequent confession, Mass, and Adoration, praying for this man I hoped to meet. I also asked God to help me with my own strength and openness to God's will for my life.

After much consideration and spiritual guidance with Fr. Tony, as well as wisdom from my parents, I made the decision to pursue a liberal arts degree at that small, Catholic college in my hometown. I felt a great shift in my focus.

This was it! It was my first day at the new school. I was twenty years old and felt ready to work on me. I was focused on my studies and committed to deepening my relationship with God. I was set on educating my whole person, not just my intellect. Since most of the men attending this school were avidly discerning the priesthood, I began to consider doing missionary work after college. Sure enough, God had other plans for me.

One day I noticed the guy I had briefly seen in passing two years before when I would go to confession. I politely said hello and little did I know, this hello would begin a deep friendship between us. Joe was an amazing man. I was inspired to watch this twenty-one year old recite the rosary, invite me for rosary walks, attend daily Mass, pray at the abortion clinic, and ask if he could sit at my table for dinner. To put it simply I was drawn to him. for the first time,

I thought there was indeed a man who was rooted in his faith and could keep bringing me closer to God. I thought, "Okay God, if this is him, GREAT!"

We courted for a year. It was so special being courted by a true gentleman. As we were moving closer to getting engaged, suddenly the only thing Joe could do was accept a job in Buffalo, New York where he had been raised.

Well now what, God? We weren't engaged and Joe felt strongly that we spend the engagement period in the same state! No jobs came up for me in Buffalo. I stayed in Texas and started a new job while I kept looking for a job in New York. I felt isolated after he left. Everyone we knew was either getting engaged or married, and we had already been together over a year at this point. Joe kept telling me we are going to get through this, something good will come of it. I began to head to daily Mass, went for runs with friends, visited friends, and looked forward to seeing Joe every other month--our commitment was making sure one of us flew in for a three-day weekend every other month. That helped to make the days and weeks go by faster. When I look back I realize, of course, that time a part was a gift to strengthen us and ultimately strengthen us in our relationship with God.

Then another big plot twist in my life story came. My mom got sick. Cancer. Again. I called Joe and he moved that very weekend. He rented an apartment and got a job at Target. This amazing man helped me care for my mom by being the supportive person I needed to lean on. My mom went into remission, and still is today, praise God!

Over those five months, I felt so close to Joe that I wondered how it could ever get better. Oh yes, how about actually getting engaged! So in the back of my mind, and my mom's for that matter, we kept wondering which special day he would propose on. On a weekend in mid-October, we drove down to Corpus Christi and visited my sister and husband and friends. On the way back to Houston, he mentioned that we should stop at Our Lady of Corpus Christi Perpetual Adoration Chapel to pray for our journey. It was there, on the steps that he said the words "Erinn, it is time." I knew in my heart he was proposing!

He asked and I said yes. It turns out that he really was the man God had prepared for me. On our way to Houston we called our parents and siblings. We picked a date, June 4th, 2005, which happened to be almost six months to the day after proposal; and even better, was the First Saturday of the month and fell on the Feast of the Immaculate Heart of Mary. How special for us, we met at a college which was founded by an order named for our Blessed Mother, and now being married on one of her feast days. God foresaw this day of Joe and me being united in the Sacrament of marriage from the beginning of time. God is truly amazing like that!

So, what did I do with the letters? I bought a card for Joe and I put them in there, and I gave them to one of my bridesmaids on the wedding day and she brought them to him. I remember him telling me during our first dance that he never knew I wrote this. He was so touched. We have been married for 13 years and we have been blessed with seven children.

Remember that saying, "Ask and you shall receive?" Well I did, and then a hundredfold!

My advice to Catholic singles. For me I felt like i had been going in circles, i can only imagine for most of you it is similar in this world. But by being specific in your prayer requests with God, I believe is what he asks of us, a good Father wants to help and give His children what they need to be closer to Him. So, my dear friends, ask and pray deeply and don't forget to unite your requests for this future spouse with our Lord in deep prayer, Adoration and frequent visitation of the Sacraments. Remember all of these are so essential.

God Knows When You're Ready

Jennifer Ringwald (E20/M21)
www.everymorningbringsnewmercy.blogspot.com

I met my husband at a time when I specifically wanted to NOT meet my husband.

Beginning in high school, I started to have crushes on boys. It would consume me, really. That was what was always on my mind. I went to college looking for a husband. Dreaming of the day I would run into him and find love at first sight, I found myself matching myself up with every guy I met. I lost interest in my classes, and wasn't faithfully going to Mass. While this was happening, my grandma passed away, my home church was going through a major renovation, I still had a tense relationship with my parents, and I simply didn't know where I belonged.

I had just finished my sophomore year of college. That first year was rough. I was living away from my family for the first time and even though they were only thirty minutes away, it was the first time I was learning to be independent. I ended up taking a full load of classes that I hated. I was constantly distracted by trying to score Mr. Right. I was struggling to balance it all in this new environment. I suffered from anxiety, depression, and eventually ended up experiencing acid reflux and panic attacks.

I ended up making bad choices in the name of "trying to find a husband." I would go to parties with my friends and make out with different guys, leading them on, but never sleeping with them. I even spent the night with one guy, but when he realized I wasn't going to sleep with him, he never contacted me again. I was heartbroken and ashamed. I needed something to snap me out of it.

I was ready for a distraction so when I was invited to come along as a chaperone with my church youth group to the Steubenville of the Rockies conference in Colorado, I jumped at the opportunity. My mother, sister, and my best friend from high school were all going, so I happily came along.

For the first time in a while, I was excited about something. I was here to focus on growing closer to God and healing some of the hurt I had experienced at college. I arrived at the church and immediately noticed there was a young adult male chaperone. Fighting my recent habits of crushing hard for guys, I turned off this part of my brain and stayed true to my mission of focusing on God.

At this point, I wasn't sure what God was calling me to do. I remember that during the retreat, I even went to Confession and told the priest that I felt called to be a sister. He asked why. After I explained what I had been going through, he recommended that I not use the convent to run away from my problems. Very Maria Von Trapp, I know. I left feeling confused but my heart was still open to experience this retreat and get the most out of it that I could.

I ended up talking to that other male counselor. His name was Richard. At this point I was convinced that no Catholic boy would really want me so we might as well be friends. Well God sure had other plans!

Richard and I really clicked! We had so much in common and I had such a wonderful time with him. I never knew men like this existed. He was so on fire for God and such a great example of how to live our faith. At first, I thought he would be a great friend to have because he seemed so nice and fun to be around! Eventually, though, I had to acknowledge the feelings that were forming. He must have felt the same because when the retreat ended, we exchanged numbers.

What happened next was a whirlwind! I was completely in puppy love with this guy! I know it went quickly but I always felt a great peace that God wanted me to spend the rest of my life with this man and that he was supposed to be the father of my children. I adored him. While I felt that our feelings were real, I wish we had been better about how far we left our physical relationship go. I regret the bad example I set for my younger siblings. I can be easy to get caught up in strong feelings of love but I wish we had been chaperoned more often so we didn't give in to those feelings before marriage.

Because our feelings for each other were so strong, and because we both knew we were meant to be together, we both wanted to get married as soon as possible. We met in June 2002, we were engaged in January, and we were married in August 2003.

My parents were a bit surprised! At first, they were happy that I was happy. But when they found out that I was going to get married before getting my degree, they were worried we were rushing things. It was very important to them that I finish school before getting married and having children. I'll admit, I was angry about their attitude for a long time.

In looking back, perhaps I wasn't making the best decisions at the time because I had fallen so hard for Richard. The fall after we started dating, I got the worst grades I have ever gotten in my life! I quit my job and would skip classes just to spend more time with Richard. He had also stopped going to college before we met because of a knee injury. After being married four years, we decided he would take a job opportunity and finish college. While we were there, I decided I should finish, too. We ended up graduating together in 2012 with three small children under five years old. It was the craziest thing we have ever done!

I know that God meant for us to be together, but our relationship hasn't been a fairy tale. We were very young when we got married and I'm not sure we really understood what we were getting ourselves into. We were constantly learning more about each other and working on our relationship.

We became pregnant with our first child after being married six months. We were so excited to welcome this blessing into our home. Sadly, at three days old, our sweet Michael passed away and went to heaven. The following two years we experienced four miscarriages. Despite being there for each other, this kind of loss also takes a big toll on marriage. It was hard to know what God wanted for our little family but we remained faithful.

Then our preemie came along. By God's grace and mercy, we are still here together, with SIX healthy kiddos! I write about our life on my blog, everymorningbringsnewmercy.blogspot.com to help other women who have suffered infant loss and miscarriage. I see that God can use our pain for great good. It's definitely been a battle to stay married. Even when God is in the middle, marriage can be a tough journey. We continue to strive to understand one another as our family grows and to keep our faith alive!

I hope to help my own children navigate their relationships. We will definitely be watchful of them and talk to them about dating, courting, marriage, sex, anything! I feel like I could've been better prepared for the intensity of dating and falling in love if I had been given more tools from my parents and mentors. When you're feeling caught up in strong feelings of love, make sure to spend time in prayer and Adoration to make sure you don't move too fast.

God Blessed the Broken Road

Laura Durant (E27/M28)
www.HealingHeartofJesus.com

The song goes, "This much I know is true. That God blessed the broken road that led me straight to you[13]." I have to admit in early 2006, I wasn't feeling much like God was leading me to a spouse. I'd had my share of heartbreak and disappointment.

That February, I made my CRHP (Christ Renews His Parish) retreat at St. Theresa's in Austin, Texas. For some, a retreat can be a quiet awakening, a gentle tug at the heart, and its greatest effects are seen after the weekend is over in the coming days and weeks. For others, it's like a shot in the arm, purifyingly painful, but at the same time, healing and transformative in a dramatic, life-changing kind of way. For me, the outcome of attending this CRHP was definitely the latter!

While I had been making my way back to the Church, albeit very slowly, my CRHP retreat weekend brought me fully back in a way that was unmistakably part of God's plan. What followed was a purging of old ways, habits, and friends who did not lead me to Christ. Then I committed to living a life more in line with God's will for me. I continued my journey with the CRHP group after the retreat. I met some lovely ladies and a month after the retreat one mentioned there was a nice guy she thought I'd really like.

I had explained to her at this point that I had sworn off dating and I needed to focus on my relationship with God. "Okay," she said, "how about instead we just all get together and go kayaking – just as friends. I really think you'd have fun with him."

She asked me a couple more times after that, and I kept telling her I would think about it. I let her know I just wasn't ready to meet anyone. To be completely honest, I was afraid. I had never truly had a healthy relationship in the past, and certainly not one with God in the center of it. I was terrified of how I would even approach it.

One night, a few weeks later, one of my friends asked if I'd like to go out to a country bar with her, as many others in our church group of friends were going. I was leaving for Canada the next day for a school conference, and I didn't feel like going. She was very persistent, however, and I finally agreed to go. Little did I know that decision would change my life forever.

Once we were there, I was glad I had come out. We were having a great time. At one point, as a couple of friends and I were sitting around a table chatting, a handsome guy walked up and said, "Would any of you ladies like to dance?" Though he made it sound like he was asking the whole table, he looked directly at me and did not look away. I accepted and we danced for a few songs.

We headed back to my table, and he recognized some of the friends with me from church. Apparently, he attended the same church as I did and we knew many of the same people! We exchanged numbers before we left, and I headed home to pack for my trip.

As I was on the plane to Canada the next morning, I told my close friend Michele about this new guy I had met. His name was John. I told her he was cute, funny, and even went to the same church as I did! However, I explained that I just didn't know if I wanted to pursue anything. I was tired of dating people and it not working out. He was Catholic (which was something I ultimately wanted in the man I married), but the whole thought of even going on a first date made me tired. Michele urged me not to give up, and that this time could be different.

Michele is one of my most trusted friends. She knows me better than most people. She has a keen intuition and a deep faith in God, which is what I value most about her. I trust her implicitly and so I decided, should John reach out to me after I got home, I wouldn't avoid him. I would trust that this time could be different.

Once I got back home, John called, and we talked a few times on the phone, getting to know each other. I learned that John was not Catholic – yet. He was going through RCIA and soon would enter the Catholic Church on Holy Saturday – which was only two weeks away.

Then came the most interesting detail. John's RCIA sponsor happened to be the husband of one of my good friends at the church – the same friend who was trying to set me up on a date a few weeks earlier! When he told me who his sponsor was, a light switch turned on. Could John possibly be the same person my friend was trying to set me up on a blind date with to go kayaking?

Immediately, I asked him, "You don't happen to like kayaking, do you?" "Sure do!" he exclaimed. I then asked if his RCIA sponsor had tried to set him up on a blind date to go kayaking, but it never happened. "Yes, how did you know?" he asked.

"Wow, God, just wow," I thought. After that conversation, I began to let my walls down and allow myself to get to know this man God had clearly intended for me to meet.

Our Courtship

Being with John as he went through the initiation into the Catholic Church was such a beautiful experience. I realized what a true blessing he was to me, with his faith in God and passion for Christ. I was re-entering the church after a long hiatus, and it was important to me to have faith in my life. He saw my being a cradle Catholic as a blessing for him as he came into the Church.

We both knew early in our courtship that we were meant for each other. When we were introduced to each other's families, it was as if we had always been a part of them. We dated for eight months before we became engaged.

Our courtship wasn't without bumps; we each came with our own baggage. However, for the first time in a relationship, I wanted to be there for John to help him work through his issues. I wanted to help him grow as a person. I desired only good for him. I desired that he get to heaven. I loved him despite all his quirks and struggles. I was okay with sticking around through it all and clearly, he felt the same for me.

I've struggled a great deal with depression and anxiety throughout my whole life, and I went through a very difficult time the summer after we met. He stuck with me through it all the way. He didn't run, and his strength helped me immensely.

I believe God guided John and I through life, each with our own unique experiences. I believe we were intended to meet when we did – and not before – so we could be prepared for each other when we met.

God had blessed our broken roads.

The love we have for each other was no doubt placed in our hearts by God. We have a love which desires the other person's good so much, we will enter into their suffering, so we can bring them into the light. This is a special type of love, a committed love, a "covenant" kind of love – where you decide, commit, and do not entertain other options beyond loving the other through their struggles. I had never had or felt that before. That's how I knew this relationship, this love, was different.

Our Marriage

The past ten years have been a progression of learning to move from seeking our own plans, hopes, and dreams, to abandoning them to God and His will for our lives. We started out with pretty typical dreams. Like many others, we wanted a house, kids, and the ability to live comfortably and to advance in our careers. We always *desired* to keep God in the center – of course! However, looking back, I see we were always holding back. We focused more on our own plans without necessarily inviting God into our decision-making.

One area where I struggled in our marriage, was putting my work first. I would justify my workaholic behavior, because at times we needed my job for stability but as I look back, I wasn't living for God. I worked harrowing hours because of my insecurity. I finally realized that what God wanted from me was total abandonment of all I thought I wanted out of life, and a total giving of self and openness to living out His will.

Another way I was closed to God's will was in family planning. Though we knew we wanted children at some point, I wanted to focus on growing my career first. I told God explicitly, *"I don't know if you want us to have children now, but I don't want to have children right now."* I certainly don't think it's wrong for a couple to wait to have children if they have discerned that it is God's will, but in my situation, I was not willing to surrender my life and my marriage to Him.

I'll never know if God wanted us to have children at that time or not. God let me have my way. I grew in my job at work though I was never truly happy. I always sought approval from others around me. I was not living out my true vocation, as it meant more to me to be the best at my job than to love John and be the wife God created me to be.

John and I have been extremely blessed in our marriage. We have been generally happy and have never had serious marital issues. As I look back on a good chunk of time throughout our marriage, however, we were like single people living together. John speaks about this time and describes it as if we were "ships passing in the night."

Two years into our marriage, we decided to start trying to have children. We would focus on trying for a few months, and then give up, because of the frustration with it all. Then, we'd wait a couple of months and begin trying again. We went to the Vitae Clinic in Austin, and I went through some of the NFP treatments and lots of tests, but ultimately, we were unable to conceive. Finally, after much prayer, and with a sense of peace, we decided to discontinue our active pursuit of pregnancy.

We are no longer charting and have decided to leave it in God's capable hands. And God, in His goodness, has provided other ways for us to live out our maternal and paternal longings through our godsons, nephews and brand-new niece, and also by providing care to John's parents and other relatives who need extra support.

Over the past year, this shift in abandoning all to God's will for our marriage has transformed our lives. One thing has become very clear – God's plans for us are greater than we could ever imagine for ourselves! Sometimes God's will does not conform to what society may dictate as normal. He may require your trust even when it may seem illogical or risky. It may feel as though you're putting yourself out on a flimsy limb.

In the past year, we've progressively given ourselves over to the Lord in great ways. We've prayerfully discerned that I leave work to stay home and provide extra support to John's parents, as well as begin work on a couple of books I've been inspired to write and continue writing for my blog. John has been inspired to create modernized Byzantine-style artwork of Jesus, Mary, and the Saints.

I find joy in making sure all John's needs are met, and he can enjoy his time at home and relax after work. If you would have spoken with me ten years ago and told me this would be the life I would be living, I would have laughed at you! Yet, here I am, living with joy and peace in my heart.

Progressively, each day, with each decision we make, we offer it to Jesus to guide us with His peace with where He'd like to lead us. We are truly working as a team to bring glory to God in a way I never dreamed imaginable and are no longer "ships passing in the night." I'm living out my vocation as a wife that loves, serves, and supports John in all the ways God intended and vice versa. There are sacrifices God asks us to make along the way, some more painful than others, to follow His will. What we find are that those sacrifices are necessary for God to fulfill His plans in our lives, and His plans *always* bring us great joy.

As God continually reminds me, when I look back on what I left behind, my work brought *me* glory, not God. What John and I are doing now brings *God* glory. It can be scary at times, as we have gone down to one income. However, we are at peace with where God is leading us at this time. Our marriage is flourishing spiritually, and we have a joint purpose, the purpose God had always intended for us. None of this would have happened without a complete and total surrender to Him, the One who created us and prepared us for each other.

Our deepening relationship with God and our devotion to the Sacred Hearts of Jesus and Mary have helped us learn how to love each other more. Experiencing God's love for me has shown me how to love John. God loves me even in my sinfulness and my brokenness. He looks at me and sees the good in me, and He sees the person He created me to be, not my woundedness. Because of this, I am able to love John in the same way. I delight in John's existence, just as God delights in mine. I am thankful for my broken road, and I fully believe God has blessed yours as well.

Advice to Those Who Are Single

Prayer. Spend time with Jesus and let Him know how you feel and what you are thinking. He already knows this, of course, but it is good for you to tell Him anyway. Trust that He desires to comfort you and guide you. He will give you all you need... the grace, the patience, the strength, the courage, and the understanding to know when the person He has prepared for you has come along.

Trust. Trust God knows you better than you know yourself. He knows exactly who and what you need. If marriage is your vocation, trust that God is preparing your soulmate for the time when you are to meet, and trust God is also preparing you as well. Trusting and believing when we cannot see is always the most difficult part, but the blessings which come from doing so are unsurpassed from any fleeting happiness we may experience from taking matters into our own hands – in any area of life, particularly this one.

Marriage - The Adventure of a Lifetime

Monica Schramer (E29/M29)

From the moment we met, our love has been one of endless adventure. After years of trying the world's way of dating and fed up with its empty promises, I finally looked to God in the search for my husband. Crying out in desperation to find my husband, I composed/brainstormed a list of the qualities he should have so that I might recognize him. Some of these were kindness, thoughtfulness, sense of adventure, joy. I also asked God that he might send me - well, NOT a fairytale prince... handsome and perfect on the outside, yet empty inside- like so many I had met. I asked for a toad prince... someone with real character- a unique and a hidden gem!

Well, there he was at the Ft. Lauderdale airport. I did not recognize him as he pretended to rifle through his bag to think of something to say to me. I said my goodbyes to my grandparents (who had come to visit from Louisiana) and headed up the escalator. He watched me go up and was upset that he did not think of something to say before I left. As I glided upstairs, a little voice (my Guardian Angel) told me to go back down. I obeyed, thinking it had to do with my grandparents and was mystified when they were not in sight and had gone through security just fine.

Then he approached. Assuming I had forgotten something, he asked me if he could bring something through airport security to my family. How thoughtful! We made small talk and I asked about him. He was a sailor, sailing into town every couple of months. First big X - I did not want a long distance relationship. What do you like to do for fun? Rock climb. Second big X- this girl comes from the flat southland and knows nothing about that. What else? Scuba diving. Okay, well, call me next time you are in town and we can go diving. It seemed so casual and despite the X's, I had goosebumps and extreme joy as I sailed up this escalator.

Later that evening, my grandparents called me to say they had made it safely home...and that they had met a nice young man named William in the airport! He had gone through security, found my grandparents, made conversation with them and asked them to put in a good word for him...and they did!

"Monica, give this young man a chance, he just might be the one for you!" they said. I couldn't believe the courage he had!

Three days later, he called and left a message on my answering machine. We started corresponding by phone. Soon I caught a cold and received a package in the mail - a can of chicken noodle soup, animal crackers, and a get well card. How sweet, thoughtful, kind, and simple!

Our first date was to be underwater diving, but as I still had that cold, sinus congestion meant going down under pressure was out. Instead, he invited me to dive in the sky. This was new to me, but as I was in my late 20's with an adventurous spirit, I thought, "Well, why not?" We went up to 14,000 feet together. As I saw him fall out of that plane, my heart sank- what if I never see him again? I followed him down and was elated to join him in this weightless free fall. This is what our love has been like!

We corresponded through handwritten letters and by phone when his ship was in range. Our next two dates, months apart due to his time away when sailing, were also big adventures. Our second date was climbing Mt. St. Helens. Our third date was diving, zip lining over cloud forests, and rafting down rapids in Costa Rica!

After three very long dates and only six months after we met, he arranged to meet my mom for the first time in New Orleans and asked her for my hand in marriage. The next day, which was All Saints Day, he flew to Ft. Lauderdale and proposed on the beach. I said "No Way!... Yes!" I was floored and honored when I found out that only the night before he was meeting secretly with my mom states away.

On our honeymoon in Belize, we almost died. We went tubing in underground caves. We were caught in a deadly hydraulic whirlpool. This force pulled us off our rafts and down under an underwater ledge, holding us underwater, and sucking us farther down. We kicked with all our might just to get a breath at the surface only to be pulled down again and again. It was as if an evil force did not want us to live, this young newly married couple. I felt our guardian angels truly with us, boistering us to the surface. We made it.

On this same trip, Will contacted a flesh eating bacteria in his leg and had high fevers, and later I was pinned under a fallen tree under a river. Finally, we both got nitrogen narcosis while accidentally diving too deep with sharks and had scary thoughts to go deeper there and die. Each time, our lives were spared. God had big plans for us!

As for the faith, I was a non-practicing Catholic at the time and he was agnostic. We had a wedding ceremony on the beach. Soon after we married, I felt a strong urging to go back to Sunday Mass. I casually invited him to come. Sometimes he would come, but most Sundays he would go surfing. I began to pray for him, for us, and now for our growing little family.

Our daughter was born and we baptized her. I began to attend weekly Adoration. I applied to have our marriage convalidated. The priest wanted to meet with Will and explain to him that we were not truly married in the eyes of the church or God. I begged him to please not counsel my Will, that this would turn him away from the faith. I took this burden on my own conscience and Father acquiesced for the sake of Will.

I cried on our new wedding day when we received the sacrament of Holy Matrimony. Now I could once more validly receive Our Lord in Holy Communion. Will did this for me, but was very confused why we were going through this second marriage ceremony.

I prayed for ten years. Most important of all, I did not push him about the faith. I loved him for who he was, this wonderful toad prince God sent me. I just kept living the faith with our daughter and now son, all the while he supported my efforts to be true to God and raise our children in the Catholic faith.

We received a newly ordained, very dynamic priest to lead our parish. He had been a husband and father, working hard to support his family in the years before his wife died and he was called to the priesthood. One evening, he and Will met up at the local pub for pizza and beer. It was during this humble night out that Will finally decided to become a Catholic. He entered RCIA and due to his weeks away sailing, met directly with our priest for his formation when he was in town.

It was through the power of prayer that he became Catholic. He had many scientific questions, many of which I was not able to answer. But he had the biggest smile on his face at that Easter Vigil and he took the name Pio as his Confirmation name.

At the reception that night, someone asked us how it was that he came to conversion. The Holy Spirit filled me with immeasurable joy as I told them of the miraculous green scapular of our Blessed Mother, revered for its power of conversion through faith in prayer, that I had slipped under his side of the mattress years ago, praying that prayer for him through the years. Along with it was a relic of Saint Padre Pio. Will was shocked to learn this and we had a great laugh when we arrived home as he looked under the mattress to see!

Today we get our thrills and adventure through the occasional travels, but mostly from just being together in our "little bubble." We have a cozy little home with lots of light streaming through, bedecked with many Holy statues and pictures, where we all enjoy being together and living the liturgical seasons. The Lord even provided us with extra land next door, which we were able to purchase.

This is our haven - our children love to dig sand caves, swing, climb into the trees to spy or read, there is a treehouse, vegetable garden, our tropical pond (which attracts many toads each spring, along with their growing toadlets!) and the many palm trees we gift one another with on our anniversaries. We have a little wooded area with a life-size statue of the Sacred Heart of Jesus that Will bought as a gift for me the Christmas before he converted that looks over all of us.

After many years of patience and prayer, joy and love, we are now a family of five, united in the faith. What a journey! So give it a try... Pray for a toad, and you might find a real Prince of God!

A Perfect Storm

Noelle O'Brien (E24/M25)

Our dating story isn't typical. We could have been the poster couple for the Rascal Flatts -- God certainly blessed the broken road that led us to each other. To be perfectly honest, I've tried writing our story a few times, and each time I've glossed over the hard bits in order to make it more appealing. Glossing over the hard parts does us and our story a disservice. We wouldn't be where we are now without the hardships, nor would we appreciate where we are now without them.

Back in August of 2000, my husband, Kevin, and I were starting new schools. He was going into the eighth grade at an all-boys Opus Dei school, and I was starting ninth grade at the sister school for girls. In general, although run by the same prelature, the Opus Dei schools and centers maintain single sex policies, but that year there was a joint school bus, and there hasn't been one since! The most significant development of us riding the bus together, was that our parents became acquainted. They discovered that we lived in the same neighborhood and attended the same parish, and when the bus was canceled the following year our families carpooled. Our parents were close friends first, which ended up being important when we started up dating ten years later.

All through high school, our circles of friends overlapped and our families got together frequently. If you'd told me then that I was driving around my future husband and the men who would become godfathers to my future children, I'd have thought you were crazy. By 2004, Kevin's family was relocated to Miami. 2004 was also the year I graduated high school and started my freshman year at Ave Maria University in Naples, Florida.

I left Ave Maria after a year and moved to Miami where I attended two more universities. The year I moved to Miami, Kevin started at Florida State University in Tallahassee, Florida. For the five years I lived in Miami, I was just down the road from Kevin's family. We went to the same grocery stores and coffee shops. When Kevin was on break from university, he worked at the movie theatre that I frequented. I worked at the same gym where his brother was a member, yet in five years we never crossed paths.

Kevin and I weren't awesome Catholics in college. We had the typical college experience of partying and dating. We each had participated in "serious" relationships, had cohabitated with our partners for periods of time. My years in Miami were some of my darkest, and during this time I ran from the Church. I was sexually assaulted, had a miscarriage, and reacted by throwing myself into unhealthy relationships and outlets, including giving in to same sex attraction. That particular temptation I'd managed to suppress within myself up until that point.

Around this time I was also diagnosed with PCOS and told I'd never be able to carry a child to term, and this was the blow that crushed me. I assumed that no man would ever want to be with a woman who wasn't able to carry his children. This was an assumption mired in self-pity, not reality.

By 2009 a perfect storm hit -- I'd been engaging in self destructive behavior for so long that my dad insisted I come back home to DC. At the same time my mom was experiencing severe heart problems and was scheduled for open heart surgery, and my grandmother's health was declining severely. I felt backed into a corner to move back home, but in hindsight Our Loving Lord in all of His mercy and understanding facilitated the move. Kevin ended up graduating a semester late from FSU and moved back to DC within a week of me.

Moving back into my parents' house was a huge transition, and it was insanely difficult. I tried living the same life I had in Miami but it was tempered by my parents' expectations and their faithfulness. Within the first month of moving home, my grandmother passed away, my mom was hospitalized because of her heart, and I was involved in a severe car accident. I began to seriously reevaluate my priorities.

Kevin's transition home was also not easy, he had a hard time finding a job and ended up waiting tables until being able to start his career.

When my mom was healthy enough before her surgery she would go to daily Mass. Kevin's mom happened to attend the same Mass. One morning they were catching up with each other and talking about us. They decided to exchange our phone numbers and set up a date in a desperate attempt to get us back onto the straight and narrow. I almost stood Kevin up on our first date, but we ended up hanging out and becoming "official". Getting back onto the straight and narrow, however, was another story.

We were definitely still very fallen away, and since I'd been diagnosed with PCOS I wasn't worried about getting pregnant. As time went on, our parents were earnestly praying for us. They knew we were having a physical relationship. They never judged, but always invited us to attend Mass and take advantage of Confession. The message eventually took hold and after not being able to come up with any more excuses, I went to Confession. It was the Saturday before Ash Wednesday. It was my first time in the box in six years. I ugly cried my sins to the priest and when I couldn't go on, Father gently and kindly counseled me. My penance was to "search for God's love within me."

A few months after we started dating, Kevin's family was relocated to Germany and he was forced to make his own way. Our relationship began to deteriorate when I started having insane mood swings which led to bigger and bigger fights. I considered finding a therapist because my mood swings were so violent they frightened me. Our biggest fight, which involved so much yelling that Kevin's roommate called the police, happened after we had been out celebrating Fat Tuesday.

We broke up, and both thought that was it and we were over. This was just three days after I'd been to Confession for the first time in six years. The next morning I woke up, filled with a combination of remorse and anger and something else -- a protruding belly. At this point in my life, I was battling an eating disorder, relying on coffee, cigarettes, and alcohol as my sustenance. I weighed about one hundred pounds, so the rounded belly sticking out was noticeable. What was alarming was how it wasn't there the day before.

My heart sank and I rushed to the store for a pregnancy test, which I took in the bathroom right after purchasing it. It was positive and my whole world came crashing down. I wasn't supposed to be able to have kids, my boyfriend and I had broken up, and I wasn't sure our relationship was able to be repaired. I also had no idea how far along I was, I was only cycling once a year or so. The fact that I had gotten pregnant was a miracle in itself.

I knew Kevin wasn't going to answer the phone if I called, so I ended up instant messaging him and telling him we needed to talk, it was important. He scathingly asked, "What, are you pregnant or something?" and I had to tell him yes. He agreed to meet up after work, back at his apartment. I remember stopping at a drug store on the way, a crying mess, and picking up a pint of his favorite ice cream and a pregnancy test so I could prove that I wasn't lying. The test was unnecessary though. When he saw my belly, he broke down into tears and we reconciled. The next two days were spent frantically trying to find an OB who would take me on. When we walked into the doctor's office we expected to see a tiny bean on the ultrasound screen. What we actually saw was a 26 week baby boy, with a functioning brain, a beating heart, kicking feet, sucking his thumb.

We were terrified that with the amount of binge drinking and chain smoking we'd been doing, along with the lack of eating, that our baby was going to suffer. The second miracle we experienced was that our son was perfectly healthy. This was the first Friday of Lent, and I definitely discovered Christ's love within me.

We knew we had to tell my parents, especially considering I had all of a sudden started to show, and weren't sure how long I'd be able to hide my belly. However, the Saturday after finding out I was pregnant was my parents' 25th wedding anniversary. They had planned a big party to celebrate their marriage, and the celebration was to start with them renewing their vows at our parish. We didn't want to get in the way of their celebration. We made it through the 5 p.m. Mass on Saturday, the vow renewal and the whole party with this news hanging over our heads.

I drank sparkling water in a champagne glass to make sure no one suspected anything. Kevin spent the night on my parents' couch so that we could tell them the next morning at breakfast. That ended up being the hardest conversation I'd had with my parents, and they were devastated that I was having a baby out of wedlock. After a few days, and seeing the pictures of their first grandson from a detailed ultrasound, my parents started transitioning from devastation to expressing what a gift and miracle this baby was going to be. It was still a hard time for all of us. I was living under my parents' roof at the time.

They pressured us to announce our engagement but we were still figuring out what our relationship was going to be. Other family members advised us that we didn't need to marry just because I was pregnant. Now that we had figured out my mood swings were due to pregnancy, Kevin and I were communicating more efficiently. Another week passed and we decided that we would meet with our pastor for council and announce our engagement.

I wasn't expecting a ring or anything, but Kevin managed a sapphire which spoke to his attention to detail -- he knew I didn't like diamonds. His proposal was just as unconventional, as it was in a parking lot at the end of my parents' street. I know, it doesn't sound romantic, but to me, it will always be one of the best moments of my life. I knew that Kevin had been uncertain about our future together initially, but the fact that he went out of his way to propose was his way of showing me he was all in.

When we started dating, the DC area was hit with a huge snowstorm and my parents' neighborhood was snowed in. When Kevin wanted to come pick me up for dates he had to park at the end of the street and walk a long block in two feet of snow. He never called to have me meet him at the car, he always walked down to come get me. He also walked me home instead of just dropping me off. One night, after parking, I opened the car door and put my foot down on a patch of ice. My foot went out from under me and I ended up flat on my back, much to my embarrassment. Kevin joked that it was where I first realized I was falling for him. It was also the spot where he proposed less than a year later.

We were at my parents' house, and he was picking me up for a date. I was rushing around finishing up some last-minute chores while Kevin was sitting down with my parents. As I passed them, I called out jokingly that he would have to ask my father's permission for my hand in marriage. Little did I know, Kevin was actually doing just that along with showing them the ring. After we walked out the door Kevin offered me his arm and suggested a walk, which caught me a little by surprise. I was also a little miffed because he knew I was hungry and we were supposed to be going out to dinner, but I took his arm and we strolled to the parking lot chatting about little things. He paused to "tie his shoe" and I continued on a few steps, still talking, totally unaware that he was trying to get my attention without interrupting me.

Finally he loudly said my name, I looked back and he was on one knee with a ring box. I was shocked into silence, and Kevin told me that when he first asked me to be his girl it was as his girlfriend, and now would I be his wife and his forever. I don't think I actually responded because of the shock and emotion, but at some point he assumed the answer was yes, the ring went on my finger and almost immediately we made an appointment to meet with our pastor.

Our pastor was wonderful. We met with him after another 5 p.m. Saturday Mass, and requested to start pre-Cana. He gently refused, and explained that being a wife and a mother were two separate roles although they were usually intertwined. At that moment, being in my third trimester with an unexpected pregnancy and not much time to prepare for the baby, he encouraged me to learn as much as I could about mothering. Once the baby was born he'd gladly baptize him, and then we could start pre-Cana to prepare us for marriage.

We signed up for the baptism class and Father gave us his blessing. In hindsight, this was a very wise decision on our pastor's part, just ten weeks after finding out about the pregnancy our son was born. We named him Liam after Kevin's father, and he was born perfectly healthy even though he was early, and I had not taken care of my health for the majority of my pregnancy. Liam is now six and a half and a wonderful little boy. We had Liam baptized eight days after he was born and started pre-Cana shortly after. On December 30th, 2011 on the feast of the Holy Family, we entered into the Covenant of marriage in front of God, our families, and friends.

Our first three years of marriage were difficult. We had committed to abstaining during our engagement, and had a massive coming back to Jesus. But we still entered into marriage with a lot of baggage. During our engagement we decided not to live together. We rented an apartment which was going to be ours, and Kevin lived there until that date. After Liam was born, we split parenting and Kevin would take him two nights a week. This was extremely difficult, and we ached for the time when we could be a family under one roof.

As hard as it was, we kept to our decision not to live together. Before dating, we had both just come out of serious relationships with people who were not good for us, and we had that baggage to deal with as well. The hardest thing to work through can be defined by the concept of "soul ties". I can't remember where I heard the term first, but essentially whenever you give yourself to another, part of yourself becomes tied to them, and vice versa. Severing all the soul ties that had come before was difficult, and every once in a while the ramifications of the decisions we made before marriage resurface.

If I knew then what I know now, I would have safeguarded myself more closely instead of giving myself to others before marriage. My husband also feels the same. I hope and pray that I can pass this lesson on to our children so they don't have to go through the heartache that we did. To be clear, I never once regretted Liam, he was truly a miracle for us, and I believe that he saved my life. If we hadn't been blessed by Liam, even as untimely as it seemed then, we'd have continued on our self-destructive paths. Having another soul to care for puts priorities into stark realization, and we knew we hadn't been living well up until then.

Our Lord saw fit to bless us with another two babies in two years. Having three babies under the age of three was a strain on our marriage but their existence made us work harder to keep our marriage together. If it hadn't been for the Covenant and both of us coming from a place where divorce was never an option, I'm not sure we would have been strong enough on our own to cling together during the hard times. In a culture where it seems so easy to just leave difficulty behind, it can seem insane to voluntarily remain in difficulty. Now that we're on the other side, I can say that the first three years of our marriage were a trial by fire. Now we know, we can make it through anything.

This past November we welcomed our fifth baby into this world, and last December we celebrated our sixth anniversary. The priest who witnessed our marriage has baptized all five of our children and he witnessed us renew our vows on our fifth anniversary in the same church where we were married. Our Loving Lord continues to bless our marriage in ways beyond what we can see, and we look forward to seeing where He will take us next. I am so grateful that He blessed us with our broken road, we have so much to teach our children and hopefully we can pass on the lessons we learned so they can learn from them. Kevin and I have worked through so much with each other, and we have seen that love never divides, it multiplies.

Where Charity and Love Are, God is There

Genie Shaw (E21/M22)
www.barefootabbey.com
IG and FB: @barefootabbey
YouTube: Genie Shaw

My husband says, "God got dropped me in his lap."

Right before my first year of high school began, after living on the island of Oahu from the age of two, my family moved back to Texas. My grandparents' health had begun to suffer and we wanted to be nearer to them to provide what support we could. I had been homeschooled since Kindergarten but started attending a public high school when we relocated. This is also when I began my fervent prayer for God to send me my "soulmate husband."

You could say I had the typical Lone Star State high school experience. The early mornings and many afternoons were filled with Drill Team practices and fall Friday nights were reserved for the state religion of football. I spent my remaining hours skimming through homework and participating in a smattering of other school-sponsored extracurricular activities. No doubt, I was having a ball, but there was a vital aspect of living in Makakilo, Hi that I desperately missed: our Church home.

My father was a Baptist minister and served as an associate pastor to a small conservative church while we lived in Hawaii. Following our return to Texas, we visited many churches but none were like the church family we had left behind. We would attend a hopeful prospect for a few months only to get discouraged by questionable theology in a week's sermon, and so the church search would commence once again. Even into my senior year of high school, our family was still in this cycle of church seeking and disappointment. Meanwhile, the weight of being without a church home gradually weighted more and more on my conscience.

I was raised with a strong sense of responsibility towards our Lord in that my life was purely a gift given at His pleasure and, therefore, it was my duty to Him to do all in my power to discern and fulfill His will for my life. And to my little INTJ heart, there was nothing passive about this process. Prayer and research (a stress coping mechanism) were constants. Not many details of God's plan for me were clear at the time, but I had always felt that it was laid on my heart to be a wife and mother. I also harbored a strong conviction that where I chose to attend college would either aid in this discernment or be a, possibly grave, detriment to my soul. With this frame of mind, my parents and I choose a small university that was Christian in name and relatively nearby in Texas terms.

My first semester of college I walked onto campus, in a completely new town, knowing no one. One of my first classes was Biology and the accompanying lab period was where I forged my first friendships of this new season. My two lab partners, Kathryn and Stephanie, and I are still friends almost fifteen years later.

As this semester went on, I became more and more disheartened. Despite my ardent prayers, I had received little male attention in high school and it appeared that the trend was set to continue for the foreseeable future. I began having doubts about whether I truly had a vocation as a wife and mother and the possibility of religious life suddenly became a realistic thought in my mind. I didn't know much about nuns besides that which I absorbed from media, namely through films like The Sound of Music and Sister Act, but to my sheltered self being a religious sister meant that you had given yourself completely over to God for His work. Naively I thought that being called to religious life would be the perfect way to make sense of my past experiences and essentially have a direct line from heaven in the future to constantly know and do the will of God for my life. This belief turned my research to the Sisters of Charity, the only sisters I knew of in real life and other convents in the area. By the end of the semester, my prayers had changed to a plea for a clear answer on which vocation I needed to pursue.

Following Christmas break, at the beginning of the next semester, Kathryn invited me to her family's home nearby home so she could do laundry. Not having transportation of my own, I jumped at the chance to leave campus even if only to complete a chore. This turned out to be one of the best decisions of my life.

That weekend Kathryn's brother, Phillip, also happened to be home for the day. We conversed and before heading back to campus we exchanged AOL screen names. LOL! Phillip and I chatted online later that night and when I mentioned needing to sign off and find something for supper, he immediately invited me out for a late dinner at a local diner an hour later. I accepted and that is when, on the Feast of St. Thomas Aquinas, our courtship was conceived.

Unbeknownst to me at the time, before our online conversation, Phillip had just arrived back at his apartment after over an hour drive from his parents home. When I agreed to dinner he remounted his stag, a white ford focus hatchback, and headed back south without hesitation.

We went on our first official date the following weekend to a local Irish pub, a nod to our shared heritage. We hit it off in the conversation right away. Being kin to my mother, a woman who's never met a stranger in her life, I didn't beat around the bush when we began sharing our dreams for our individual lives. And when I mentioned my hope for a huge family Phillip didn't bat an eye. He went on to share with me about the near-fatal electrocution that he had experienced when he was twelve years old and how the months of recovery in the hospital following that accident had helped him cement the priorities and aspirations in his own life. On the top of his list was to be a father. As the meal went on, it was a delightful surprise to see that we shared so many of the same life ambitions. These similarities were also so a confirmation that the physical attraction we both experienced had the support of an even deeper foundation of mutual understanding. Our courtship was a long-distance whirlwind from there. Two weeks later, we knew we loved each other.

I have Phillip to thank for my formal introduction to the truth of Catholicism. The Mass was more like my old Baptist church than all the other congregations we had visited throughout my high school days. The comfortable hymns were present, but also the less familiar, ethereal chant that takes you halfway to heaven with each melisma. The reverence was present, but in a tangible way felt acutely in both your body, through the physical postures, and your soul, as you ponder the spoken word. But there was also so much more that had been missing before, the history that takes you back to Christ himself, your brothers and sisters the saints that graciously share wisdom and courage for the trials of this world through their writings and examples, and our Blessed Mother, the solace of sinners and precious intercessor that transforms the meager dandelions of our offerings into a fragrant bouquet fit for the eyes of our Lord. I continued reading while my brain continued to decipher the ancient truth my soul perceived from the start.

Due to class schedules, we spent the weekdays apart and only saw each other on the weekends. On Saturday mornings, we would usually attend Mass in the morning followed by breakfast club with friends at the same diner from our first dinner together. The next semester, as our schedules opened up, we were able to start meeting for prayer on Thursdays, which we called death day because it was the dat the abortionist was at a local abortion clinic.

That December, before Midnight Mass, under the tree at his family's Christmas Eve gathering, Phillip surprised me with a promise ring and asked if I'd be his bride once we graduated. Over the next two years, until we were married, our relationship was strengthened as we supported each other through the hardships of my father's two heart attacks and the loss of Phillip's grandfather. The experience we gained from those difficult times of our courtship has been invaluable in our marriage.

After Phillip graduated, we were married on the Feast of Our Lady Help of all Christians, May 24th, 2008. For our Nuptial Mass, we used the vows and blessings from the Sarum Use, the rite used in England during the Middle Ages until the Reformation, and William Byrd's Mass for 5 verses for the musical setting. The ancient words of our vows serve as a reminder to us of the purpose and daily sacrifice of our shared vocation, "With this ring, I thee wed, this gold and silver I thee give, and with my body I thee worship, and with all my worldly cathel I thee endow."

After taking a semester off when my father had his second heart attack, I graduated in December, the same year we got married. The next year we welcomed our first son at the beginning of April. His middle name is Aquinas. Three years after we were married, on the Feast of St. Hildegard, I was received into the Catholic Church. This year we will be celebrating our tenth wedding anniversary. We now have six living children and still occasionally take them to the same dinner where we first began our journey through life together so many years ago.

In The Long Run

Diana C. Murphy (E29/M30)
www.luckoftheirishtwinmom.wordpress.com
Twitter/Instagram: @dianachristine3

The alarm went off at 3:15 am. It was still pitch dark outside. I got out of bed, put on my racing gear that I had set up only hours before, and ate something that settled in my nervous stomach. I went downstairs to the hotel lobby and caught a shuttle to the start line.

The entire world felt surreal. It was the middle of the night and I was surrounded by palm trees and people in matching purple singlets. The shuttle dropped us off somewhere and we had to walk the rest of the way. Almost everyone needed to use the bathroom. Coach Anne gave us a pep talk and tried to calm our nerves. The lines to the porta-potties were ridiculous. I had to rush to drop off my gear bag and get to my starting corral. I was in corral 20, somewhere in the middle of 30,000 runners. The race officially started at 6:15 am, but it was 6:31 by the time I got to the start line.

And then I ran a marathon.

I'm not entirely sure how they got my contact information, but sometime in my mid-20s I started getting brochures from run-for-charity organizations in the mail almost weekly. More often than not, these mailings would end up in the trash or recycling bin. I liked doing workout videos and making the occasional trip to the gym, but I hated running and the act of it made me physically ill. Besides, I was much too busy sleeping in on weekend mornings after late nights in the city with my boyfriend to have time to train for a marathon.

I was in love with said boyfriend, which was unfortunate because he was completely wrong for me. He – let's call him Joe – kept saying that he didn't want to get married for another ten years, which of course was cause for alarm for someone with a biological clock. Joe was also an atheist, and while he respected and was fascinated by the tradition of my Catholic faith, he had no intention whatsoever of becoming Catholic himself. He may have been a good person and we had a good time together, but there was something fundamentally lacking and wrong in the very foundation of our relationship.

On top of that, I found that being with someone who didn't make going to Mass a priority led me to make my faith less of a priority. I was a cradle Catholic who started going to Mass every Sunday before I can even remember. I was in a great youth group in high school and a solid campus ministry in college. After college, I did a volunteer year with the Capuchin Franciscans at a teenage retreat center. I struggled after moving back home to Long Island when the volunteer year was over, though. I had lost the strong Catholic community I'd had through those high school and college years. Community is so important to Catholic faith, but none of my local friends were practicing Catholics, and none of the guys I dated were either. Especially Joe.

Still, I clung to Joe in an unhealthy way until I couldn't anymore – until he broke up with me one evening shortly after New Year's Day when I was 25 years old. I became a complete mess of heartbreak and emotions and confusion and lack of direction, and in this state I stumbled upon one of those run-for-charity brochures and hesitated before throwing it out.

That's how someone who hated running signed up to run 26.2 miles for the Leukemia & Lymphoma Society through an organization called Team in Training. LLS has a long history of fighting blood cancers, and although I didn't know anyone with blood cancer, it seemed like a good cause. As an added bonus, it turned out that training for a full marathon and raising thousands of dollars for charity was so time consuming that it was a good distraction from breakup pain.

It was a different kind of pain I felt instead. Before I started training, I didn't know that long distance running is a full body exercise; I assumed it would only work my leg muscles. But after a long training run, I felt sore in every single muscle of my body. I had a toenail turn black and blue and almost fall off. I had blisters on my toes and feet that seemed almost permanent. I was fatigued from setting my alarm for 5:15 every morning to do my training runs before work, and to attend the early morning group training runs on Saturdays. I also learned some important lessons, such as never, ever wear a brand new sports bra during a long training run.

Still, learning the stories of others who were battling cancer made my aches and pains seem miniscule in comparison. I began to appreciate how lucky I was to have a strong body capable of running a marathon. And partaking in those Saturday morning group training runs and listening to the "mission moments" of those affected by cancer, gave me perspective and a cause outside of myself to focus on. The organization also gave me a sense of community similar to the one I had felt when I was more active in my church and youth ministry.

Most importantly, running gave me back the confidence that had been stripped away by a messy breakup. While you can train with others, running is a mostly independent sport, and actually more mental than it is physical. You need the discipline to do your training runs every day, and you have to believe that your body is capable of running for hours on end. As with most things in life, believing in yourself is half the battle. Perseverance, dedication and self-confidence are great qualities to cultivate when you're aiming for a successful marriage as well.

I traveled almost 3,000 miles to San Diego to run the marathon, and it was an amazing experience. Getting to mile twenty-five and realizing that I was about to finish a full marathon, that I had really done it, was incredibly life-affirming. It gave me this overwhelming feeling of awe that I've since felt only three other times in my life: the moment when my husband proposed, and the moments when each of my two children were born. I didn't even mind that it took me seventeen minutes longer than my goal time to finish.

Unfortunately, running a marathon didn't work in helping me in my main goal – I ended up getting back together with Joe again. And then breaking up with him again. And then getting back together with him again. Sometimes a bad relationship is like sin. You keep going back to it no matter how hard you try.

Joe and I broke up for the last time in March of the next year. This time, I was more mentally and emotionally ready for the breakup. Even though I wanted to be with Joe, I knew I wanted marriage and babies more, and I would never have them with Joe. I also felt more trusting for the first time that God had someone better in mind for me.

At the time I was experimenting with prayer journaling again. I've kept prayer journals on and off over the years, and this one ended up lasting a total of nine days. Two nights after I broke up with my ex for the last time, I wrote in this prayer journal, "God, please let me meet the man I'm supposed to marry, and please let him love You too."

I think I realized then that how much I wanted my faith to be part of any relationship I pursued. I had gotten back into volunteering in youth ministry since running the marathon, and had met some examples of couples who shared the same Catholic beliefs. To them, marriage was more than just a good relationship and a piece of paper; it was the sacrament of matrimony. Out of all of the guys I had dated throughout my teen years and college through my mid-20s, not one of them had been a practicing Catholic. Practicing male Catholics in my generation seem to be few and far between.

Still, I prayed because I believed that this could be the missing element that would make a good relationship strong enough to last in the long run. I wanted a guy who would go to church with me, and I prayed that God would help me find him. I met him the very next night.

It was a Friday night and I was supposed to be hanging out with a few girlfriends I had met through the marathon, but the plans fell through at the last minute. Terrified at the thought of a Friday night home alone with my thoughts, the first Friday since breaking up officially with Joe, I scrambled to make other plans. I found them on a website called Meetup.com, an online platform for local events based on certain interests. I had been to meetup events before, like running meetups and writing meetups (I had actually met Joe at the latter). This night, I chose to go to a Catholic young adults meetup at a church a few towns away.

The event started with Adoration and then a group discussion in the church basement. What did we discuss? I don't remember, but I do remember seeing my future husband for the first time in a seat across the circle from me and thinking, "Hmmm. Maybe."

After the group discussion, everyone went to a local diner and sat together at a long row of tables. My future husband, Patrick, ended up sitting right next to me.

Patrick seemed a little shy but intrigued by my constant chatter and friendliness that night. He sent me a Facebook message the next day and our friendship grew from there. It helped that this Catholic young adults group had a bunch of meetup events planned, which gave us stress-free opportunities to see each other again. Our first non-group hangout was actually going to a Good Friday service at my church and then talking for hours afterward. I was initially hesitant to jump into something serious so soon after breaking up with Joe, but something told me that I shouldn't miss a good opportunity just because of the timing.

One night not long after we started dating, I could tell there was something on his mind. "I have something to tell you," he said, and I prepared myself for the worst.

But it turned out to be something slightly ironic. He told me he has chronic myeloid leukemia – also known as CML – but that his condition is controlled by a drug called Gleevec. Thanks to Gleevec, he never had to undergo radiation or chemotherapy. He just takes a daily pill and he is able to live a normal, otherwise healthy life with a normal life expectancy. The research and development of Gleevec was majorly funded by the Leukemia & Lymphoma Society – the same organization I had raised thousands of dollars and ran hundreds of miles for.

Coincidence? Maybe. Maybe not. Patrick was afraid that this information might dissuade me from pursuing a more serious relationship with him. And perhaps it was because of my experience with blood cancers through Team in Training, but it didn't. At all. Instead I just said, "I ran a marathon for you."

I continued seeing Patrick but it wasn't until I ran my next marathon for LLS that I realized I was in love with him. It was a drizzly September morning, and Patrick was a total rock star that day. He drove me almost two hours to the start line. He took pictures of me and my teammates and coaches. He cheered for me as the race began, and then drove to different points along the course to cheer some more at moments I needed it most. He scavenged up a bottle of water and banana for me at the finish line. And when we returned to his car, I found a rose and teddy bear waiting for me. The teddy bear was wearing a shirt that said, "You are amazing."

I didn't say I love you just yet, but that's when I started to feel it. That's when I started to look at him and trust that this was a man who could take care of me for the rest of my life. A man I wanted to take care of, too. A man who shared my vision of a future with the sacrament of matrimony and children – and soon.

Sometimes I wish I had met Patrick when we were younger so that we'd have more time together. But the truth is, if I had met Patrick when we were younger I might have thought he wasn't my type. I wouldn't have known all of the things I didn't want in a relationship by experiencing them with the wrong guys, and I wouldn't have fully appreciated the right relationship when it was finally there. I wouldn't have been as grateful as I am now to have a guy to hold my hand during a homily (though let's be honest. These days we can't hold hands during mass anymore because we're too busy trying to keep our one-year-old and two-year-old from escaping the pew.) The family my husband and I are building has become the strongest little Catholic community I could ever hope to be a part of, and my most important relationship – the one with God – is thriving in a way it never has before.

I haven't really run in years because my body went through the equally difficult experience of back-to-back pregnancies. But I recently got exciting news – after years of trying, I finally got into the New York City Marathon through the lottery drawing. I had a less than 15 percent chance of getting picked, but this year I was lucky. I've decided I'm going to run the marathon with Team in Training.

My advice to singles is to view the path to a marriage vocation like training for a marathon. You simply can't run a marathon without properly training for it first, so prepare yourself to be ready for the right relationship when it does come. Focus on making yourself a stronger person and honing the qualities that will make you a good spouse. Look at your missteps as learning experiences. And just keep moving, no matter how slowly you're going, and no matter how much you're hurting.

There is a bigger picture and you will get to that finish line eventually, even if it's not exactly within your goal time; in a marathon, every finisher gets the same medal in the end. Trust that God is guiding your steps, even when you get a little off course. Sometimes the destination isn't what you thought it would be, but it's actually so much better.

A Second Chance

Aneesa Plumey (E25/M26)

On a weekend in May of 1992, my mother packed my bags and took me to our parish of San Isidro Catholic Church in Pompano Beach, Florida for a retreat. She waved goodbye to me as the bus pulled from the parking lot. I sulked in the second to last seat. I was not prepared for the way that God would radically change my life that weekend, but that's the way God usually works!

The very first person to pray with me on this retreat was a wonderful woman named Isabel Plumey. She would later become one of my most favorite women, as well as an amazing support and my personal prayer warrior. I remember her praying with me on the first night of retreat. When she was done, she looked at me and said "Aneesa, I don't know why but I feel like God is telling me that you are going to be a part of my life for a very long time." Of course, being a skeptical teenager, I didn't believe her for one minute.

On that retreat weekend, I also met two of Isabel's three children. Her daughter was funny and welcoming. Her son, Javier, was nice and also very serious about his faith. He was also a couple of years younger than me so, I just looked at him as Isabel's sweet son. I began to develop a friendship with the Plumey family that weekend and came home ready to deepen my relationship with God and my new friends. I got involved with San Isidro's Youth Group after that retreat and remained involved throughout High School. At the same time my friendship deepened with the entire Plumey family.

After graduating from High School and starting college, I drifted away from the church and my friends. I got involved in a relationship which eventually led to marriage. On July 10, 1995, with my family and friends including the Plumeys as witnesses, I got married. I was a happy bride but also very young and scared. I went into the marriage with doubt and even some unwillingness to have children.

We were married for four and a half years, and after all of the pain, bitterness, hurt, and resentment we caused one another, we decided to separate in November of 1999. I was left broken and depressed and my mom knew that I needed someone to talk to. She reached out to Isabel and asked her to pray for me. Isabel took it one step further by calling me and inviting me over to lunch on a Sunday in April of 2000.

I was so happy to see her after losing touch for some time and we picked up right where we left off. We talked for hours that day and it felt wonderful to be with my "other mother." About two hours after I arrived, Javier came out of his room where he had been the entire time, to say hello. I didn't even realize he was there! It was great to see him as well and it was so nice to chat with him after all this time. We talked until late into the evening and I told both Javier and Isabel about my failed marriage and all that I had been experiencing. They both promised to pray for me and to keep in touch.

About two months later, my divorce was finalized, just shy of what would have been our fifth anniversary. Shortly after, Javier called me to "check in" and see how I was doing. By this point I had been seeing a therapist and taking an antidepressant. He asked me how I felt about going back to church and I told him that it was something I was open to. It had been years since I had been to church and confession so he was kind enough to say that he would go with me.

That weekend, he picked me up and drove me to confession, my first in over five years. I came out feeling so loved by God. I was able to let go of a lot of hurt and pain and found it in my heart to forgive my ex-husband. I even joined Javier and his parents for Mass the next day! And so began the story of us. I stopped taking medication shortly after going to confession.

Javier and I became closer as the months went by, often meeting for prayer or Mass, going to grab a bite to eat, or just hanging out with his mom. It was a sweet and special time in our friendship and it helped with my healing process. After about three months, Javier and I began to talk about taking our relationship a step further and explore the possibility of dating. I couldn't bring myself to say "courting" because I knew I would have to be granted an annulment in order to be married again in the Catholic Church.

I began the annulment process though my parish in October of 2000 with Javier's help. It was a painful process that brought back feelings of hurt and resentment but also one that was very vital for me to move on. I was able to petition for the annulment because on the day of my wedding, I was on birth control and therefore not open to life. I felt shame explaining that I was never open to having children with my ex. Javier was so incredibly supportive every step of the way and his presence and prayers kept me positive during the long waiting period.

After we received our first approval from the Archdiocese of Miami and my case was sent to the Archdiocese of Philadelphia for a second review, Javier proposed to me in April of 2001. He even told me that all those months earlier, as I sat and talked with his mom, he knew we were going to get married! We began planning our wedding and our future together. I was certain of one thing though, if I was not granted the annulment, we agreed that we would end our engagement because I did not want to take the opportunity to participate in the sacrament of marriage away from Javier.

In May of 2002, I received a letter granting me an Annulment and therefore allowing me to be married in the Catholic Church! We were married on July 27, 2002 at San Isidro Catholic Church. On that day, while I waited in the sacristy to walk down the aisle, my future mother-in-law Isabel came in, held my hands, looked at me with so much love and said, "See Aneesa, God is so good! He knew you would be in my life for a very long time." It was a beautiful day and I was a truly happy and blessed bride. I said my vows, with no doubts in my mind and no lies on my lips. I knew that I wanted to share a full life with Javier.

This year, Javier and I will celebrate our 16th wedding anniversary. Together we live out our Sacrament daily and share our crazy, wonderful, and perfectly imperfect lives with our two sons, Lucas and Alex along with our sweet puppy Luna. We've had our ups and downs but there's no one I'd rather share my life and my love with. God is so, so good and He has truly moved mountains for us to be together.

The Blessing of a Breakup

Katelynne Hendrick (E21/M22)
stumblingtowardsainthood.com
Twitter @SainthoodOrBust

I met my husband the night before I got dumped by the man I thought I was going to marry.

Friendship
Every year, my university hosts Orientation Week. The week kicking off my sophomore year, my boyfriend at the time and I started arguing quite a bit. That Saturday, things totally blew up between us. We were supposed to go on a camping trip with a group of friends, but I was so upset with how he brushed off my concerns that I decided to stay back. Instead, I went to a free swing dancing class on campus hoping some exercise and learning something new would help take my mind off of the fight.

Ben was starting his freshman year. He was already getting sick of playing video games and decided to look for a fun activity to do. Ben saw a chalk advertisement for a free swing dance lesson and thought it would be a good way to meet girls on a campus with a 3:1 ratio of men to women. I guess he was right.

I don't remember meeting Ben that night. Thoughts of the earlier fight preoccupied my mind, and we rotated dance partners so often that none of the people I danced with really stuck anyways. The next morning, my boyfriend dumped me right after Mass leaving me hurt but also aware that this was a good thing because he treated me so poorly.

Both Ben and I continued attending swing dance lessons on campus. After the lessons, during free dance time, we almost always danced together. I suspected he was interested in me because though there was a shortage of men in the club, he only ever asked me to dance. Despite my initial attraction to him, I wanted to be careful. I didn't want to treat him like a rebound, and I didn't want to risk getting hurt again. So we just kept building a friendship.

Conversations between Ben and I flowed naturally; we talked about music and the outdoors. Ben's involvement in his dorm's Bible study and search for a church in town piqued my interest.

Though I was a barely-practicing Catholic, I wanted to date a Christian. Admittedly, neither of my relationships with Catholic men worked out, but one of the main reasons I broke up with the other guy I had dated in high school was that his skepticism of Christianity caused some internal conflict for me. If you asked me why I wanted to date a Christian or why I thought it was important, my answer would have probably been pretty lame. I just knew there was something important about both people, at the very least, believing in God and that Jesus is God. Though I often relegated God into small compartments of my life, His presence in my life and the life of the man I would date was necessary.

Eventually, it got to the point where I wanted to see Ben more than the weekly swing dance lessons, but I was too nervous to ask for his number or give him my own. I knew he liked music and helping others, so he seemed like a great fit for a service organization I was involved with. I decided to invite him to a cookout we were hosting. Afterwards, I looked over the sign-up sheet so I could learn his last name and find him on Facebook. I'll admit this was a little stalker-y, but it turns out he was happy I did it.

Once Ben and I connected on Facebook, we talked a lot more. We'd spend hours talking both online and in person. We spent several weeks awkwardly trying to hint we were interested in each other and inviting the other to hang out, but neither of us had the guts to actually ask the other out.

Ben eventually took me on what he now refers to as a "pre-date." Our campus would play movies on the weekends, and he invited me to see a movie with him. I wasn't totally sure what to do. I was definitely interested in him, but I didn't know if it was wise to start a relationship yet. I agreed, telling him my friends and I would meet him there. If there was any doubt in my mind about whether or not he liked me, it was banished the second I saw the huge smile that broke across his face as soon as he saw me. Throughout the evening, I still couldn't figure out if it was a date, but I enjoyed my time with Ben. We ended up just walking around campus, talking for hours after the movie.

We kept hanging out, and I was pleasantly surprised at how open he was to the different activities. Whether it was swing dancing, playing board games with some friends, watching a chick flick, or just hanging out and chatting, we had fun spending time together. Eventually, I determined I was ready to date again.

Love

I can't remember the exact moment I knew I wanted our friendship to be a romantic relationship, but I do remember I was determined that I wouldn't be the one to bring up the "define the relationship" talk.

An oblivious friend thwarted that plan when he questioned me repeatedly about the state of my relationship with Ben...in front of Ben and a large group of people. With the help of some other friends, we uncomfortably changed the subject. Later that night, Ben and I walked around campus together. I apologized profusely for the awkwardness (and was internally convinced that Ben would never want to hang out with me again). We stopped in one of the music practice rooms on campus, and I listened to him play the piano.

He sat down next to me on the floor and put his arm around me. In my mind, I told myself I wouldn't try to define the relationship. I would just let things happen naturally. I could be patient. I could wait until he brought it up. But I couldn't hold it in any more. I blurted out the most romantic line conceivable "So what are we exactly? Because I feel like we're more than friends." Smooth, right?

Fortunately, Ben's response was just as eloquent: "Do you want to give it a shot?"

I said "Sure." I asked if he wanted to "give it a shot", and we started dating.

I had no desire to convert Ben to Catholicism. My faith was mostly portioned off into Sundays, choir practice, and praying each night. It was not a priority to me, so it certainly wasn't important to me that the man I was dating was also Catholic. As I said before, my qualification for a Christian boyfriend was belief in Jesus Christ. If that checkbox was marked, we were good to go.

Ben ended up converting to Catholicism about a year and a half later, but it had nothing to do with me. All credit goes to the Holy Spirit on that one.

Ben visited me our first Christmas together, and I asked if he wanted to join my family for Christmas Eve Mass or if he wanted me to also attend a Protestant service with him. He chose the former, and the beauty of the Mass spoke to him (though I didn't know that at the time). While I was on an internship that spring, I learned Ben attended Mass each Sunday because my friend was texting me about it. I didn't want Ben's conversion to be motivated by me in any way, so I didn't bother bringing it up to him. We didn't discuss our faith much anyways, so it wasn't unusual that the topic didn't come up.

One day, Ben texted me saying he was going to start going to RCIA classes the next year. I asked if it was because he wanted to learn more or if he was thinking about becoming Catholic. To my surprise, he was interested in becoming Catholic. After a number of conversations assuring that this was his own decision and not because of me, I happily supported him in his spiritual journey. Ben was confirmed into the Catholic Church a year later.

It was a pretty standard committed relationship for two college students. We spent a lot of time together and found ways to continue growing closer despite long distance. We had the same values, enjoyed similar things, and loved spending time together. My parents loved Ben, and his parents loved me. We traded off holidays and road-tripped together.

Our relationship was pretty serious, and we started making future plans.

It was the most in love either of us had ever been with another person. Unfortunately, we learned the very difficult lesson that love on its own isn't enough to sustain a relationship.

Break-Up

Like any relationship, things didn't go as smoothly as they had in the beginning. After over two years of dating, Ben broke up with me.

Those months were the worst in my life, but looking back, I can see how necessary they were for the health of our relationship and for our own good as individuals. This incredibly painful time helped me address a lot of weaknesses I hadn't noticed until post-breakup or had underestimated the depths of.

The months apart also pushed Ben and I closer to God.

Towards the end of our breakup, I attended a huge Catholic university student conference. On the last night there, the familiar, bitter sense of loneliness overwhelmed me. I went to the makeshift

Eucharistic Adoration chapel in the hotel and sat down. I admitted to God (and to myself), that I knew that if I was going to get married, Ben was meant to be my spouse. I literally told God that it was either Ben or I was going to become a religious sister.

I know that this is a terrible way to "discern" your vocation, and that being a religious sister isn't a back-up plan for not having a husband, but that was where I was at in that moment. I begged God for an answer. That's when I "heard" God's voice. It wasn't really a perception of sound. Instead, the words completely took over my mind, blocking out every other thought and sensory process.

"You are mine."

"Ok, God, that's great, but what am I supposed to do now?"

"You are mine, and that is enough."

I had wanted a clear answer-marriage or religious life - but God gave me the most important answer of all. That my purpose hinges on being His daughter. I needed that understanding, that acceptance of His love, before I was able to be in a healthy relationship.

I didn't recognize this at the time, but God was the missing piece in my relationship with Ben. We shared the same morals and values, had similarly aligned goals, and were committed to one another. These are all critically important things in a relationship, but when you place the burden of the perfect love for which we were made on an imperfect person, you are going to be disappointed.

True Love

After about three months apart, Ben and I started dating again. We reconnected by talking about our faith, and we addressed the problems that had caused us to break up. Because we centered our relationship on God instead of each other, we were able to work through the issues prior to the break-up and heal from the trust issues that developed from the break-up.

We were engaged a few months later (it was fun explaining to my co-workers that I hadn't only been dating my fiance for three months).

During that time, we navigated the stress of learning to live with a new chronic illness, surprise surgery, succeeding in classes, job-hunting, and planning for our future. We arguably had much more difficult challenges to face this time, but we were much more equipped to handle them because we kept Christ at the centerpoint.

We still had a lot more growth to do when it came to our in-dividual faith journeys (on my part, I was still trying to figure out which religion really was true), but now we were doing it together. I talked to Ben about articles I read, and Ben would share what he heard on podcasts he listened to. We talked about the hard questions when it came to our faith, and we encouraged each other to continue seeking the truth.

Marriage prep also brought up some difficult issues, and I will be forever grateful to Sr. Ellen and Fr. Ben for helping us work through those topics. As we planned our wedding day, we determined our priorities were as follows:

1. We receive the Sacrament of Holy Matrimony.
2. No one gets hurt.
3. We have fun.

On July 9, 2016, Ben and I got married in the church where Ben was confirmed and which had been such an important space for our spiritual growth. So many people warned me that my wedding day would be super stressful, but because we were focused on the big picture - the Sacramental union- all the little "oops" moments didn't seem to matter.

We've only been married about two years and haven't experienced the blessing of children yet.

I know my outlook may be rose-tinted by newlywed naivety. I know there are days we will fight. I know finances can cause a strain. I know having children (if it's God's will) will change our relationship dynamics. I know we will face challenges that we can't even conceive of. And I know there are days we might not love each other and want to give up entirely. But I also know that God's love is so much greater than all of that. I know that if we turn to God, He will give us the grace to lovingly work through the challenges we will most certainly encounter.

God's Dreams Were Better Than Mine

Leslie Sholly (E21/M22)
www.lifeineverylimb.com
FB: /lifeineverylimb
Twitter: @LeslieSholly
Instagram: @Leslie Sholly

Once upon a time, when I was eighteen years old, I had everything figured out. I was going to go to college and find a husband. He was going to be Catholic, and eventually become a lawyer. Everyone knows lawyers are rich so we would have plenty of money so that I could stay home with the ten kids we were going to have—whose names I had already picked out!

Well, I got about two-thirds of what I wanted, but it took a while.

I grew up as the product of what they used to call a "mixed marriage." My father was not Catholic. Back when my parents were married, he had to sign something promising to raise the kids Catholic, and they had to be married on the outside of the altar rail. My mother's sister was also married to a non-Catholic, as was their mother. So I grew up in an environment where church was a woman's thing, and I didn't want that for my family.

Because I wanted a Catholic husband, I picked a Catholic university—Georgetown—and planned to only date Catholic boys. I remember explaining this to some of my friends my freshman year. They thought that was crazy, but I believed (and still do) that you should never start dating anyone who you wouldn't consider to be potential marriage material, because despite your good intentions, feelings have a way of escaping your control, especially when you are young!

I met John in September 1985. We were introduced by my roommate, who knew him from French class, while he was delivering mail to our dorm. Delivering mail was his work-study job throughout college, and he used to amaze new acquaintances by reciting their P.O. Box number! We were friendly acquaintances that first year, and my first impression of him—recorded in my diary at that time—was that he was a "very funny guy."

My roommate and I were placed together at random but we chose to live together all four years. She and I ended up becoming good friends with John our sophomore year, spending most weekends going to the on-campus movies, hanging out at his apartment, drinking strange and potent alcoholic concoctions he brewed up, or going to Alfredo and Miriam's. This Georgetown pizza place was open until the wee hours and featured a middle-aged singer with a thick Italian accent whose signature pieces were "Volare" and Bruce Springsteen's "I'm on Fire."

I had known since late freshman year that my roommate had a crush on John, and I was happy for her when he asked her to a dance in the Fall of our sophomore year and they became a couple. The three of us continued to hang out together, and this didn't change even after he broke up with her a short time later. When the sparks began to fly between John and me, we did have a difficult few months.

By the second semester of my sophomore year, it was becoming increasingly obvious that John was interested in me. At the start of Presidents Day weekend, he asked me if I would have some time to talk with him on Monday when he returned from a quick visit home to Baltimore. My friends and I—because of course, being 19-year-old girls, we all discussed it—were pretty sure what he was going to say.

Sure enough, on February 16, 1987—a date I will never forget because we've celebrated it every year since—John asked if I would like to go out with him. To be honest, I had never thought of John romantically before he started showing interest in me. I'd been too used to thinking of him as my roommate's guy to consider him in that light. But by now the chemistry was working on me, and I had wanted a boyfriend for a long time so despite the roommate issue I said yes and the adventure began.

I'm happy to say that we were able to work through the awkwardness in time. My roommate was eventually glad to be my maid of honor and we are all friends to this day.

I was free to fall for John and I fell hard. If you've ever been infatuated with someone, you know how it goes—I lost weight because I wasn't interested in eating! I would try to study, reading an entire Platonic dialogue without taking in a word. We wrote love letters daily. We were trading declarations of love in the space of a week, long before we really understood what love really was or what it would demand of us.

We were eating brunch when I first looked across the table at John and asked myself how I felt about staring at him across a breakfast table every morning for the rest of my life. I decided I was okay with that.

I only went home for a short time that summer since I planned to work in D.C. during the holiday. John came down to Knoxville with me to meet my family. It was late one night during his visit when we had a very important conversation. I'm not sure he appreciated at the time how important—how pivotal—that conversation was. Even though we'd only been dating for a few months, I'd already been thinking a lot about how and when to approach this topic. Because whether John knew it or not, the future of our relationship hinged on the outcome of this talk we were about to have.

You see, despite all my grand plans about who I was going to date and who I was going to marry and how my life was going to turn out, I had fallen in love with a non-Catholic. I had traveled from Knoxville, Tennessee, where I was one of the 2% of Catholics surrounded by mostly Southern Baptists (including over half my own relatives) to a Catholic college hoping to find a nice Catholic boy to marry. Instead I met a boy from Baltimore, one of the most Catholic cities in America, who happened to be a SOUTHERN BAPTIST.

John's father, who had died less than two years before we met, was nominally Presbyterian but didn't care about organized religion. His mother was raised Southern Baptist but didn't go to church because her husband didn't want to go. So John was essentially unchurched as a child, but he had made the decision on his own to be baptized at nineteen, not long before we met. He had a lot of predictable ideas and misconceptions about Catholicism, but thank God he was curious and intelligent and willing to listen and learn.

Although we may have discussed religion casually in our friendship, I'd never had any reason until now to tell him that it was a non-negotiable requirement for me that my children be raised Catholic. I know a mixed-religion family where the boys go to a Catholic church with their father and the girls attend a Protestant church with their mother. I've heard of families who attend both churches every Sunday, or switch off each week. And there are families who don't do anything and let the children grow up to make their own choices. I think John initially believed we might be able to compromise on this issue—maybe meet in the middle and go to an Episcopal church or something. Not being raised a Catholic, he just didn't understand, and I knew I had to make him understand.

By the end of that night I had obtained his promise that any children we might theoretically have—and this was all VERY theoretical to him because he was imagining the one or two kids he thought we might have maybe ten years down the road—could be raised Catholic as long as he could tell them what parts of the faith he disagreed with. I went along with that, figuring we would cross that particular bridge when we came to it!

Although our theologies were different, we both agreed strongly that a married couple should attend church together. Because he'd been attending a Catholic college and respected the Jesuits who had been his teachers, John was willing to try going to Mass with me. We are both very stubborn people but I had been Catholic all my life whereas the regular practice of religion was new to him. Had he practiced all his life I think winning him over to all of this would have been a lot harder.

Another thing we both agreed on strongly was the permanence of marriage. Because we both believed marriage was a commitment that would require hard work, even while we were still a relatively new couple, we started doing some of that work by having deep discussions and hashing out these disagreements rather than ignoring them in favor of maintaining harmony.

When I was a high school junior, part of our religion curriculum was a relationship component based on an ancient workbook—my used copy was already falling apart when I purchased it—called *Relating*[14]. It was full of checklists, quizzes, and advice about Christian relationships. I specifically remember a section called "The Ten Hallmarks of Love vs. Infatuation" and another section that introduced us to the concepts of fighting fairly. I am not the only person I know who dragged that textbook out during college to evaluate a romantic relationship! I brought it along on a road trip we took during the summer and while John drove I shared its wisdom with him. We took the various relationship quizzes. We had been dating six months by this time and the results encouraged me to believe that our relationship was on strong footing.

One of the hallmarks of love vs. infatuation is that your grades tend to suffer if you are only infatuated—and in truth my grades during our first few months of courtship were the worst I'd ever made! When I made straight A's the following semester, I felt vindicated! That was my junior and John's senior year. We lived in the same dorm on separate floors, and spent pretty much every spare moment together. We even took a class together—20th Century Protestant Theology! My roommate and I had always been inseparable, but she had a boyfriend, who would later become her husband, so she did not feel abandoned.

I majored in English and minored in Theology, and that year I took a class that was life-changing for both of us—Christian Marriage. *Humanae Vitae*[15] and *The Art of Natural Family Planning*[16] were two of the required texts for this class, which was taught by a Jesuit.

Of course I knew that the Church was against the use of artificial birth control. We even watched a film on NFP in high school. But no one had ever told me WHY. I thought this was some old-fashioned notion that could be safely ignored. Until I read *Humanae Vitae*. I remember well how increasingly uncomfortable I grew, page by page, as it became obvious that there WERE reasons, that they made sense, and that I was not going to be able to ignore this teaching. I knew we were in for a very uncomfortable conversation and that it wasn't going to be easy to convince John that we were going to have to follow MY conscience in this matter.

When we did discuss it, he remained unconvinced by the theology but somewhat persuaded by the science behind NFP plus its aesthetic appeal, and he agreed that when the time came we would try it my way. I started charting a year before we were married so that I would have lots of practice and as luck or perhaps Providence would have it, Phase III began on the day of our wedding.

We became engaged in the summer of 1988, after John had graduated, moved across the river, and started his first real job with the Office of Federal Investigations. My senior year was divided between school, spending most of my spare time with John, and wedding planning. My roommate and I left our Friday schedules free so that we could drive all around the D.C. area trying on wedding and bridesmaid dresses! It was a busy and exciting time. I was working two jobs and taking five classes and excelling at all of it which seemed like a good sign to me.

We were married in my parish church in August 1989 by a Jesuit whom we had come to know at Georgetown. He was John's Intro to Philosophy professor, and was one of the priests associated with the Catholic student group my roommate and I were active in. Our ceremony was a Catholic one, but without a Mass. John refused to kneel and insisted that we say the Protestant version of the Our Father but I felt those were small concessions to make, considering I was marrying a man whose uncle handed him an anti-Catholic pamphlet on the wedding day, saying "I just want to make sure you know what you are getting into."

I'll be honest, we didn't go to church every, or even most, Sundays the first year we were married. But when we did, we went to Catholic churches. And when we moved to Knoxville a year later, we did begin going weekly, checking out various parishes at John's request before ending up back at my home parish.

Our less-than-perfect-practice of the principles of NFP landed us with three babies in four years. We found out that #3 was on the way when #2 was only five months old, and just days before John was to take the bar exam. Our circumstances at that time were far from ideal! But that wasn't the only surprise coming.

We told our family and friends about the upcoming new baby in August 1994 at a party after #2's baptism. Then John announced that he had been offered his first post-law school job. My mother said something like, "So many surprises! The next thing you know you'll be telling us you are becoming Catholic!" To which John replied, "Well, as a matter of fact ..."

You see, just a few days before he had shared with me his intention of starting RCIA classes in the fall. I NEVER saw it coming. I never pressured him—never did anything other than pray. God worked on him through his weekly Mass attendance. He grew to want to be a real part of the church where he worshipped every week. We had a pastor at that time who gave him the grace to continue to have doubts and questions as he began the process and he has grown in faith and fidelity since, from just wanting to believe to really believing.

John entered the Church at Easter 1995. None of our children remember a time when their father wasn't Catholic. John always says our wedding day was the happiest of his life, but for me nothing will match the day he became Catholic.

Just a short while later John attended his first Knights of Columbus meeting. He'd grown up around men who were involved in the

Masons and other fraternal orders and was very excited to become a Knight. He came home that evening and told me that at the end of the meeting, as he knelt with the other men to say the rosary, he thought to himself: "How did this happen?"

He's been Catholic for 23 years now, and went on to be the KOC Grand Knight several times, the Color Corps Commander for the Fourth Degree, a KOC District Deputy, a two-time Pastoral Council member, and a Lector—not to mention the father of five. Most people are shocked to learn that he isn't a cradle Catholic.

My "mixed marriage" story had the happiest of endings. And many people are able to have happy marriages even when their spouse never converts. But that doesn't mean my opinion has changed. I still think that my initial reluctance to date anyone who wasn't Catholic was a good impulse. I would still recommend looking for your future spouse in a Catholic environment. I would still never advise you date someone you think you'd never want to marry.

Even though the Lord works in mysterious ways, and even though He had a sense of humor in guiding me to marry a Southern Baptist after I traveled so far to find a Catholic, it was HARD. And marriage is hard enough already. If you want a good one, it's going to take a lot of work even if you are both coming from the same faith tradition. It's hard having to explain and justify everything about your beliefs, it's hard having to negotiate everything, and it's REALLY hard to maintain a completely chaste relationship when you are young and in love and only one of you is committed to waiting.

But if you do find yourself in a serious relationship with a non-Catholic, I have two recommendations. The first is to know your faith. And if you don't know it already, study it. Be able to answer your partner's questions. The Church really does have all the answers! You don't have to make them up or figure them out on your own. The second is to know—and STICK TO—what is non-negotiable for you. Your kids must be baptized Catholic, but maybe they don't have to attend parochial school. You have to go to Mass every Sunday, but maybe your spouse can stay home or attend a different church. Don't let yourself be pushed into anything that's wrong for you, but don't insist on having your way about every last thing when there is room to consider your partner's feelings.

Back to the beginning of my story . . . I met my husband in college, and he is Catholic now. He's a lawyer, but most of his work is with indigent clients and we are not rich! We have five living children and a sixth who was miscarried, and most of their names were not on the list I had before I met him. I've been a stay-at-home mother since my second child was six months old, but I currently work at home. John had planned to date many women before settling down in his 30s and having one or two kids, so we still ended up with most of what I wanted—and I'm pretty sure he's not sorry it turned out that way!

The Waiting Game

Kimberly Cook (E30/M31)
Author, Blogger, Artist
www.thelionofdesign.com

An Early Revelation

From a very early age, I drew close to our Lord, and although I was not from a very devout household, I found myself speaking with the Lord often throughout my childhood. Among these years of childhood innocence, there were a few very distinct spiritual revelations from him – one of which was about my future vocation.

I remember running to tell my mom about this particular revelation, around the age of seven. "Mommy," I said, "I am not going to meet my husband until I am thirty." My mother smiled at me amusedly and asked where I had heard such a thing. "Jesus told me," I said plainly and excitedly, although I had no idea what that meant, or where age thirty fell in relation to the course of my lifetime.

Perhaps what I remember most about that experience, was the startling shock on my mother's face at the mention of the unfamiliar spiritual mysticism I had encountered. "Don't worry honey," she comforted, "You will be married long before age thirty." I was temporarily satisfied with that, and as the years went on, the memory of this experience faded into the recesses of my childhood memories.

Without God

By high school, all connections to religion had been severed. My family no longer practiced our Catholic faith, and I found myself plunged into the darkness of teenage angst, amongst my public-school peers - all of whom had been exposed to much more than I ever had.

That first year was a battle for my innocence and purity. Everything seemed to be moving so quickly around me – information, relationships, hormones, expectations! And everyone seemed to be angry, depressed, and had some great cause and need for rebellion. I found myself greatly isolated in this new miniature teenage society.

At long last, the battle within me was lost, as little-by-little I gave in to the pressure of these temptations floating about. At first there was a constant nagging - sickening me at the thought of every sin. I tried in vain to push it away. After all, God was no longer present in these darkest and most dismal years. My spiritual affection for him only surfaced at times of greatest darkness, like the cry of a wounded animal who knew it was trapped.

Return to Him

Thankfully, the good Lord spared me the injustice of being "lukewarm." I can certainly say that I was always either icy cold or burning hot - and those sentiments he could work with! I ran back to his loving embrace shortly after high school, and after a profoundly miraculous experience ushered in by Our Lady, I turned away from my past, received confirmation, and headed off to the Catholic haven of Franciscan University of Steubenville.

There, at college, in the heart of a community striving for sainthood, I found the true freedom my heart had longed for. As my original childhood faith once again increased, I recalled those whisperings of my heart. Still, I doubted the message that stated so clearly that I would meet my husband at age thirty, and rather hoped I would find my spouse among one of the deeply spiritual men attending the University.

I met many of these upright and holy men while attending college, and I formed wonderful friendships with some of them. Yet, there was no peace to be found in moving forward in one of these relationships. Religious life presented a great and beautiful attraction to me, but I knew it was not meant to be my vocation.

Turbulent Times and Limbo

Integrating back into daily life after my time of sanctuary at Franciscan University was not easy. Shortly after returning home, I ended up back in a turbulent relationship, which quickly escalated to a marriage proposal. Although every grain of common sense within me opposed the proposal – I said "yes" anyway.

That engagement lasted for a total of a month, before we both had to face the reality that it was not in the Lord's plan for us. A great depression fell over me, and although I plunged myself into meaningful work, study, and friendships over the following years, I couldn't help feeling that something was missing. There was a missing piece of my heart, which I knew the Lord wanted to fill in this lifetime. And I knew that promise of sacrificial service – my personal path to heaven, was the love of a husband and children.

So, throughout the remainder of my twenties I clung to that promise, as I watched the dwindling remnant of my single friends enter happily into marriages of their own. I can't tell you exactly how lonely it became, I can only describe to you that it produced such a vivid spiritual and mental anguish that I felt my heart was actually screaming out to the Lord in Adoration as the tears burned down my cheeks.

Something was missing, I knew something was missing. I just couldn't understand why the Lord was making me wait so long. Guided by a spiritual director, I began to "prepare" for marriage by reducing frivolous time and focusing instead on increasing strengths to bring to a marriage. I cooked and cleaned more, tried to serve others, focused on my prayer life, and began to pray a rosary every day for my future spouse. I knew that if he was truly out there, I wanted to shower him with prayers now, rather than wait until I met him. Somehow, I had the sense that he needed the prayers now. The Lord put this devotion on my heart, and I would find out soon enough why he did.

Turning 30

As I mournfully accepted my thirtieth birthday, I was not at all at peace with where I was in my life. My career was uncertain, as I held a very stressful and non-maintainable teaching position. The romantic relationship I had been trying to hang onto for the past year had recently ended, leaving me with no prospects in sight. I had no certainty of the future in any direction, and yet there remained an unexplainable tiny glimmer of hope within me. All I could do was surrender the desires of my heart over and over again to my heavenly Father. Thinking back on this now is bitter-sweet.

It was at a Halloween party hosted by Catholic young adults in the DC area that I first "met" my husband. I emphasize "met" because it truly was a brief two-minute meeting. My roommate called me over to introduce me to a few people, one of which was Cory. As my roommate was extremely social and always introducing me to new people, I thought absolutely nothing of our first meeting, and neither did he. In fact, if my roommate hadn't gone on to invite him to several events at our house, I may never have seen him again. But God had other plans.

He was *nothing* at all like I had imagined my future spouse to be – a deeply rooted Catholic from a big family, perhaps raised on a farm or the side of a beautiful mountain somewhere. In fact, he had been raised in a small agnostic household, and only converted to Catholicism as a senior in college, at a secular university.

How it all Changed

As I prepared to retake the GRE, in hopes of improving my hopeless math score for entrance into graduate school, I knew I would have to cut out almost all social time. Against my will, my well-intentioned roommate took the liberty of asking Cory to tutor me in math, considering that he was an engineer and very proficient in math. He agreed, and she set the whole thing up - none of us knowing it would lead to anything more than a better score.

I should mention that my second score was somehow worse *after* he tutored me, which should say something about our focus. At first, I was frustrated my roommate had set up the tutoring, and I prepared for a very awkward first session, after which I had decided I would kindly tell him was all the help I needed.

But as we sat down at Panera with a hot drink and a math textbook between us, the hours passed quickly. We laughed easily and comfortably with one another and our personalities and intellects balanced one another quite well. I discovered that his lack of Catholic community after coming into the Church had led him along many rocky paths over the years - something he was working avidly to remedy. In fact, it was over the past few years (when I was praying the rosary for him) that he really felt a saving grace call him back into the fold of Mother Church!

By the end of that first tutoring session, we had struck a deal. As I was a theology student who needed to learn math, and he was an engineer who wanted to learn theology, we would continue the tutoring sessions, splitting them between the study of math and the study of theology.

For many months our relationship was nothing more than a friendship we both appreciated. God still had not opened either of our eyes to the chosen one he had placed before us. In fact, I still prayed fervently and longed for God to reveal my future spouse.

Then, all at once, it changed. One night, Cory looked at me from across a crowded room, and as he recalls; the Holy Spirit stirred such a strong and powerful love in his heart, that he was overcome. It seemed ridiculous to him that he couldn't have seen it all along, and he knew that my heart would be his.

The Fast Track

Something was also stirring in my own heart, but I made every effort to resist it. This was primarily due to a complicated situation, which involved not wanting to hurt a dear friend who had begun to develop feelings for him. I'm so thankful now for spiritual direction, because it clearly untangled the virtue from the vice, and laid out a clear path forward – with Cory.

When I finally said "yes" to a relationship with Cory, we knew very quickly that we were on the fast track to marriage! We both knew that we were called to an abundant vocation of marriage and children, deeply rooted in the Catholic Church. We were also building upon a year-long friendship that had developed gradually and naturally over time.

I remember how overwhelmed I was with joy on our wedding day. After the Mass, I went to the back of the basilica and wept like a baby. I felt overcome with emotion, to the point of wanting to burst with joy. It could not have been better if I had experienced a miracle right before my eyes, for I knew that the Lord fulfilled his promise to me, and that he is not outdone in generosity when he promises the desires of our heart.

God Redeems

Donna Belleville (E23/M24)

Fred's Story (Written by Donna's husband)

The church teaches that I must be willing to give myself to a woman the same way Jesus gave of himself for the church. I must sacrifice my life for the spiritual health of my wife. It took me a long time to really understand what this meant. Before telling our story, I want to discuss the brokenness that God had to heal in order to create a person worthy of love, relationship, and marriage.

For years, I treated women as objects. At the age of eight I was exposed to pornography. That began a warped mentality toward women and relationships. I didn't know love was possible outside the emotions of eroticism. This thinking led me down some dark paths and deep despair. Drinking, of course, accompanied this way of life which only made the descent gain speed.

When I was in my early twenties, I tried to find this feeling of love through sex with a teenager. This was the point where my life drastically changed. After much treatment and incarceration, I sought the spiritual help from the church. After eighteen months of jail, I was given a second chance at life on probation.

I started attending Mass weekly with my mom and a very kind priest began to look out for me. There was a one-day seminar put on by the church called Theology of the Body presented by Christopher West. My mom invited me to attend and for whatever reason, I was willing. It was the first time I was ever told the God given calling of men and women and of marriage. Or, at least, it was the first time I was willing to listen. Something changed in me that day.

I bought that man's book and went up to him after to get him to sign it. All I could do was cry. He gave me a big hug and told me to cry out to the Lord, "All will be okay," he said. I walked away with hope and a new purpose in my life. I tried to read *Theology of the Body*[17] every day. The more I read, the more I realized how much work I had to do.

I tried to always think of women as children of God. I tried to date, but with very little success. Women would take my lack of desire for sex two ways; I was either a religious nut who was living in the past or they just figured I did not like them since I didn't want to use them. An alcohol recovery program teaches that if we are having difficulty in any area of life, we need to get involved into serving others.

I started to bring meetings into treatment facilities and attended many meetings. I volunteered to put a on a BBQ to help raise money and awareness. It was during the planning of this BBQ that I first met Donna. We went out to dinner and I was completely honest with her. I told her of my horrible past, but most importantly how I am trying to live my life today. I told her I had returned to my Catholic roots and I wanted God to be at the center of my life today.

Our evening ended. I walked her to her car and gave her a hug. I assumed that it all would have been enough to scare her off for good. As it turned out, God had us both go through some more godless relationships to prepare us for what was to come.

About a year after that dinner, I received a text from Donna asking if I was seeing anyone. This would begin the greatest chapter in our book. Donna and I began to talk endlessly about *Theology of the Body*[18] and the Catholic Church. We attempted to understand how to date while trusting in all the church teaches. After about a year of dating, chastity, and reconciliation from a loving God, we decided to get married.

During preparation for marriage we learned about Natural Family Planning. I also learned about the Church's teaching on being open to life, a teaching that I definitely struggled with. I had many fears about being a father. I was convinced that I was not good enough and because of my past, it would be far too difficult on a child. As we approached our wedding day, we learned that Donna would be fertile during our honeymoon.

This was something that gave me great anxiety. I prayed daily to be open to life. I went to Adoration often with this one intention in mind, but whenever I would think about being a parent, the anxiety would return. It wasn't until the day before our wedding that I would get some relief. During my prayer time, on that very day, I thought about being a parent again but this time an incredible peace washed over me. I know that God had, once again, given me the grace to follow his will. Wouldn't you know it, he gave us a beautiful child on that honeymoon.

Donna's Story

From my earliest memories I struggled with depression, self-loathing, and an obsession with doing the next thing to feel okay in my own skin. I was always trying to fill that 'God-shaped hole' in my heart with anything but. This led me down a path of alcoholism, promiscuity, and drug addiction. This lifestyle began to change, however, when I got clean and sober at nineteen years old.

Through my recovery, I had discovered a relationship with a God of my understanding but had not returned to my Catholic roots. When I met Fred, I would not have considered myself a Catholic. We met doing service work. At that time, I was in another relationship. On that first day of service, we went out after a work meeting to a sandwich shop.

He laid out his story. His honesty was refreshing and attractive. He was an open book. There was nothing to hide. It wasn't until about a year later that we started actually dating. Over the course of that year I slowly began learning more about the God I had grown up with. I began going to church and every once in a while, I would see Fred from across the church. At 6'4", he stood up above the crowd and was easy to spot. He wasn't the reason I kept going back but I did enjoy seeing him.

I continued to stay in an unhealthy relationship for the next year. One Sunday at Mass, I heard God speak loud and clear to my heart, "It's time." I knew I couldn't continue in a relationship based on nothing of importance. I wanted to be wanted and loved, but God was calling me to so much more then what I was settling for. That day I reached out, in faith, to Fred.

The beginning of our relationship was a lot of talking about what the Catholic Church taught regarding sexuality. He was so honest and forthright with me regarding his past. I felt a spark of light in this new way of thinking. It was intriguing to me, but I couldn't understand why living according to the *Theology of the Body* was better than the way I had learned to live from the culture.

We had a lot of deep conversations about sexuality and the human body. Naturally, he directed me to reading *Theology of the Body for Beginners*[19] by Christopher West. I would sit in Adoration and soak up the material. This book rocked my world! All that Fred had been talking about started making sense in light of Pope St. John

Paul II's teachings of *Theology of the Body*. There was a beauty in this that I had never known. I felt like I had discovered the secret we are all searching for - that desire to be wanted and loved was a God-given desire. I realized it was my own distortion of it, my sinfulness, that had led to so many problems. I saw through my brokenness and came to understand my true essence as good and beautiful.

Dating Fred was a whole new experience for me. We strived in all things to live out a chaste relationship. We went to Mass and Adoration together frequently. God was in the middle of our relationship from the beginning. Fred proposed on our one year dating anniversary and we were married six months later.

Our Story

We married on August 15, 2009 (the Feast of the Assumption of Mary). Pope Saint John Paul II has always been a patron for us. Following the church's teachings and prayerfully being open to life, God blessed us with five children over the next seven years. During this time, Fred started his own business and Donna has been able to stay home to care for the kids.

There have been many ups and down over the years. Because of Fred's past, he has to limit his involvement in parish life and events at the children's school. The road of recovery has been a difficult one for both of us, but through the grace of God, we have risen above each trial, stronger as a result. We continue to keep God at the center of our marriage which gives us a strength we would not have on our own.

We work on our spiritual health by going to monthly confession and weekly Adoration. We keep 'us' a priority through regular date nights, lunch dates, and attending marriage seminars and retreats. We both meet with spiritual directors.

During our eighth year of marriage we had the opportunity to attend a marriage retreat put on by Christopher West. It was an honor to be able to go up to him at the end of the seminar to thank him for introducing us to these life changing teachings. He prayed with us, encouraging us to continue diving deeper into these teachings and fighting for this goodness God has given us in our marriage and our beautiful family.

Our past brokenness and life experiences have made us who we are today. We are able to use our past to help others through experience, strength and hope. It's difficult to regret past mistakes when God has used them to create such a beautiful present. We live our lives today grateful for a life we surely do not deserve, devoted to our family and Christ's teachings.

An Unlikely Matchmaker, My Brother

Lori Mierzejewski (E26/M27)

Sometimes a love story starts before you even know it's being written. This was the case with my husband and me. My brother, Tony, had been best friends with Jim, my future husband, since elementary school. At first they played at school. Then they played in Little League together, opposite teams, but they had fun teasing each other and playing ball together. When it was time to move onto middle school, Jim made the school team and Tony would cheer his friend on from the sidelines.

By the time high school rolled around, they formed a team with their other friends and played recreational basketball and softball. All the while joking and enjoying whatever they were doing. They had similar interests and liked spending time together. It was when Tony and Jim were freshman in high school that I had my first face to face meeting with Jim.

We lived down the street from the high school so our house was the natural meeting place. He knocked on the door. I ran to answer not knowing it was a friend of Tony's. When I saw this cute guy at the door with a killer smile I turned three shades of red. He asked if Tony was home. I called to my brother. My mother showed up first and asked me to invite Jim in.

Stumbling in the kitchen I became very aware of my surroundings. I knew of Jim but had never actually met him. My brother strolled in and casually said, "Oh Jim, this is my sister Lori." He smiled and I melted. This would be the extent of my exposure to him for the next few years. He'd knock on the door, we'd do small talk in the kitchen, my brother would show up, I'd smile like a silly schoolgirl, he'd give me a cute chuckle, and the boys would head off.

Before we knew it, I was starting my freshman year of high school. I had all kinds of crushes on various guys but at this point, I had never considered Jim a crush. I never fantasized about dating him, I just thought he was nice and of course cute. After all, he was my brother's friend so anything but being the kid sister was out of the question. All the while he was so gentle and sweet when he spoke to me. He made me feel special. I was able to let my true self out without worrying about drama.

I would always be the younger sister and he would always be my brother's friend -- end of story. There was zero chance of anything ever going further and besides, he already had a girlfriend. What would he see in me anyway? Unbeknownst to me, he enjoyed our kitchen chats and actually looked forward to the whole three seconds we would talk and stare at each other smiling the whole time. Well, Jim smiled, I turned beet red and tried to act natural. Over time, I became very relaxed around him. He fell into this strange quasi-friend zone. I fell into a quasi-little sister zone for him.

I was sitting with my mother one day and I was down in the dumps feeling very unloved. I was telling her my tale of woe about no one liking me. She said, "Lori, really? No one likes you?"

I said, "Not in a boyfriend/girlfriend way."

She hugged me and said, "Honey, the boys know you are special. Boys don't want special now, they want special when they marry."

I said, "If you are trying to make me feel better, it is not working." I smiled and added, "I know mom but can't someone just ask me to a movie or something?"

She replied as she often did, "God has a plan. He knows who you will marry someday. When you least expect it your future husband will appear. In fact, you may just marry a friend of your brother's one day."

"Eww!" I said. "No Mom, not a friend of Tony's. They are all gross!"

She laughed and walked out of the room saying, "You'll see... when you least expect it." Cue my eye roll and sigh.

Did you ever stop and think why certain people are always in the background of your life? Just there lurking. They are living their life and you are living yours, but for some unexplained reason your lives are always crossing paths? Now that I think about it, Jim was that person for me and I was that for him.

He was just always in the right place at the right time for me. There was this one time, I must have been 21 or 22 years old driving my new car around feeling cool when I turned my head and saw Tony being carried into an ambulance. I had a mild anxiety attack as I pulled over and ran to see what was happening. Tony had gone to a picnic at his friend Mark's house. Mark's picnics were legendary, lots of horsing around, swimming and some drinking. Tony dislocated his shoulder messing around in the pool.

As always, Jim was there. He saw me run over to see what happened to my brother. He hugged me and told me what happened. He made sure I was calm before getting into the car and let my parents know what happened. Driving away I smiled and thought what a nice guy!

Jim was there when I moved into my apartment the next year. He just happened to be free and volunteered to help move my stuff. He had a BIG Chevy Blazer that was able to fit my bed, dressers and loveseat. Not only did he give up a whole day to help me move, but he helped my roommates too! When we threw a thank you party, Tony and his friends were invited. Jim came alone and stayed late into the night laughing and talking with me.

Our paths would cross often, some of the time I was dating someone and other times he was dating someone. It seemed we took turns being unavailable. We were moving closer and closer but the timing was not right. We did our fair share of flirting and laughing whenever we saw each other. One thing that never changed was how much we liked spending time together. It didn't hurt that I thought he was so cute with those blue/green eyes, his dimples, and his laugh which always made me smile.

Things seemed to change a bit after Tony got married. Yes, we were both in the wedding and yes, we danced a fair amount too. The next day there was a picnic for family and close friends of the bride and groom. After a few glasses of wine, I worked up the courage to say, "Jim, I know you like me. Why not just ask me out?"

He replied, "Really?" Then he added, "You could ask me out too."

I tossed my head and said, "Not on your life!" and walked away. All the while I was chastising myself. *Why oh why did you make a fool out of yourself and say something!* I was totally embarrassed. Meanwhile, Jim felt very good about himself saying softly, "Hmmm... maybe... just maybe."

The timing still wasn't right but things started changing slowly. Jim had just landed a job he was gunning for at a utility company. Now, he could finally think about settling down with just the right person. Could this be the right timing?

He starting showing up at places he knew I would be like basketball games for my much younger brother who was still in high school. Supporting my little brother, I would show up after work, walk in the gym, and low and behold, Jim and Tony were sitting on the bleachers smiling and waving me over. The three of us would sit together and watch the game. At least Tony watched the game.

Jim and I flirted and watched each other. We sat together the entire season. After the first few games, Jim would come by himself and wait for me. I would walk in, look for him, and we would sit and watch the games. At this point, it was very clear that he liked me. Both of us were very shy about how "in like" we were. One thing was for sure, I was not going to make the first move. I thought he was playing it cool but everyone else at the games (i.e. my parents, relatives and family friends) saw Jim following me around like a little puppy. They all saw a budding romance.

Tony knew he had to do something to nudge us forward so he threw a New Year's Eve party. And what a coincidence... Jim and I were the only single guests! I walked into the house and saw a room full of married people and Jim, who sat all alone. I blushed but smiled at the obvious setup. Jim and I sat across from each other. We smiled and laughed all night. At midnight Jim went in for a kiss.

Ring, ring my heart sang or something like that song goes. Well, we were both goners. Finally, the timing was right! My mom was right, when you least expect it, God surprises you. I was indeed surprised. When God has a plan he executes it with perfect timing. Jim and I started dating right after New Year's and by that July were engaged and married the following April. April 2018 we celebrated our 30th wedding anniversary.

Okay, I know you are probably thinking I got married a little fast? If I were you, I might think the same thing EXCEPT Jim and I had known each other for most of our lives. Falling in love was the easy part once we stopped denying how much we cared for each other. Again, timing, God's timing.

We just clicked in every way. He knew all my good and not so good parts and I knew his. We would be there for each other just like we always were. We just made it official. I was made for him and he was made for me.

Our love and commitment has been tested many times these 30 years but we always stood firm in our love. We have raised two amazing children, survived my three cancer diagnoses and the death of his parents. I was there for him and he was there for me. This story is far from over and in some ways is only just beginning. I hear GOD say to me the best is yet to come. Just wait and see.

Be Satisfied With Me

Stephanie Gervais (E22/M23)

Our love story started way back in 2008. The date was August 8, 2008, and let's face it, 08/08/08 is a pretty unforgettable date! After hanging out at a friend's backyard bonfire, my friend Josh offered to walk me home. We had been friends for years and had both recently come out of longer relationships but that didn't stop my eighteen-year-old self from getting all "bubbly" around him. I guess he must have felt something similar because when we got to my back door, he kissed me!

For the next few weeks, things were very exciting, as they often are with new feelings. We spent lots of time that month hanging out and flirting. Then one night, he sat me down and said "Steff, I think you're great and I always have so much fun with you, but it almost seems like this is too good to be true."

I couldn't believe my ears. I really thought we were going somewhere. I think he had some other excuses about how he wasn't ready to start dating again but at that point, I had completely drowned out everything else he was saying and replied with something along the lines of: "Oh, yeah, you're right. I'm not ready either." I think I even had the guts to mention another guy that was interested in me as well.

Suffice it to say, I was a little heartbroken and definitely not over him. That next year was a mess for us. We had a lot of mutual friends so we saw each other often. We would still flirt and dance together when we would be at the same parties or events. It was hard for me trying to protect my heart from him when he was so obviously flirting and dancing with me all the time. I dated other guys in an attempt to get over him but seeing him still made me melt a bit and hearing about him dating other girls made me so jealous. I knew I wasn't over him and I needed to really distance myself from him if I had any chance of really letting go.

The next summer, I worked at a Catholic summer camp for a few weeks. I had worked at the camp in the summers prior but this year was different. I had a close friend of mine, Emily, working with me there and I learned a lot that summer about letting God love me. One of the staff members there was someone who, I believe, had a deep faith. He would often just walk into a room and thank me for "being me" or "being beautiful." At first, this weirded me right out.

Slowly, he kind of chipped away at my hardened heart and I started to really take his comments more seriously. He was thanking me for allowing God to work in and through me. I was changing. Emily and I spent more time singing and praying in the little chapel and talking about bigger things instead of just talking about the guys we liked and our weekend plans. She was preparing to leave on a year-long mission trip and I was finding myself secretly inspired by that idea.

After the summer, I went back to university for a second year but I was still feeling pulled in another direction. I began to discern ministry work and found an organization in Ireland that really stuck out to me. When I went to the airport to say goodbye to Emily, she hugged me and said, "Go to Ireland!" It was the final push I needed. I still remember going home after the airport and emailing the application forms to my mom at her work because we didn't have a printer at home!

By March of 2010, I was accepted to go and spend a year in Ireland starting in August. I was dating someone at the time that I was accepted and broke up with him because I had made the decision that I was giving this year to God. I decided that I would spend my time in Ireland learning how to give my heart to God and then He would be the one to give my heart to the right man when the right time came. That was my simple, straightforward plan.

About one month after being accepted, I was hanging out with a friend of mine and he was planning on going to a bonfire at Josh's house that evening for his birthday. I tagged along – I hadn't seen or heard from Josh in a good six or seven months at that point so I figured going to a casual birthday party wouldn't be too much of an issue. Plus, my heart was "closed to all human men until further notice."

It was really great to see him again and be able to wish him a happy birthday from a totally, in my opinion, platonic place. The night was great, and I left having had a great visit with friends and no regrets. A few weeks later, I stopped by a local coffee shop to grab a coffee for a night of exam cramming and who else was studying there but Josh!

I sat down with him for a bit and he thanked me for coming to his birthday. We caught up a little bit and before I left he asked me if I wanted to go see a "Kenny Chesney Live" movie with him because he wanted to go and didn't have many friends who liked country music. He made it pretty clear that it was just a friend thing and so I said yes. I will be honest, it was a total weak moment for me. I did like country music but I wasn't really into Kenny Chesney. The desire to spend time with him snuck up on me and before I could think twice I heard myself agreeing to go with him! I barely remember that concert but what I do remember is that little "friend date" set off a bit of a chain of events for us.

We started hanging out again, just the two of us. We went for a walk one day and hashed out everything that had happened that past year and a half. We apologized and forgave each other for the hurts we had caused. It felt so good to finally be honest with each other and to also start putting things behind us. Shortly after this talk, we went out for dinner with some friends of ours for sushi. I don't know if this was set up or not but after our dinner, the other couple took off, saying they had somewhere to be. That left Josh and me on our own for the rest of our Saturday night.

We decided to rent a movie and go back to his place to watch it. While we were watching the movie, we were having our own "classic movie scene." All of a sudden, our hands were touching and getting closer and closer until finally, our fingers found each other and we were holding hands. Obviously, at this point, I was no longer watching the movie but just sitting there, almost numb, trying to guess where this was going next. Luckily, I didn't have to keep guessing for long because Josh looked at me and told me he had feelings for me. Like, real feelings this time.

I felt a million emotions at the same time: Excitement – my dream guy finally liked me! Anger and frustration – he told me he wasn't interested and then when I finally got over him he decides to swoop in and try and win me again? Confusion – I was about to leave for almost a year and I had made a promise to myself and God about this exact situation NOT happening.

Luckily for me, Josh followed up his shocking profession by telling me that he didn't want to get in between me and my year away. He said he really couldn't help but tell me how he felt but also understood where I was at and encouraged me not to start dating him.

Who was this guy?! It was clear that we had both grown up a little bit over the past few years. We decided that we would continue to spend time together rebuilding our friendship but we would not pursue a dating relationship until after I returned from Ireland.

The few months before I left were hard. It was a really weird in-between feeling of starting a new relationship, or at least knowing we both liked each other but trying not to actually start anything. I tried to keep my distance from him as much as I could and surround myself with my girlfriends while I prepared to leave but, in all honesty, we still spent time together. We tried our best not to be too exclusive but there was a really fine line for us between building a friendship and building a relationship. Long story short, by the time I was actually leaving for Ireland, I felt like I was leaving behind more than just one of my friends.

I barely remember being at the airport and saying goodbye to everyone. I do remember being the girl sitting at the airport gate crying before she boarded the plane. By the time I reached Ireland, my tears had dried up and I was full of adrenaline and excitement about finally being there. I made it to my host home but aside from the fact that I couldn't figure out my host mom's very Irish name, I don't remember a whole lot between the jet lag and exhaustion all catching up to me.

Once I got settled into my host home, I pulled out my Bible and found that Josh had actually stolen it at some point and had written a whole bunch of tiny notes among some of his favorite bible verses. Of course, I started crying, but this time it was in consolation. I knew I had made the right decision to give this year to God and now that I wasn't in the same city as Josh, I could really put this into practice. I also realized that as much as I needed a year with God, Josh did too.

Things in Ireland got pretty exciting and busy for me almost right away. I didn't have much time to miss anyone for the first little while and I was able to really focus on the present and everything I was experiencing and learning at training. Once the year really got started, Josh and I would touch base through emails every so often and the odd Skype date.

I made sure to tell the girls on my team about him – half because I wanted to talk about him and half because I wanted them to hold me accountable. I am so thankful for those women and their prayers. We would often pray St. Anthony of Padua's prayer called "Be Satisfied with Me."[20] I prayed that prayer constantly throughout my year in Ireland – I sent it to Josh because I was so moved by it.

Halfway through the year, Josh and his friend took a Europe trip so he conveniently planned that his flights to and from Canada would be at the Dublin Airport. It was so special that he could come and visit me and see me in my element. I was so excited to introduce him to the people I was living with and he got along great with everyone. My team leader was amazing and made sure I had some time to go on little outings with him while he was there. We went for sushi, just like old times, spent some time on the beach and even tried deep-fried Mars bars. We still talk about how good they were! We had so much fun and it made me all the more excited to get back home and really start dating him and building our relationship.

One moment that will forever stand out for me from my year in Ireland was a conversation I had with one of the girls on my team while we were traveling one day. We were talking about if we had ever had a surprise party thrown for us and I was telling her how much I loved surprises. While I was saying that, a bible verse popped into my head from 1 Corinthians 2:9: "However, as it is written: "What no eye has seen, what no ear has heard, and what no human mind has conceived"- the things God has prepared for those who love Him." It hit me out of nowhere that God knows how much I love surprises and He was asking me to allow Him to surprise me in my life. Josh was a huge surprise for me already, and I felt consolation that if I continued to trust and give God my heart, more would come.

At the end of our year of ministry, we had a week of wrap up. We each got certificates and were recognized for specific things we had accomplished over the year. My accomplishment, written by my supervisor, was that I had strived to always give my heart to God. I don't remember ever telling her about my little rule for the year, but I know she wouldn't have given me recognition for it, were it not true. It was so comforting and consoling that I had truly carried out my goal that year. I was headed back home with my heart in His Heart and was so excited to see the surprises that lay ahead.

The night I got home, Josh met me at the airport with my favorite Canadian doughnuts and a huge smile on his face. That night, he brought me back home and we talked and caught up and by the end of the night he was finally my boyfriend! We dated for a year and a half and then got engaged and were married in August of 2013 – five years and many ups and downs after that first kiss. And just to make things extra cute, we spent our honeymoon back in Ireland for a few weeks!

Be Satisfied with Me

By St. Anthony of Padua's Prayer:

Everyone longs to give themselves completely to someone, to have a deep soul relationship with another, to be loved thoroughly and exclusively. But God, to a Christian, says, "No, not until you are satisfied, fulfilled and content with being loved by Me alone, with giving yourself totally and unreservedly to Me, with having an intensely personal and unique relationship with Me alone. Discovering that only in Me is your satisfaction to be found, will you be capable of the perfect human relationship that I have planned for you. You will never be united with another until you are united with Me alone, exclusive of anyone or anything else, exclusive of any other desires or longings.

I want you to stop planning, stop wishing, and allow Me to give you the most thrilling plan existing, one that you cannot imagine. Please allow Me to bring it to you. You just keep watching Me, expecting the greatest things. Keep experiencing the satisfaction that I Am. Keep listening and learning the things I tell you. You just wait. That's all. Don't be anxious. Don't worry. Don't look at the things you think you want; You just keep looking off and away up to Me, or you'll miss what I want to show you. And then when you are ready, I'll surprise you with a love far more wonderful than any you could dream of. You see, until you are ready and until the one I have for you is ready (I am working even at this moment to have you both ready at the same time), until you are both satisfied exclusively with Me and the life I prepared for you, you won't be able to experience the love that exemplified your relationship with Me. And this is the perfect love.

And dear one, I want you to have this most wonderful love, I want you to see in the flesh a picture of your relationship with Me, and to enjoy materially and concretely the everlasting union of beauty, perfection and love that I offer you with Myself. Know that I love utterly. I Am God. Believe it and be satisfied.

A History of Love

Regina Mc Guire (E19/M20)

When I was born, I was literally a cradle Catholic. I had been born weighing less than two pounds and at least ten weeks early. I was my parents' fourth child to be born three months early. My other three siblings had all died within 24 hours of birth. Since we were all born in a Catholic hospital they were all baptized as soon as it became evident they were in danger of death. In my case, they knew that I was likely to die so the hospital chaplain baptized me within minutes.

Eventually, my parents were blessed with three children who survived, three girls. We grew up going to our parish Catholic school and attended Mass on Sundays. My parents prayed the rosary with us in the evening. We celebrated Advent with our own wreath, made sacrifices during Lent, and put coins in our Lenten boxes. It was a very happy, though somewhat sheltered, environment. We lived in Southern California in the 60's.

I was close to God in my early teens, but the confusion in the church that followed the implementation of Vatican II affected my religious education. We got some solid teaching but also a lot of pop psychology and some important things just plain weren't mentioned at all. I had no church history and no scripture training.

My parents taught CCD, read the Bible on their own, and went to religious conferences and talks. Religion was one of the things that got talked about at the dinner table. It was important in my family life and I was aware that my parents prayed together.

My parents had an exceptionally close loving relationship. The trial of losing four of seven children to miscarriage was heavy, but it drew them closer to each other and God. When I got older, both of my parents talked to me about how it had affected them. My mother talked to me about her vocation to marriage. She was thirteen when Pearl Harbor happened and quite rightly believed that her future husband would be involved in the war. She started praying to St. Anne to protect him.

My father enlisted at eighteen in 1942 because he knew he would be drafted. He wanted to be an engineer and knew his parents couldn't afford a college education for him. He went through boot camp and was sent to accelerated classes just for soldiers in New York. The classes went twice as fast—if he had finished he would have had his degree in two years. But the invasion of Normandy was in the works and he and his classmates were reassigned. He ended up a sniper in the European campaign and one day his outfit got a little too forward.

They retreated over a mile to reach safety and when he sat down he couldn't stand up. His Achilles tendon had been severed by a bullet. It is not medically possible to run with a severed Achilles tendon but he did. My mom's prayers were answered. These and other family stories from people who were not in the least superstitious helped overcome the "science is God and change is necessary" mentality around me that prevailed in the 60's.

Because of my mother's experience praying to St. Anne, I invoked her intercession from the age of seven, on and off, when I thought of marriage. I specifically asked for the spiritual and physical safety of my future husband. My First Communion preparation included the suggestion that we pray about our future vocation because Jesus loved the prayers of children and often let them know what he wanted them to do. I had done that and believed from an early age that I was not called to religious life.

I dreamed about a future husband, highly influenced by my family's "library full of books." But I was in California. Dating was not what it had been for my parents and my experiences at two secular colleges had taught me that what most of the men I met were interested in was not a Catholic marriage. They weren't even necessarily interested in a long-term relationship. When I found that out I dropped them. I had become discouraged by the whole process. I was looking for a husband, but the men I dated were not looking for wives.

Sometime during college, I had become even more convinced that God was real and very important. I began to see that my religious education had been very deficient and I knew little about being an adult Catholic. I had been taught the Ten Commandments in my First Communion preparation but not much was said later. Jesus and His church were important to me but going to a state university, I didn't know how to meet like-minded people. I went to school with people interested in science and mathematics. Nobody mentioned religion. I decided to stop dating and get serious about my faith again. I understood that I had to get my relationship with Christ straight first. I fell in love with Jesus all over again and at the time, I didn't know how a man fit in with my deep religious passion.

So here I was, it was my junior year in college and I was studying mathematics. I had just re-established a serious prayer life after being a very nominal Catholic for a few years. I wasn't dating anyone or looking to start a relationship.

And that is precisely when I met my future husband... while I was washing dishes at my friend Dee Ann's house.

Dee Ann and her husband George had just moved into our parish. She had visited our prayer group to meet some new friends. She used a wheelchair most of the time, and they hadn't had time to hire a housekeeper. I was working part-time and going to college, but I had time to lend, so I had come over to help out. George, Dee Ann and I were planning to have one of George's famous spaghetti dinners and go to a regional charismatic Mass at one of the local parishes. They had invited George's high school friend Eugene and since he didn't drive, George went to pick him up. When I saw Eugene the first time it struck me that he had the saddest and most compelling brown eyes I had ever seen. I felt very drawn to this dark-haired, bearded man with glasses because I didn't want him to be so sad.

To set the scene, it's important to know a little more about Eugene before he arrived at the spaghetti dinner that night. Eugene is like a man from a foreign country! He had grown up in West Virginia. His mother's family was Southern Baptist and his father's family was mostly committed sinners, which was an actual social class in West Virginia in the 50's. Most people went to church somewhere. His mother's father was a deacon and both his mother and grandmother were teachers in the two-room local elementary school. He literally grew up in church and school as I had, with the addition of being related to half the county.

Throughout high school, he had been friends with several Catholics and even had an unofficial Catholic girlfriend. She never gave him an indication that she wanted to marry him and when college came, their ways separated. He had been to Catholic Mass, studied the liturgy, and even thought about becoming Catholic but his mother had talked him out of it. He was attending a Foursquare church in the San Fernando Valley when he found himself surprisingly rejected! They made it sound like he had to be healed before he could get married. Things got weird and he decided to leave.

He asked himself where he wanted to go to church and decided to go to a Catholic church. He had believed in the real presence for years. He had only just recently discovered that his church didn't. He stayed up all night using his Thompson chain reference bible to discover if the papacy was scriptural. He decided it was. When he met me that day in April, he had already made the decision to become Catholic on Easter Sunday. He had even talked to a priest but he hadn't communicated it to all his friends and family yet.

So here we are: Eugene's just barely dipping his toes into Catholicism after being rejected not only by women who weren't looking for a serious relationship, but also from his Protestant church as well, and me feeling as if there are no serious Catholic men out there having sworn off dating.

As we sat and ate spaghetti, we talked about various things, one of which was Catholic places we wanted to visit. We all four agreed that we wanted to visit Lourdes and I remember thinking that this man could do so much with his life if he had someone to help him. During Mass that evening, I was distracted by watching Eugene pray. Even though he didn't walk, he knelt in prayer for part of the Mass. There was such intensity in his prayer. I was very interested in this man but had no thought of a romantic relationship. I had sworn off dating.

I was trying to do God's will, finish my college degree, and see what He had for me next. But inside I was very lonely. Eugene gave me his phone number and on Sunday I called him. We talked for 2 ½ hours. I am not a person who likes to make phone calls but we had so much to talk about: Christ, the church, our families, and books. Most of the men I knew did not read fiction or express any interest in Christ. I had even tried to learn philosophy on my own by reading the encyclopedia and my parents' set of Great Books. I didn't have the necessary background to understand but here was a man who did.

His disability had kept him from much outdoor play with his friends, so he learned to read early and well. He did not read fiction newer than one hundred years old at a certain part of his life so he had familiarity with books I had heard of but not read. We continued to meet at his friend's house for the next week or two. He was done with college and had not been able to find a job. As we spent time talking, helping his friends settle into their new house, and going to church together, we both realized something was happening.

Later he told me that he knew right when he met me that I was the one but it scared him so much he didn't admit it even to himself. It took three more days for him to admit it to himself. I noticed his cheerfulness return right away. I soon learned that this was his real personality. It took 2 ½ weeks for me to realize that I wanted to marry him. I remember praying in bed one night "Jesus, if you don't want me to marry this guy, you better let me know pretty quick." This was totally unlike me. I normally take a very long time to make up my mind as anyone who has watched me order in a restaurant can tell you. I like to have rational reasons for what I do and well-thought-out explanations.

My parents had an exceptionally happy marriage. I wanted no less than a Catholic man who would care about me as my father did my mother. I had asked my mother why she had married my dad. She said because he treated his mother and sisters so well she was sure he would treat his wife with respect and love. My mom was right.

My relationship with Jesus was growing. I was experiencing joy even in the midst of trials. I became more confident and at peace. But what was I supposed to do about this Eugene? I wasn't sure he was serious about me and he was distracting me from my faith. I didn't want a relationship with any person pulling me away from Jesus. A month after we met, I decided I was going to stop seeing him.

I had been invited to a Tupperware party at Dee Ann's house and he was going to be there. We sat together on the couch with several other people and listened to the joys of owning a pickle keeper. When the party was over, I stayed to help Dee Ann clean up but I was also hoping to talk to Eugene alone. I told him that we needed to talk. He said that he had something to say to me too.

I told him to go first. He did... and I said "Yes!"

I started bouncing around the room which was very uncharacteristic of me. That started a happy but tumultuous year. We didn't tell my parents at once because I was afraid they wouldn't approve. They didn't. They weren't sure that Eugene was really going to become Catholic and they were very worried about his difficulties finding work.

His parents were also reserved about it. His mother and his recently Christian father weren't sure a Catholic woman was Christian. They too worried about his ability to provide. We continued to go to Mass and prayer meetings together and spent time with each other. We didn't go on many formal dates because of economic concerns and time constraints. Eugene was busy learning about the church and looking for work. He got a full-time job and in fall started RCIA which was brand new in Los Angeles.

We were supposed to be married in January but I started dragging my feet. My communication with my parents was poor and I felt overwhelmed with marriage planning on top of school and work. We scheduled our wedding in April and I took a semester off of school to help deal with my stress level and the increasing workload at work. Before Christmas Eve Mass, he gave me my Christmas present—a ruby engagement ring. I was distracted the whole Mass.

We spent New Year's Eve with a group of Christian friends celebrating and praying. One night at a prayer meeting, Eugene pulled me into the vestibule of the church. He told me he didn't think God wanted us to get married. I started crying and one of the prayer group leaders came out to see what was wrong. He counseled us that God wanted us married and the resistance we were dealing with was from people who didn't understand what God wanted. We were quickly re-engaged but we still had questions.

Then we went to our Engaged Encounter weekend. It was Valentine's Day weekend and it poured the whole time we were there. It meant no walks in the gardens but we didn't care. As we poured out our hearts to each other on paper and prayed, it became clear that yes, in spite of our problems, God wanted us to get married. My parents helped us with the wedding. One year and one day from when we met, we were married.

Eugene joined the church a year later at the Easter Vigil because the RCIA process at St. Jane Frances took two years. It has been 38 years, we are happily married and we now have five living children and four grandchildren.

We took the road less traveled and it has made all the difference.

My Advice

First, get a real relationship with Jesus. It's hard to hear what God wants you to do about a life-changing decision if you are not listening to Him about the everyday ones. Frequent the sacraments, read the Bible, pray the Rosary, and go to Eucharistic Adoration. Try to spend as much time listening as talking.

Second, try to discern what God wants from you now. I didn't help my friend because I expected to find my husband there. I wanted to serve those around me and God just happened to show up there. By being faithful you are preparing yourself for whatever God sends.

Third, pray for your future husband and don't stop there. Pray for those you know who are married, those preparing to be married, and those trying to discern their vocation.

Fourth, don't get too attached to your idea of Mr. Right. God may have other ideas. I thought I would marry someone who was born Catholic. I did marry someone who ended up being Catholic, and his previous faith tradition has brought many blessings to our lives together.

Never Say Never

Sophia Hart (E42/M43)

Now they were both old, and far advanced in years. . .The Lord said to
Abraham: Why did Sara laugh, saying: Shall I who am an old woman
bear a child indeed? Is there any thing hard to God?
— Gen 18:11, 13-14

Fiat mihi secundum verbum tuum.
— Luke 1:38

"Hey Sophie, how is it going? I see your mom at Mass sometimes."
That was it, just a post on my Facebook wall and a friend request attached to a half-remembered name. It took me a full two
minutes to unearth Matt Hart from my long-term memory bank.
In fairness, it had been approximately a quarter century since last
I heard it, and another ten years prior to that since I had seen the
face I now associated with it.

In spite of misgivings, I had joined Facebook a couple of years
earlier at the urging of a friend. Matt had to be cajoled into joining
as well. His best friend's wife ended up creating his profile ("You
never know who might be out there!" – God bless her matchmaking
heart).

I was scrolling my FB feed from San Diego, California, where I
had been thriving since my early thirties. But now I was 40, unem-
ployed, and living in a converted garage behind someone's house,
with half my belongings in storage. I was at one of the lowest points
of my life. After years of working at a meaningful career, I had bot-
tomed out. The initial lines of *Dante's Inferno*[21] kept reverberating:
"Midway through the journey of life I found myself in a dark wood,
for I had lost the straight path."

For me, as I suspect for many women, hitting that 40-year mark
without a family or a partner is unbearably hard. A good job can
make single life easier, even enjoyable, and Providence had blessed
me with great friendships and an extraordinary community of
Catholics—both single and married—in Southern California. Sev-
en months of unemployment had taken a toll. Though I refused to
give much credence to the notion of the "ticking biological clock,"

I suppose the inevitable hormonal shifts that take place as a body gives way to middle age were at work as well. The result: an old, unwanted houseguest, depression, had returned and taken up residence.

Such is the story leading up to a single line on a social network that forever altered the course of two lives—two hearts—and eternally etched upon each soul the simple truth that nothing is impossible for God. My initial reaction to the post, once I had recalled the poster, was to remember a lanky, curly-haired kid from grade school who was kind of quiet.

"Oh, Matt. I remember seeing his family at Mass some Sundays. Good heavens, is he still going to the same church? Poor guy never made it out." That condescending thought was prompted by the knowledge that my mother, and Matt and his, were still attending the parish that Matt and I had known as schoolchildren.

We met in the second grade and were in the same class almost every year. In middle school, we didn't see much of each other, unsurprisingly (at that age I thought boys were akin to insects). Matt's memories of high school and mine are somewhat divergent. He says we used to have lunch together frequently, often joined by other friends; I just vaguely recall a few encounters. As time marched ahead, Matt faded from view and from my memory. But as it turned out, I didn't fade from his.

After joining Facebook, he decided to look me up. His mother had pointed out my mother at Mass one day, and he got to wondering where I was and what I was doing. In Matt's mind, I was always the "cute" girl with the dimples he recalled from elementary school. He had never asked me out, but during our courtship, he admitted the thought had crossed his mind on a few occasions. Many years and sorrows later, he took a chance and tossed out a line across the miles. He caught a lot more than he bargained for!

Matt's life had taken some unexpected turns. He had spent many years in a relationship but never married. Sadly, his partner succumbed to a medical crisis which left her requiring round-the-clock care in a nursing home. While able to breathe on her own, she had limited awareness and could not move without aid. Matt had left his business behind in east Texas to enable her to be near her family. When he reached out to me, he was still visiting her every day, as he had for the past decade. But his heart was telling him it was time to move on. He had also returned to the Church after drifting away.

I found all this out not long after that initial contact. I had replied lightly to the message, thinking I wouldn't hear much more from him (as was the case with a lot of Facebook reconnections). But he would consistently comment on my posts, and then we started sending messages to each other. When Matt opened up about his life, I was moved. I had been learning about the theology of the body while living the single life in San Diego. Hearing of his unwavering support of someone who could no longer reciprocate in any way seemed to me a profound version of St. John Paul II's teachings on the true nature of love: an act of the will, not a feeling expressed.

Such were my thoughts. Entering into a relationship with someone, however admirable, who lived in a place I had gladly departed years earlier did not enter my thoughts. Even so, I agreed to meet up with Matt the following Christmas during a family visit to Texas. I didn't think of going out with him as a date. Indeed, I very deliberately characterized it to friends and family (who by this point were quite curious about Matt and me) as nothing more than a high school reunion.

What actually transpired surprised me. Matt picked me up from my mother's home in his flame-red 1998 Chevy Corvette convertible, a car he had recently purchased and detailed himself—so that he would be driving something that would impress me (he told me this some time later). At my sister's suggestion, we went to the Perot Museum in downtown Dallas. Quelle surprise: I discovered I was having a good time.

I felt at ease in Matt's presence, which wasn't typical for me. I had always been uncomfortable with dating and invariably ill at ease on a first date. I think it helped that I had talked myself into the idea that this was not a date. There was a sense of familiarity with this man, in spite of the passage of decades. I trusted him. I never felt as though he had any ulterior motive beyond a desire to reconnect. After the museum, I proposed we head to a nearby music/restaurant venue for a bite to eat and a drink.

As we sat at the bar, I asked Matt how his life was going. His answer was noncommittal, but his expression and body language suggested a man who was not in a place he would have liked to be.

I understood how he felt. Even though I had been living well in San Diego, with friends and family and good times, I wasn't truly fulfilled. I wasn't living a vocation—I was living for myself, without a sense of purpose or mission.

None of this occurred to me in the moment of course. Matt and I stayed a bit longer and chatted, then I said I had better be getting back because my mother was ill. He took me home. I thanked him, bid him goodnight, and we exchanged Christmas presents. I had bought a small memento of San Diego for him, a keychain I had picked up in the gift shop at the mission church. Matt sheepishly handed over a small Macy's box, saying he hadn't a clue what to give me, so he just got me a gift card. I didn't look at it then, which was a good thing. When I opened it the next day and discovered it was worth more than $100, I was stunned.

I was also confronted with an ethical quandary. What to do? All I could think was this is completely inappropriate—what is this man thinking? Is he after something? My first instinct was to return it with a polite note. A trustworthy friend convinced me to keep the gift. She told me to think of accepting as an act of humility. Over time, I would come to understand Matt was generous by nature. He had a reputation among his own community for giving: not just gifts but time, support, financial assistance—even, on occasion, accommodations to the needy.

After Christmas, I returned to San Diego. By now I was in a very different place than I had been six months earlier. Some weeks after Matt's initial contact, I had landed a great job as a textbook editor for an online university. I had moved out of the garage into a comfortable apartment in a nice part of town. And I figured the encounter with Matt, while enjoyable enough, was just another social engagement to reminisce over and catalogue in a cell phone camera album.

As is His way, God had something else in mind. But before His plans could begin to take shape, I had to undergo a bit of a "road to Damascus" moment. Suffice it to say, I experienced a rather unsettling event, one which threw my whole life into sharp relief. I came to see all the decisions and relationships of adulthood—most especially those having to do with romantic pursuits (and the lack of them)—in a starkly different light. That new light helped me to understand that I had in fact, been dishonest with myself for my entire adult life. Ultimately that realization was followed by another, very simple one: I had to let go of control and yield every part of my life, even the parts that I was most terrified to surrender, to Christ. If that seems fairly straightforward, it was anything but. It took work and humility and admitting to the people closest to me that I was not all right, that in fact, I needed serious healing. Now, with room to work, the Divine Gardener began to uproot the weeds in the garden of my soul.

Where was Matt during all this self-reckoning? Where he had been all along: back in Texas, working his job and taking care of the people in his life. He was also still emailing me about stories of his trips to Six Flags, adventures in car repair, and silly grade-school-level humor. All things that were plain and true—a calm port in a stormy time. I didn't share much of my interior struggle with him then, but I wrote him about my work, my friends in San Diego, movies we had seen and liked. For the most part, I thought of him as a pen pal. Matt, on the other hand, was craftier than he seemed. He was playing out his fishing line by inches.

The summer after, I went back to Texas to celebrate my mom's 75th birthday. She and Matt happened to be born on the same date, so he invited me to attend his birthday dinner with his family a few days after my mother's party. Of course, he planned ahead and made sure we had time before the dinner to "do some fun stuff"—a wax museum, a civic sculpture well known from my childhood. Having fun was a hallmark of our relationship, and this too became part of my healing, as I recovered a sense of childlike joy that I had been sorely missing. The birthday dinner was well attended. Matt has six siblings, four of them local; a bevy of nephews and nieces; and close friends with kids. All of them were in attendance that night. Overwhelming? Yep—but more than anything I was impressed by the goodwill and respect for him that were on display. And one of my biggest takeaways from that night was this thought: wow, he really should be a father—he is so great with kids. I hope he finds a wife who can give him some.

After I returned home, Matt e-mailed me right away. "I enjoyed every minute with you" were his precise words, and I began to feel something new. Something deep down was beginning to take hold. Sometime later that summer, he lamented that he wasn't able to join his family for a vacation on the Texas coast, a tradition he had enjoyed for many years. "Well," I responded in my message, "We have beaches out here too. Come on out!" I wasn't speaking too earnestly because I honestly never imagined he would take me up.

But he did that October. A man who hadn't been on an airplane in more than a decade bought his tickets, rented a car, and booked a motel. In five days we had as much fun as two people can in Southern California (which is a lot). We frequented museums, a play, the beach, dinner with my sister and her family, and Disneyland. During the late night drive back from Disneyland, when it had become clear to me where Matt's heart was, I opened up to him about everything. I was exhausted and emotionally raw but I knew I had to be completely honest. It was now or never.

"I can't be in a relationship right now. I have to heal, and it's not fair to ask you to hang around while I sort myself out. You should just go ahead and live your life." That was the message, more or less. It was a lot to unload on a guy, especially one who had come to San Diego with the express purpose of courting a woman who surely was a tough get. But Matt, in his stoic way, just listened and bore it all—a steady rock more than capable of withstanding the roiling waters around him. When he returned home he wrote me in his plain way, just to let me know that he was in love with me and didn't mind waiting around; he wasn't occupied with much of anything else.

I decided to go back to Dallas for Thanksgiving. I knew I had to test the waters a bit more, regardless of what I'd said to him. Yes, there was still work to be done, and yes, I knew that I was taking a risk even stepping onto the road to a relationship. I was praying, and I asked Matt to pray; others were praying too. The Saturday after Thanksgiving, Matt picked me up for a marathon, all-out, four-hour date. During the course of it, I came to see how he was fiercely pro-life, a passionate defender of the most vulnerable—values that were of paramount importance to me. At the end of the date, we were a couple. I flew home with a full heart and, of course, the sticky question of a long-distance relationship.

The answer to that question came sooner than expected. For the next two months, we corresponded regularly via e-mail, text, and the occasional phone call. I put the whole thing in God's hands, as I had been trying to do with everything. God sorted it out fairly efficiently. After 18 months at my new job, I was shown the door as part of a company layoff. "There," Providence said, "I've given you a push. Are you prepared to go where I ask?" I thought I might be, but I realized I had to view all these turns of fortune as part of a larger plan, one that was not my own. For the first time in my life, I needed to ask if I was called to a vocation of marriage. That was a question I had never been willing to put to God, myself, or anyone. Now, at the age of 42, I finally did.

I moved back to Texas with the idea that I would just explore the relationship, see if it was, in fact, part of God's plan. If it wasn't, California would welcome me back. But I felt sure of the answer before I boarded the plane, and as it took off, I knew I was saying goodbye for good. Matt met me at baggage claim with yellow roses.

Three months later, we did make a trip to the Texas coast, staying in a beach rental with Matt's extended family. I had my suspicions but was still caught by surprise when he proposed to me at the top of a Ferris wheel in Galveston. "Yes!" was my second answer—I had to tease him a little with the first by asking for a week to think it over. We married on April 25, 2015.

The call had come, and we both had answered in fairly rapid fashion. But God hadn't yet shown all His cards. As we had courted, I raised the issue of children and told Matt that while they weren't out of the question, conception would be chancy at best (and deep down I ruled out the possibility). Much to our surprise, we found ourselves expecting just nine months after our wedding. Due to pregnancy complications, our daughter Phoebe was born eight weeks preterm but healthy. We got on our knees and thanked God for His everlasting mercy. And because God loves to keep His children guessing, he blessed us again just over a year later. As of this writing, I am six weeks from the arrival of our second child, a son.

Marriage—to say nothing of parenting!—at our age brings challenges young marrieds don't always encounter. Drastic change at this age is a rarity, so we have to be much more accepting of each other—flaws and tics and habits and all. Both of us had rather chaotic childhoods, which manifests sometimes in how we respond to a crisis (i.e. not always with the coolest of heads). Also, we expect to be mistaken for our children's grandparents for our whole lives. On the other hand, we have a sense of humor about things that younger newlyweds might not, and we tend to be fairly quick to forgive each other because we are so familiar with our own shortcomings.

In short, we face all the difficulties and joys and intricacies of married life. We're still having fun too, just of a different kind. We do it all with gratitude, for we know God looked at our two souls and saw that we were not yet the persons He intends us to become. We needed the one-flesh union to be sanctified, but not when we expected. His timing, it turns out, is everything.

Finding Love, Twice

Kristen Proctor (E21/M23, E28/M29)
www.proctorsadopt.blogspot.com/

Warning: The author's first husband dies in this story. It is a beautiful story but can be emotionally difficult to read!

I met Chris in January 2000, our freshman year of high school, in the Driver's Ed classroom. Our large high school of 2,500 students was fed by two different middle schools, so we had not been at the same school until that year. Our sophomore year we had three classes together and became good friends, while we each dated someone else. Right after school let out, we went on our first date in June 2001 and were together from then on.

We dated the final two years of high school, but after graduating in 2003 we went to two different state schools that were a two-hour drive apart. Our parents cautioned us that long distance and changes at college would probably be the end of our relationship, but we knew they were wrong. I did not have a cell phone for my first year at college, so I had to call him from my dorm using a calling card on the landline phone.

I was studying architecture in an incredibly intense program, often at the studio until the wee hours of the morning, so it was difficult for us to connect. I did not have a car on campus, so Chris would often drive across the state to see me for just a few hours and a meal before heading back to his campus. The first year of college was probably the most difficult year in our relationship because we had so much less time and communication with each other.

After we made it through our first year of long distance apart at school, I knew we could make it through college. Chris gave me a promise ring in June 2004. I got my first cell phone that summer, too, which made keeping in touch while at school a lot easier. Chris proposed to me in June 2006 – he did manage to surprise me, even though I knew we would get married, because I thought we would have an eighteen-month engagement, not a two-year engagement.

That summer we were both doing internships downtown in our hometown and were able to commute together, which was such a nice chance to spend that hour a day together, and often the evenings after work. Chris was in a standard four-year program at college but my program was a five-year program, so he graduated in May 2007 and then started working at the firm where he had interned the summer before. I was working on wedding planning and my thesis, which was incredibly stressful, but Chris was able to drive up to visit me more often on the weekends now that he was not also in school.

Our wedding in June 2008 was picture perfect, the wedding of our dreams, and went off without a hitch. We were 23 and had everything going for us. We went on a Mediterranean cruise for our honeymoon and had the most amazing time. When we returned, we had three days to load up all of our wedding gifts, everything from his apartment, and everything of mine from college from my parents' house, and then we drove a moving truck, towing our car, 1000 miles across the country to Florida, where I had found a job with the firm I had interned with the summer before. Chris easily found a job at a firm on the other side of Tampa Bay, and we settled into married life in our apartment.

We lived in Florida from July 2008 to July 2011, and they were blissful years full of friends, family visits, and traveling. We joined the small Lutheran church near our apartment and quickly became involved with the church council, leading the youth group, leading a Bible study in our home, and Chris was on the school board for the school at our church. We were busy with all of that plus work but had a very happy marriage and time together. Chris and I had practically grown up together and were very evenly matched in temperaments.

In June 2011, Chris was offered a job with his old firm back in Indianapolis. We had planned on living in Florida for 3-5 years but wanted to wait to start having children until we were back near our families. When this opportunity landed in his lap, we felt like it was a sign and decided to move home. We moved back in July 2011, bought a house, and started trying to get pregnant. Chris studied for and passed his Professional Engineers exam on the first try, at age 26 – the youngest age possible. This came with a promotion at work, which he was incredibly excited about. I was offered a contract position at a firm where a friend of mine from college was working and started working there in December 2011.

Everything was going perfectly in our lives: we had a lovely house a 15 minute drive from all of our parents, Chris had a job he loved and could support us on his salary alone, I had a new job that I was really enjoying, but it was temporary and could stop working to be a stay at home mom once I got pregnant. We were living the dream.

On February 9, 2012, Chris headed out for a meeting in the morning, I gave him a hug and a kiss goodbye, called him while I was driving to work a little later, and then had a busy morning at the office. I texted Chris a couple of times but knew he was in a meeting all morning and did not hear back from him. We had a friend from Florida coming to stay with us that day for a job interview the next morning, and we had left him a key outside the door so he could let himself in, as his flight arrived before we would be home.

After a series of confusing texts and then phone calls with our friend, I came to understand that he had found Chris dead in our home when he came into the house. My boss of less than three months drove me home to find multiple emergency vehicles at our house, and a chaplain who told me that my sweet Chris was dead. I was asked questions by detectives that did not make any sense, but they told me that Chris had killed himself.

Even now, years later, it still makes no sense to me. Chris had no history of depression or mental illness, he had zero of the warning signs of suicide, and I have no idea what happened that day. We had everything going for us in our lives, and I have no idea what was bothering him, or if he just had a sudden chemical imbalance in his brain that day. Many of the details are etched into my mind, crystal clear, while some details are just a fog and a blur. At 27 years old, I was a widow. I would never have children that looked just like Chris, with his freckles or dark hair. The memories of our life together would die with me.

The first few months after Chris' death are mostly a blur. The shock took a while to wear off, and the new reality that I was all alone took a while to set in. I found a grief counselor and began weekly counseling sessions with her. The grief and depression took a hold of me, as I found myself unable to see any sort of future for myself. Everything I had wanted and dreamed of were impossible now, so what was the point of a life without Chris? I thankfully was hired on as a full-time employee at my firm, and they were beyond wonderful to me, allowing me to adjust my schedule to fit in counseling sessions and did not seem to care that I was sobbing silently at my desk all day.

I was able to keep my house, despite being completely screwed over by the life insurance company because of a suicide clause in Chris' policy that denied me the claim. I stopped going to church. I could not stand to be in the sanctuary where our wedding had been, where his funeral was, where everyone looked at me with pity eyes. No one knew what to say to me, how to help. I felt like there was a glass wall between me and the rest of the world like I was just looking in on everyone else's lives moving forward, and I was trapped all alone, unable to move. The grief was crippling and isolating.

After the one year anniversary of his death, I started to despair that at 28, I would never find someone my age who would consider dating a widow, and the baggage that that entails. I have a good relationship with Chris' mother and siblings that I wanted to keep open, so that added another layer of complication to the idea of dating.

I decided to join ChristianMingle.com in the spring of 2013 because it allowed me to put my story out there, and then if someone could not handle all of my "stuff", then they could just click on by and not waste my time or emotional energy. I had a surprising number of interested people, though sadly a lot of 50 and 60-year-old widowers – creepy! I dated a guy for about a month in May of 2013. He could not actually handle everything, though, and I knew I could not continue to see him.

On June 30th, I found Andy's profile online and thought, this guy sounds great, so I messaged him. We messaged back and forth a lot, then spoke on the phone for a week for hours at a time. My sister's wedding was the next weekend, so we met in person for our first date on Monday, July 8, 2013. We just clicked, and I told him the full version of my story with Chris that very evening. He was not scared off. We went on another date that Wednesday and again on Friday. He met my parents before we had known each other a week, and I met his whole family a week after that. I do not know how to describe it, but we just clicked.

It sounds crazy, I know, but I just knew he was the one for me.

I went to Mass with him for the first time after we had been seeing each other for about two weeks. He was cantoring at Mass, and

I had not been to church in months, probably since Easter with my family. Andy had been in the seminary for six years before discerning out, so I knew that he would not convert for me – if I wanted our future family to go to church together, I would have to convert to Catholicism, though he didn't pressure me or even ask me to do so.

I joined RCIA in September, right after we bought a ring. He proposed to me on October 5, 2013, less than three months after our first date, and we were married in April 2014, the week after I joined the Catholic Church at Easter. Our wedding was a beautiful, perfect day. As we always say, when you know, you know! Our relationship grew fast, but we were older and had been through some life experiences before meeting each other.

We started trying to get pregnant right away. After a year of no success, I started researching international adoption. I had always wanted to adopt from China, and Chris and I had started saving money for that, but after Chris died, I did not qualify by myself. Andy and I would not qualify to adopt from China until we had been married for five years, which is a common requirement for international adoption. I found an agency located in our city, which worked with eight different countries at that time.

The week that I found them, they had an open house on that Saturday for prospective parents, and it happened to be the only Saturday in the next two months that we did not have plans and could attend. I considered this to be a sign. We went and found that even only being married for a year, we qualified for several different countries, and of those, we selected an Eastern European program that had travel times that best fit with our availability. We signed the contract to start the paperwork chase in August 2015.

Three days later we found out I was pregnant! Our crazy story continues! Our beautiful daughter was born in April 2016, on the date I joined the Catholic Church two years prior. We are currently waiting for a referral for our adoptive child(ren) from Eastern Europe. We look forward to seeing our family and love story grow, hopefully through biological as well as adoptive children.

My love story has not turned out the way I thought it would when I started dating Chris at sixteen. Losing Chris was devastating and the grief of that loss continues today and always will. God blessed me with a chapter two in my love story, a second chance at love in Andy, and a chance to become a mother for which I am so grateful.

Goin' to the Chapel and We're Gonna Get Married!

Emily Ricci (E22/M23)
www.gloriammarketing.com

I often tell my husband that I wish God would allow us to freeze frame parts of our lives and just take a moment to point out that what we are experiencing is a huge turning point.

Like the day you see a job listing online that will turn out to be your lifelong career. Or when you realize you drove by your future home every day for years before you bought it.

Or the day you meet your future spouse and become friends in the very same chapel you'll one day get married in.

On days like those, I always imagine God sitting up in heaven, almost giddy, waiting as we approach this pivotal moment and knowing how it will all play out in our lives, while we think it's just another day.

What if I'd gotten that flash forward insight? If I had, I think it would have looked something like this...

*   *   *

It was February 26, 2012. I was a senior in high school, attending New Student Day at one of my top choice colleges when I spotted a friend from a retreat my family attended each year. We squealed in delight and hugged, gushing over the fact that we didn't know we were both considering this school. She had to go to another table, but we promised we'd meet up later.

Later in the day, I spotted her in the gym for the College Bowl, a series of games and contests that would allow us to win college gear in exchange for making fools out of ourselves. We picked a spot in the bleachers, and that's when this thin blonde guy walked over and sat down near us.

"Oh, Emily," my friend said, "This is Aaron; he and I are in youth group together."

You would think that the earth would shake, the lights would go dim, or SOMETHING amazing would happen the first time I ever looked in my future husband's eyes.

Nope.

"Hi," we both said lamely, and then awkwardly avoided speaking to each other the rest of the time. No fireworks, no heart flutterings – in fact, the only reason he and I even remember that this encounter happened was from the photo evidence! There was a crowd shot from that day where you can see really blurry images of him and I sitting next to our mutual friend.

As fate (or God!) would have it, we both ended up attending that same school. We didn't see each other again until move-in day when we passed each other on the street and waved. The day after we moved in was a Sunday, and even though I'd already gone to Mass the night before, I decided I was going to be super religious and go again. My primary motive may or may not have been to see if there were any cute guys who I hadn't seen the night before. Sorry, Lord. Aaron hadn't gone to Mass yet that weekend, so he and I ended up going together for the first time in our college's chapel.

In the beginning, our relationship was purely platonic. I soon found out that his dorm room was directly above mine so naturally, I would try to annoy him by bouncing a rubber ball off of my ceiling at night. We ended up becoming part of the same freshman friend group for that first semester. Slowly though, our friend group began to dwindle until Aaron and I were the only two who consistently hung out with one another, without really knowing why. We were an unlikely pair of friends – he was a shy, outdoorsy tech guy and I was an outgoing reading and writing fanatic – but we had one very solid thing in common: our faith.

We had both grown up in devout Catholic families but had been worried we wouldn't be able to find anyone on campus who shared our deep faith. What we were afraid didn't exist on our campus, we found in one another. We began to go to daily Mass together and quickly became good friends with all of the Campus Ministry regulars. And so our friendship grew rapidly as we spent hours upon hours together in that college chapel.

It wasn't long before all of these friends were telling us that we were going to get married someday. I always laughed it off and insisted that we'd drive each other nuts if we were ever in a relationship. I just didn't feel any romantic attachment to him. In fact, I used to ask him for advice about a different guy I had a crush on! Still, he quickly became my best friend and partner-in-crime. We were pretty much inseparable.

Every once in a while, I'd wonder if Aaron had feelings for me, but I was never sure if he was flirting or just being friendly. Neither of us had ever been in a relationship before, so we had no clue what we were doing. I'd usually shrug off the feeling though because I didn't know how I felt about him and anyway, I was pretty sure he didn't like me that way.

We didn't see each other for three and a half months during our first summer break, but we talked through Facebook Messenger almost every day and Skyped a few times. There was one day when we were so bored that we planned an entire fake wedding to each other, spurred on by a joke from his sister about me. We made up our imaginary guest list, bridesmaid dresses, honeymoon destination, and first dance song. Spoiler alert: we ended up having that exact song as the first dance at our real wedding four years later!

With the distance, I took the time to try to figure out my feelings for him, and by the end of the summer, I concluded... definitively... that I did just want to be friends. Looking back, I realize that was all out of fear – his friendship and presence in my life were too important for me to risk.

I should have known that wasn't going to work on the first day of sophomore year. That day, I wasn't feeling well and was just generally grumpy. The only thing keeping me going was that I'd get to see Aaron again after so long. I'd had a countdown going on my phone as to the exact minute I'd get to see him, and I tried to convince myself that I was not spending more time than usual picking out what I was going to wear that day just because I was going to see him. When I finally saw him, I burst into a sprint and grabbed him into a big hug, my grumpiness instantly evaporating. But yeah, we were totally just friends. *Eye roll.*

One night about two weeks into the semester, I was lying in bed, staring at the ceiling, trying to fall asleep and talking to God. I was telling Him how I wanted to marry someone like Aaron – someone who was steady, responsible, fun to be around, and a devout Catholic. Suddenly, it was like a bolt of lightning hit me, and I literally jolted up as I realized that I didn't just want to marry someone *like* Aaron; I wanted to marry *him*.

I truly went from "just friends" ... to having a crush... to wanting to marry him in about 10 seconds. After that realization, resistance was futile. It was exactly how the character Hazel reflects on her relationship with her best friend in *The Fault in Our Stars* – "I fell in love like you fall asleep: slowly, and then all at once[22] ."

There was just one teensy little problem – the second I realized I had a crush on him, I was immediately convinced that he would never go out with me. The more I evaluated his attitude towards me, the more I realized it was just one of deep friendship. I tried to bury my feelings and move on.

On September 11, 2013, Aaron and I were hanging out in the Campus Ministry office for the afternoon, pretending to do homework but really just socializing while we waited around for the annual 9/11 memorial, which we were going to be singing at together with the church choir. My best friend Meg came in after class, and she and I went to grab food at the café down the hall. As we were waiting in line, I casually mentioned that I loved the shirt that Aaron was wearing; it was a bright blue color that we both loved. She commented that she thought I was going to say that I loved Aaron and so I took a breath and said, "Maybe I do."

Lots of girly squealing ensued since she'd always been the biggest proponent of us going out in the first place, but something about the way Meg was talking to me, very distractedly, made me curious. "Do you know something I don't know?" I asked her quizzically. She insisted that she didn't, but something seemed suspicious and I wondered what she wasn't telling me.

That night, we were all getting dinner together before the service, and I was watching Aaron out of the corner of my eye. While he got up from the table, my heart was doing somersaults. I was kicking myself for never noticing before how handsome he was.

Suddenly, Meg burst out, "I lied to you. I do know something you don't know – Aaron likes you too, he was going to ask you out today." My mouth dropped open.

She continued, "But look normal! He's coming back and you're not supposed to know!"

Yeah, okay, act normal. Sure, no problem.

I don't know how I got through the 9/11 service that night or the next few days as I tried to find opportunities to be alone with him so he could ask me out. I didn't really want to be the one to bring it up since I technically wasn't supposed to know. Later I found out that he was still so nervous I'd say no that he kept avoiding it whenever possible.

Finally, it was the afternoon of Friday, September 13, 2013. Aaron and I spent over two hours basically not talking to each other as both of us were trying to figure out how to initiate the relationship. He was commuting at the time, so he finally said that he needed to leave. My heart sank as I realized that I was going to have to sit with this for the entire weekend, so I finally blurted out, "Would you please just say something?"

He stopped and looked at me like a deer in the headlights as he suddenly realized that I knew. "I think we both know what's going on here."

For most people, saying "those three little words" is a moment of great weight, preceded by hours upon hours of thought and agony about when and how to say it. For me, though, it just kind of popped out.

So, I started our relationship with what usually takes a much longer time – "I love you," I finally admitted.

He burst into a relieved smile, one that I'll never forget – "I love you too."

I don't know what most couples do when they first start going out, but we ended up going to the chapel, the same chapel where our friendship had developed, to pray together.

Ladies – if you ever want assurance that the guy you just agreed to date is the right one, just wait until he asks you to pray with him moments after asking you out. I guarantee it will put your mind at ease.

When we got there, Aaron began to open his heart to God and myself, asking for His blessing over our relationship and guiding us through whatever path it would take us, especially if that path was going to lead to marriage. I was blown away by his candor, and knew our relationship was destined to be special with a beginning like that.

*   *   *

My peek into the future speeds up for a bit, with images of fun dates, study sessions, and sacristy antics flashing by until it slows down again in May of 2015.

Just before Aaron and I started dating, I realized that I could complete my undergraduate degree in three years due to some extra credits, so I ended up graduating a year before him. During the year and a half we were dating while in school, we spent just about every minute we could together – Daily Mass, church choir, college choir, Honors Council, Campus Ministry trips. We loved our core group of friends, but we were totally fine just being the two of us. Some of my favorite times in school were just meeting him for lunch or dinner in the dining hall or when he would surprise me by sneaking up on me while I was studying in the library.

Dating during college was simple and a natural continuation of our friendship. We weren't really doing anything that different than we had before, except now we would hold hands and text each other "I love you" at night. During the breaks in between semesters, we would revert to long distance, which was always really hard. But soon enough, the countdown timer on my phone would be back to zero, and we'd have another three and a half months to make more memories.

But all of that ease and simplicity changed when I graduated. Suddenly, we weren't seeing each other every day, and although we only lived an hour away from each other, it was just enough distance to be a pain and make planning time together a project.

Right before I left campus on my graduation day, we stopped at the chapel again, asking God to guide us as we entered this new season of our relationship. After about two weeks of dating, we had already started talking about marriage, and I'd known before we even dated that I wanted to marry him someday. Still, it was the conviction of a girl who had never dated anyone else before, and I honestly thought that being long distance would make us fizzle out and die. Leaving the chapel that day was bittersweet as I wondered if I'd ever get to pray there with him again.

Boy was I wrong. Although long distance was the hardest thing I've ever done in my life, I think the long distance time in our relationship is what actually made us get married in the end. Being long distance forced us to learn how to communicate and to value the time we spent together. It challenged us to find creative ways to work at showing our love and growing our relationship. It proved that we weren't just together because it was easy or convenient while we were at school, but because we actually loved each other and truly wanted to be together.

SMITTEN

One thing that was pivotal to the long distance season of our relationship was prayer. We made it a habit to Skype each night, and at the end of our call, we would say a short prayer together, one we would make up for each season of our lives. We had one for when we first started long distance, one for once Aaron graduated, one as we approached engagement, etc. Sometimes, after a conversation that was riddled with misunderstanding and lost video connection, that prayer would be what would get us through and remind us of why we were roughing it out through that period of long distance.

Over the next year, our relationship matured and my desire to marry him got stronger with each day as I learned to value his kindness, his dedication to me and our relationship, and our deepening faith. It wasn't long before I realized that my childhood hopes of marrying the only guy I'd ever kissed or dated were suddenly a eality as I became fully convinced that Aaron was the man I wanted to spend the rest of my life with.

By July 2016, after Aaron had graduated and we were both beginning full-time work, I was definitely on high alert for an engagement ring. Each time we were together, I'd look at his pockets to see if I could catch a glimpse of a ring box sticking out. Still, I wasn't really thinking that the engagement would be coming imminently, just probably sometime in the next year or so.

Around the beginning of August 2016, Aaron casually mentioned that he'd be working out of the office near our college (where I now worked) that coming Friday and wanted to know if I wanted to eat lunch together that day. He knew I only had a half hour for lunch, but said he would come and meet me at the college and we could eat together, and he made some comment about going to the chapel first so we could say grace, to which I agreed.

That day, he picked me up and we drove to the chapel together. We walked about halfway up the aisle to go in and pray when Aaron stopped and grabbed my hands, facing me in the middle of the aisle. There was a look in his eye that made me cock my head and ask him "What?"

He just smiled and took my hands. "We've just been through so much together and I just love you so much." I smiled.

"I love you too!" I replied.

He hugged me and then continued looking at me with that gleam in his eye. Suddenly, he gave the tiniest little sigh, let go of my hands,...and got down on one knee!

Cue the instantaneous crying.

I always thought I'd be very calm and collected when he proposed, at least at first. I figured it would take at least 30 seconds to process before I'd be emotional.

Nope.

I'm not even sure if he actually hit the ground before I was all-out sobbing. As a result, I have almost no memory of the actual proposal because I sounded like someone was murdering a seal. The one part I got, which is the important part, was the "Will you marry me, my wonderful darling friend?" (a line from one of my favorite Jane Austen novels, *Emma*, whose story reminded me so much of ours. Apparently, I had once remarked off-hand that it would be cool if he proposed using that line). I don't remember much else except my hysterical sobbing.

And then I realized I was actually supposed to respond to the "Will you marry me" question, to which I then managed to choke out a "yes!"

After a lot of hugs and tears, we sat down in the very same pew we had three and a half years earlier when we took the leap from friends to boyfriend and girlfriend, now about to take a new leap of faith. Aaron prayed again, asking God to continue to bless us as we entered yet another new chapter, and I ended with a hearty "ditto!" because I may or may not have still been crying my eyes out (for joy, of course!).

It was 307 days later and I found myself kneeling on the floor of that very same chapel. It was the night before our wedding, and my father-in-law, who will become a deacon this June, had exposed the Blessed Sacrament for us before our rehearsal. Our wedding party was joining us in the Rosary, and I caught myself looking around the room in nostalgia. Every corner of the small, 200-seater chapel held a piece of Aaron's and my story – the chairs where we used to sit for church choir, the pew where we first started dating and where he proposed, the chalice and ciboria we'd spent hours cleaning in the sacristy as freshman friends...it was all right here, right in this one place, and it hit me that this was what God had envisioned all along, since the very first time we'd walked into that place to-gether to now.

On June 16, 2017, I walked down that aisle that I'd trekked so many times in the last five years, but this time, I was wearing a white dress and Aaron was waiting for me at the other end. We stood at the altar where we had prayed on our first day of dating and watched our whole journey come full circle as we said our vows and became husband and wife, just where we had asked God to lead us if He so willed. Our family and friends packed the pews that we once sat in together as freshmen five years before, totally unaware of what this room would come to mean to us.

For me today, almost a year later, my college's chapel isn't just where I used to go to Mass or even simply the place where I got married, but rather, it is a standing reminder to myself to trust. Every time I walk in and feel the flood of memories come back that write our love story, I remember to trust in God's greater plan for my life, because if He can write a love story like ours so far into the future, then He must have crazy plans for my whole life.

* * *

The sounds of cheering bring me back, and I'm suddenly sitting in the bleachers again, senior year of high school, unsure of all the twists and turns about to come in life. I look at the sandy-haired boy next to me, but still have no idea of how intertwined our lives are about to become.

What would I say to myself, if I could go back to that day and tell myself everything?

Probably nothing.

Because in the end, I think God said it better.

Advice for singles:
My advice is two-fold: The first is to trust. I was only single until I was nineteen, but prior to that, I'd never dated anyone before. I felt like I was unlovable, that I would never find someone who could possibly want to be with me because I was too religious and no one would want to keep up with that. The truth is, at nineteen, I'd only just barely begun to meet people, and the second I stopped looking, God showed me that "the one" had been there all along, in the last

person I would have expected. I know that trusting is really hard, but I promise you, His plan will be so much greater than anything you could have come up with.

Second, marriage is beautiful for completely different reasons than I had imagined when I was single or even dating. At our wedding, Meg said during her maid-of-honor speech that she wanted to say "I told you so" for having predicted this day so many years before, but had realized that we had, in fact, told her so. We had always insisted that our friendship had to come first, and it had. Aaron is still to this day my best friend, and I can see the fruits of Aaron's and my initial friendship still bearing fruit in our marriage. The best parts of marriage aren't the moments that can be captured by a cell phone and shared on social media. They're the impromptu dance parties in the living room, the security of a good morning snuggle, the sacrifice of doing chores while the other person is sick, a "boring" Saturday night staying home and watching a movie together. That's marriage, and that's what makes it beautiful.

The Call of the Spirit

Erin Gillard (E21/M22)

My name is Erin and I live in Sydney, Australia with my beautiful husband Kiel and our two children, Amelia and James. True love exists. Our story is one of hope, love, patience, and trust in God's divine providence. I hope you enjoy it and that it brings you hope.

From my earliest memories, I have always been a hopeless romantic. I love stories of princesses being swept off their feet by a handsome and charming prince. As a teenager and young adult, I loved romantic movies and books... always looking for, hoping for that happy ending. Inside I was always hoping and yearning for that myself as well.

I was constantly on the lookout for a potential boyfriend. Could it be him? Maybe this one? I went to an all-girls Catholic high school, so the only exposure we had to boys was at the train station before school or at dances held once a term. My friends always had boyfriends. Me? Well, I was the 'best friend', you know... always in the friend zone.

One of my friends challenged me to write down every quality I wanted in a boyfriend/husband and then to let go and let God. I had some very high ideals and qualities. I knew this was a good thing because of the positive and loving relationship I had with my own father. I was also blessed with good guy friends in my life. So I did it! I let GO and Let God.

University came along and with that a great exposure to all different types of men. I chose to surround myself with Catholic friends through the university Catholic society. Here, I met a wonderful Catholic man. He fulfilled almost all of the qualities on my list. I quickly fell in love with this guy who had become my best friend, but those feelings of love weren't reciprocated in a romantic way.

In January 2009, I attended a Catholic youth conference in Bathurst NSW which is in Outback Australia. There were over five hundred young people. I was going to attend this conference with my boyfriend at the time. He was a nice Catholic boy who had been considering joining the priesthood. Unfortunately, the day before we were supposed to leave, he became ill and couldn't come. I was still up for going by myself but didn't have any way of getting to the conference. He was the one who was going to drive us to Bathurst from Sydney. At this point, I considered not going. I wouldn't really know anyone else there and I didn't have a way of getting there or back home.

The Holy Spirit had other plans for me. My parents kindly decided to help me out and they drove me the 400 km (250 miles) round trip.

So there I was in the bush, only knowing one other person among the crowds. I was scared to speak to anyone. I did my best to get involved but I began despairing. On one particular day, I went to pray the rosary and then headed down to the dining hall to have an early lunch by myself. Everyone was still in their classes/workshops so I sat alone in the massive hall with my schnitzel. With tears in my eyes, my heart cried out, "Lord, why have you brought me here, all alone? I don't want to be here. I want to go home."

In that exact moment, a young man in a black shirt and shorts walked down the long hall and over to me with his lunch. He asked to join me. Of course, I said yes and we sat enjoying our lunch as two strangers. I discovered his name was Kiel, he was a computer programmer, and that this was his first time here too. I remember having seen him at some of the rallies and he looked like a pro at all the praise and worship moments so I was surprised to learn he was a first timer too.

A little voice wondered in my head, as it always did, maybe he could be my boyfriend... with a few style changes, of course! Yes, he would do just fine! We had a great chat and I bumped into him here and there over the days to come. We even attended the same class on discerning vocations. What a great chuckle God must have been having to himself.

While I was seeing coincidences and feeling butterflies, Kiel was at the conference with his girlfriend... the love of his life for over five years.

On the final night of the conference, I got another chance to have a decent talk with Kiel. He came and sat next to me earlier in the night while a talent show was on. I was introduced to his girlfriend who had been singing in the show. She had to run off but Kiel told me about the great love he had for her. He told me that he had been planning to propose but was giving her time while she was discerning her vocation. During that conversation, I felt a massive change in my heart.

I fell in love with the LOVE Kiel had for his girlfriend. He had all the qualities I was wanting in a husband and a father. I wanted to be loved in the exact way that Kiel loved his girlfriend, a reflection of how Christ loved the church. I walked away with tears in my eyes, heart overwhelming, praising God. "Thank you, Lord for showing me such a love and passion exists. That men like Kiel exist. I know now that it is possible for this kind of love to still exist and I know I need to wait for someone just like Kiel. Thank you, Lord!"

We stayed in contact via Facebook and the odd phone call here and there over the next eighteen months. During that time I continued to search for love. Unfortunately, I was badly hurt by a wolf in sheep's clothing. I thought it was a Catholic relationship but it wasn't really. I know God was just as hurt and upset as I was about how badly it all turned out.

On the eve of my 21st birthday, Kiel came along to my high tea birthday party. He traveled a very long way to come and knew no one except for me there. The party kicked on into the evening with pizza back at my house. As people headed home for the night, Kiel remained. We watched a movie together, his favorite, *Stardust*.[23] He began to make his move, trying to hold my hand. The movie ended and my last guest decided to head home. Kiel remained.

When we were finally alone Kiel professed his love for me and we shared our first kiss which literally shifted gravity. I knew in that very instant I was going to marry this man, however Kiel, at this point, was now discerning a vocation to the priesthood. In fact, the day after our first date he was at the seminary for a seminarian retreat!

This was the start of our whirlwind romance and courtship. Dates, outings, long phone calls, letters, and messaging. We had our own code word that would pop up everywhere. S.H.M.I.L.Y See How Much I Love You. A month after we started dating, Kiel went on a pilgrimage to the Holy Land for a month to discern his vocation. He had originally booked this trip to discern a call to the priesthood, however, it became a trip to discern a vocation to the priesthood or marriage. SHMILY was drawn in the rocky ground on top of Mt. Sinai, out on a boat in the river Jordan, on top of the Mount of Beatitudes and in Ephesus.

A month after Kiel came back I was backpacking through Europe for a month with my best friend. SHMILY popped up in front of the Eiffel Tower, on top of the highest mountain in Europe, at the Vatican. At every hotel I would arrive at Kiel would have left a message for me to receive which was fun because English wasn't always the strongest language of the staff receiving the messages. Things were often lost in translation. The whole tour bus would wait to hear the love messages sent to me from across the world.

We were absolutely, totally, and completely in love. I was ready for Kiel to propose after two weeks of dating. In fact, I thought Kiel was going to propose on one particular evening just after we started dating. There were candles throughout the house along with a candlelit dinner that he made! Kiel didn't propose until two days before my 22nd birthday, although I have since learned that he carried the ring around with him in his bag for months beforehand.

Kiel proposed in front of a crackling fire on a cold winter's night, down on one knee in the Blue Mountains. He had seen that I liked this particular bed and breakfast's cozy accommodation and set about making this dream come true. I, of course, saw it coming from a mile away and was so very excited. The speech he made was beautiful and the ring, divine, just as our love was.

Three days later, we met with our priest and booked our wedding reception. We wouldn't marry though until eleven months later, July 14, 2012. Our nuptial Mass was so very blessed and our wedding reception was so full of love and light. We were blessed to get pregnant on our honeymoon but miscarried our baby early on. Our daughter Amelia was only a few weeks behind her sibling on joining our family. When Amelia was 3.5 years old we were blessed again with our son James.

This year we celebrate being married for six years and together for eight. SHMILY notes still appear, our love has matured and deepened and we journey together ever closer through parenthood. We now mentor engaged couples on their journey towards marriage and hope to be a witness of married life and love to our community.

I named our story The Call of the Spirit because of one very special thing. Although this call from the spirit didn't happen to me, it happened to Kiel. When he saw the lonely girl sitting in the massive dining room he heard something deep within him say, "That's your wife right there." Since Kiel was at the conference with his girl-friend who he had been waiting to propose to, this call made Kiel very uneasy and rattled him for a long time after.

"That's my wife right there? How can that be Lord? She's not the girl I'm dating."

It just goes to show that the plans we have for our life and the plans that God has for our lives aren't always the same. At so many points along our journey, Kiel and I could have gone very different ways. So many obstacles presented themselves to prevent me from even attending the conference. Had I not have gone, I would never have met Kiel.

Even if Kiel and I were never meant to be, I was forever changed because I encountered the Christ within him. He showed me the sheer love Christ has for each and every one of us. He helped me see the passion, patience, the romance, the overwhelming, all-consuming love. God wants us all to experience it because it foreshadows the divine love He has for us and is the smallest glimpse of heaven we get to have. At a silent retreat, alone in the church, I felt God speak to me of the love he has for us:

"Allow me to romance you, allow me to woo your heart,
The love that I provide sustains and always lasts.
I promise to be beside you, each step you take each day.
Come discover a love like no other. A romance to blow you away"

Men, love your wife with passion and reverence just as Christ loved the church, whether or not you have met her yet. Women, wait for the man who will love you with such passion, who will lay his life down for you as Christ did. Do not settle for anything less than the divine, perfect love that Christ modeled for us. And if it isn't marriage you are called to, Christ may be calling you into the great passionate love affair with him as a Bride of Christ or men, to marry his Bride of Christ.

Open your heart to God and he will fill it to abundance with blessings and direct you to where he knows you will be the most fulfilled and best able to taste the glory and promise of eternal life with him in heaven.

A Winter's Tale

Bridgette Fargason (E24/M24)
www.hailmarry.org

Before I tell you my story, let me share that my husband is not Catholic. This presents a unique set of challenges in our marriage. I get a lot of interesting responses from people when they learn of it. Some people choose to tell me about their own husband's conversion stories. Some are visibly shocked and can't seem to understand how I could have made the choice to marry outside the faith. Others react as though I'd said he was blonde or something superficial. While I love him a great deal, it is by no means a superficial difference between us.

I truly believe that God created this man and designed us for each other. It has not been without some ups and downs but as I look back, I can see God's fingerprints all over our relationship.

I recall praying as a young girl and making a list of the kind of man I wanted to marry. The only things I can remember from that list are that he needed to be funny, older than me by a couple years, taller than me, blue-eyed and that we needed to have an established friendship before a romantic one developed. And I've always liked the name "Josh." Not the most stellar of lists, I know, but in my young mind, those seemed like important features to have in a spouse.

I don't remember the first time I met my husband, but I do remember very clearly the first time I had heard his name. My older brother had come home from school and was complaining about a classmate he was sharing a role with in the school play. He called him "arrogant", among other things, and I remember thinking to myself, "He can't be that bad."

I would meet this classmate a year later during another school play and I didn't find him arrogant at all. In fact, I actually enjoyed feeding his ego. He was charming and funny, we shared a love of theatre and performing, we both came from large military families, and my mother loved him. My mother used to say we would get married, but I didn't see him in that way at all and would almost roll my eyes.

Then one night after he graduated, he planned a group get together to see the movie *Gladiator*[24] and I was invited. As it turned out, everyone else ended up canceling for one reason or another. I will never forget my best friend calling to inform me of this and asking if I would be ok. I laughed and said, "It's Josh! Of course, I'll be ok." Then I ran up to my room and changed clothes.

He called and asked if we were still on for the movie and that's how a group outing turned into our first date. It was perfect.

It was casual and fun. We didn't have to impress each other because we were already such good friends. He was also a perfect gentleman. He didn't even kiss me goodnight which really set him apart from all the other guys I dated previously. I felt loved and really cherished for who I was.

We kept in touch over AOL Instant Messenger throughout my early college years, and then one summer my best friend and I took a road trip to visit him. Seeing him again after so many years was almost magical. We'd spent the night at his house and the next day we all just hung out. While playing a game of Twister I looked up at him and very clearly heard the Holy Spirit whisper to me, "You're going to marry him someday."

To say it took me off-guard would be an understatement. I mean, we had been friends for years and except for that one spontaneous movie date, we had always dated other people. I had never really thought about him in that way but one doesn't just brush off a Holy Spirit experience like that!

I sat down and thought about our history so far:

- I looked back on closing night of our spring musical my freshman year of high school and remembered how I cried because I thought he was graduating, and then how elated I was to discover he was a junior and he'd be around another year.
- I looked back on how I would run and jump in his arms whenever I saw him in the hallway at school, especially after he graduated.
- I looked back on our accidental date and how sweet he had been.
- I looked back on the list I had made as a young girl and how he fit every criterion!

Though I was knocked over by this experience, I wasn't dismayed or to be honest, even surprised. It was as if someone had pointed out something I had known deep down all along.

We began a serious long-distance courtship that included regular phone calls and him writing me letters and poetry, usually Shakespeare. He would send me little gifts of things that made him think of me, like costume butterfly wings or a keychain that looked like a ballet slipper. By Thanksgiving of that year, we were in a committed, long-distance relationship.

Most love stories don't play out perfectly without any bumps. In January of the next year, I decided to take a break. I'd lost sight of what God had told me and in my confusion, I thought I needed space.

After some time, it became clear that I really wanted to be with Josh but by the time I had figured this out, I learned he had moved on. I thought that was it; we were over. I'd taken too long to make up my mind and there was no getting him back. It began a dark time for me.

I fell into the Dark Side. I became manipulative, selfish, and learned how to use people. I stopped going to Mass because of my class load. I still prayed though I wasn't positive God was listening anymore. I lost sight of who I was and who God was. I needed my Savior.

Then one day He showed up. I saw a flyer for auditions for a dance company near where Josh was living. I was seriously trying to start my career as a ballet dancer and because all of my other auditions had ended in rejection letters, I decided to travel for this one. I saw Josh while I was in town, but things were awkward.

When I got hired, he helped me get settled in the area and we began to reestablish our friendship. Even though it felt awkward considering what had passed between us, the love we'd fostered in the early years of our friendship hadn't faded. We were still close and comfortable together, we just needed time to heal the hurt.

The healing process took about a year for both of us. He helped me to unlearn all the destructive behaviors I had cultivated after our falling out and slowly trust was rebuilt. By the time we were ready to start dating again, we both knew this time was going to be more serious. Josh looked at his life and decided joining the military would be the best thing for him. He knew that having grown up a military dependent that I did not want that life for my kids.

One day he asked me, "Would you marry me if I joined the military?"

I didn't have to stop and think. The thought of being without Josh again was far worse than military life could ever be. I can't say I didn't stomp my feet and pout a bit at the idea of being a military dependent again but I had so much love for this man, I was willing to trust him and to trust God.

Josh joined the military. In God's mercy, he would only be two hours away from me during training, which helped us get through that time. When I saw him again after Basic Training, I knew this was the life God wanted us to have together. He proposed to me over Christmas break and two weeks later, we were married by a retired judge in her living room with one of my new brothers-in-law as a witness.

I knew Josh wasn't Catholic, but at the time we got married, I didn't think the differences in our theology would be an issue. He was Christian, after all. We started going to church together and once we got settled into our first duty station, I started attending both Protestant and Catholic Bible study groups. I learned so much about Christianity that I had never known before.

When I was younger, my life felt very compartmentalized. I had my school friends, my dance friends, and my faith life but they felt very separate. Though both my parents were cradle Catholics, they never really explained to me that not all Christians are Catholic. I learned that on my own in high school as most of my friends went to many different churches.

Through those years, despite meeting people of various denominations, I didn't recognize the differences in our theologies. I didn't understand the significance of the differences between Protestantism and Catholicism. To be honest, even if I had, I don't think it would have kept me from choosing to marry my husband. I had felt so moved by the Holy Spirit to marry him that it didn't feel like a choice I made on my own.

I have come so far in my knowledge about my Catholic faith. There were so many things I had taken for granted before. I have come to see the deeper and more beautiful meaning in so much that our faith has to offer.

My husband is now out of the military and our two darling children won't have the military childhood that I grew up with. We are doing our best navigating the struggles of an unequally yoked marriage, but our love for each other keeps getting stronger. Our faith in God and His promises continues to grow as we have come through so many crazy challenges together! I'm talking about better and worse, sickness and health, richer and poorer, the whole nine yards.

I firmly believe that Josh is the man God wanted me to marry, and God is equipping me every chance I allow Him to be the wife Josh needs.

God works in mysterious ways and He can work all things for His glory and our good. He knows our path to Heaven and He knows the plans and dreams He has for each one of His children.

Being in an unequally yoked marriage isn't easy. There are struggles I wish no one had to share, but that's really true of every marriage. All struggles are opportunities to grow in virtue and holiness. Of course, that doesn't mean we should go looking for hardship, but if you hear God's voice and know He is calling you to a vocation, trust that He knows what He is doing. It may not look like you had envisioned, but if you prayerfully consider all the options and conform your will to His, you will find blessings beyond anything you could dream of.

Love At First Click: An Unruly Catholic Story

Brittany (Maldonado) Seeley (E21/M22)

It has taken a lot of courage and humility for me to write my story. It's filled with trials and some decisions I'm not proud of, but this is the story of how I fell in love with my husband and how God can redeem us through the sacraments. I had been on Catholic-Match.com for a month when I received a message that said, "Happy birthday!" That is how it all started, with a birthday greeting.

My to-be husband, Matthew, was sweet to reach out to me, but I wasn't so sure we would be compatible. He was passionately into movies and video games. Me, not so much. I kept scrolling through profiles, but I returned back to Matthew's. He did seem like a faithful Catholic guy plus he was cute so, I figured "why not?" After all, I did like going to the theater and using my Wii so maybe we had enough in common.

We chatted online and not before long, we were talking on the phone and video chatting. Not only did a screen separate us, but we were also states away. I was in Arizona and he was in California. We had an immediate connection so while we were planning an in-person visit, we continued to video chat daily. Our conversations were so frequent and so intimate that before long, we fell into some inappropriate online behavior. We would engage in provocative language and gestures and eventually masturbate online.

I don't say this to be shocking, but I share it because I think it's all too common. When you love someone and you want to feel close to them, it can be so easy to do what feels good and to believe that makes your relationship stronger. In our culture, it's easy to think that you're making good choices simply by not having sex but the truth is, even things like naughty online chatting or pornography, can stain your relationship and lead to worse things down the line.

I was not a virgin before meeting and marrying Matthew. I had a brief time when I wasn't living a truly faithful Catholic life and I was acting out sexually. I am so grateful that he waited for me and that he did not see me as damaged goods. He has shown me some of God's mercy and forgiveness. To this day, I feel sad and remorseful that my husband wasn't my first and only. Honestly, I wish I could take back those other experiences because they didn't prepare me in any helpful way for marriage.

As our in-person visit was quickly approaching, we continued to talk and video chat and got to know one another. Finally, I drove eight hours to California to meet this wonderful person I had been getting to know. I remember when I pulled up to the driveway, Matthew was waiting for me with a bouquet of flowers and the biggest smile. He was so happy and excited to see me and I felt exactly the same way. It's one of my most cherished memories of our relationship.

Without hesitation, I ran into his arms and we shared our first kiss. It was magical. It was love at first sight. I truly felt connected to him and in that moment, we both knew we were meant to be.

I was there for the whole weekend and we went out on many dates. We had such a strong connection and we had so much fun! Despite the short time we had known each other, we felt ready to take our relationship to the next level. He proposed to me and I said yes!

At the time, Matthew was living with his parents so we shared this exciting news with them. Not surprisingly, we were met with apprehension and doubt. Despite their misgivings, we were undeterred. We knew in our hearts that we were meant to spend the rest of our lives together.

Feeling overcome with love and the excitement of our whirlwind, romantic weekend, we got caught up in our emotions and we had sex. Though we were so in love, when I look back, I really lament this decision. I felt conflicted because it was as if I had finally met this amazing man and it felt so right to be with him and yet so morally wrong at the same time. I engaged in premarital sex because I wanted Matthew to know I was with him all the way.

For Matthew, he had struggled with an addiction to pornography. This is so common in young men now, though it is still often unaddressed. We really consider pornography as sort of a gateway drug to our having sex. It made it easier to slip into that behavior.

This temporary bliss led to a spiral of unchastity in our relationship. The new closeness I felt to Matthew made it very difficult for me to go back to Arizona when the weekend came to a close. Once home, we continued our phone calls and video chatting.

Matthew came for a visit to Arizona and because of what we had done before, it was all too easy to give into weakness. We engaged in more sexual activity and not only did this make us feel guilty, but it also made it so painful for us to part. You would think we should have just gotten married right then and there. But the truth of the matter is we would have gotten pushback from unsupportive family members. It was a "damned if you do, damned if you don't" situation. Plus, I did not want to elope.

I wanted to have my mom and sisters present. I wanted to plan a wedding, pick out a dress, try cake samples, and DIY party favors, which I eventually got to do. Most importantly, I wanted to get married in the Catholic Church. It sounds a little hypocritical, doesn't it? Wanting a church wedding when I was not always in good standing with Her. But this is where the sacraments come into play.

Accepting that we had to continue our relationship long-distance, we tried hard to talk often and be loving and supportive of each other through phone calls and video chatting. Then, a huge bomb dropped.

Matthew's mother found out we had sex while prying on his phone. It was a whirlwind of chaos and sadness. Matthew's parents said he could no longer live at home and I found myself driving to California a second time to pick him up. We packed his belongings and he moved in with me in Arizona. This was just two months after we had been matched online.

We lived together for three months before we found separate apartments in student housing since I was a senior finishing up my undergraduate studies. Though we each had roommates and jobs to focus on, we still fell into our bad habits. We slept together many times. Reflecting back on this time in our life, I am disgusted and we both felt horrible because we knew better.

As Catholics, we knew the church's teaching on premarital relations but were consumed by the world's pleasures. But we turned to the Lord. We confessed our sins many times and were forgiven. I am so grateful for the sacraments of Reconciliation and Holy Communion.

At the time, I had not been educated about Natural Family Planning and we found ourselves unexpectedly pregnant. Sadly, we lost that baby early during pregnancy.

Three months before we were set to get married, we made a serious commitment to live chastely until our wedding. We wanted the best start to our marriage, even though it began a bit tumultuously. We leaned on the great love and forgiveness of Jesus.

Our total relationship from the start of being a couple to being married was sixteen months. Some said our relationship went by too quickly, especially since we got engaged when we met one another for the first time! But we knew we were meant to be together. We loved each other very much.

This year we are coming up on our third wedding anniversary. We are celebrating our daughter's second birthday. We have grieved the early loss of another baby. And through it all, we continue to put the focus of our lives always on our Lord.

As I am older now, I can see that a lot of my poor choices go back to being brought up by a widow and not having any real male influence or father figure around. During the time of me acting out sexually, I was looking for that closeness, love, and security from a man. But I did not find it. It actually hurt me later when I brought a lot of baggage from my past into my marriage and sex life. I wish I had learned to lean on the love of the Lord instead. Even if you don't understand what that means, go try and find out right now by asking questions online or at your local parish.

Premarital sex negatively affected my sex life in marriage. There are times when I am being intimate with my husband or Matthew does something that reminds me of my past, I get flashbacks of ex-boyfriends, the things I did with them, the bad things they did to me. It's quite traumatizing at times. I try to push it out of my mind and wish it wasn't engraved in my brain.

Sometimes I struggle with scrupulosity of ensuring that my past sexual sins are wiped clean. They may be forgiven, but they are definitely not forgotten and it makes me feel so unworthy of myself, Matthew, and especially Jesus. Because I knew better. Before I started having sex, I talked to peers about my desire to have sex and I was met with "It's your decision. God will forgive you anyway." And I chose myself over Him, even though He is greater than I.

My husband and I definitely think that all the physical things we did together before marriage negatively affected our married sex life. Because premarital sex was fun and spontaneous and easy, now that we are married, expectations about sex have had to change. Sometimes it is not as easy and wild as it has been in the past and it may not ever be like that again due to health, children, NFP, exhaustion, etc. Having these before/after ideas about sex sometimes takes a toll on our marriage and sex life.

My advice to all Catholic couples is to wait for your spouse. I am still deeply saddened that I did not wait to have sex until marriage. Go to the sacraments often. Surround yourself with His grace to help keep you strong. It is in Jesus that we are forgiven, loved, and healed.

Despite unwanted comments or negativity around your relationship, make sure to put Jesus first. Listen to the wisdom of others but don't let them dictate your relationship. Know that your actions, whether positive or negative, have natural consequences. You have the power to build up your relationship or to create additional obstacles to your own love story.

Marriage is not easy. You will likely find that it is based on trial and error, as it has been for us, as you learn to live a life together. No matter what, center your marriage on Jesus and his teachings, and your marriage is sure to be blessed.

Two Worlds Collide

Maria Cecilia Escobedo (E25/M26)
www.hairbows4life.com
@mercyrunsonlove

Marriage and babies! That is all I wanted in life. I knew early on that my vocation would be marriage and family life. Yet, there was a time that I thought that might not ever happen due to the fact that I was almost 24 and I was still single. There was no sign of my soul mate. My mother and older sister married at a young age of 21 and so by the time I turned 24, I felt like it was over for me and there was no marriage in my future.

One night after another disappointed Catholic Young Adult outing, I felt called to check out AveMariaSingleCatholics.com. I felt that God was really calling me to try this out. That I had to look beyond the old fashion method and try this out. I really liked how in depth the questionnaire was. I hoped that if it asked that many questions, there was a chance it could really match me with someone special. I also appreciated that you had to pay to be part of the site. After all, I wanted to get married and I figured if someone wanted to get married, they would be serious enough to pay.

After a few emails from different gentlemen, I came across one that got my attention. His name was Gonzalo. I decided to be brave and email him. The date was July 8th, 2000. We started to email back and forth and I really began to enjoy our conversations. We seemed to have a lot in common but yet we came from different worlds.

Gonzalo comes from a small family with one sister. They lived in the middle of Mexico City. I come from a large family with two sisters and four brothers. I was born in Costa Rica. My parents are Cuban and I was raised in South Florida. Gonzalo got his PhD in Chemical Engineering and is a talented violin player. I got my BS in Early Childhood Education and Development and played soccer for about twenty years. Though we were very different, we did share our love for the Catholic Church, classical music, and family.

Even though I was having a good time emailing and getting to know Gonzalo better, I felt the need to know sooner rather than later if this was meant to go on further. I decided to hit up the saint of the impossible causes because at this point, I really felt like marriage was an impossible case for me! St. Jude to the rescue! Off I went on to complete a nine-day novena. Every day I headed to the local Adoration chapel to say my novena prayers. I specifically ask St. Jude on the ninth day to somehow let me know whether I should continue to pursue this relationship or not. I asked him to be very clear since I was a slow learner!

On the ninth and final day of the novena, I received an email from Gonzalo. By this time, we were writing daily emails. It was nothing unusual and I responded like normal. That day I also had to travel from school to visit my sister so I was preoccupied and didn't think much of the email. When I got to her house, I had asked her if I could check my email for something for school not expecting another email from Gonzalo since he had never written me twice in one day. To my surprise, I saw that he had emailed me back already!

An even bigger surprise was that in his second email, he had written that a good friend of his in Delaware had a brother who was a priest in the Opus Dei movement. This very same priest happened to be a family priest who had been friends with my family for at least fifteen years! I was shocked. Here I was living in South Florida writing to a guy from Mexico who was getting his Ph.D. in Delaware and yet we had family friends in common. I guess St. Jude knew how to get my attention for sure.

Gonzalo and I started to talk on the phone at least twice a week for hours at a time. It was like we were going on real dates even though we never left the phone. This gave us an opportunity to really get to know each other due to the lack of distractions. We knew that we had to finally meet to really see if this was meant to be or not. Since I had to travel to New York City for a conference, we decided to meet up at the St. Patrick Cathedral on October 8th, 2000. It really was love at first sight! We had an amazing weekend. Neither of us wanted it to end, but we had to go our separate ways back home. I went back to Florida and he went to Delaware.

We continued our relationship and once again, I knew I had to call upon one of my favorite saints for guidance, St. Therese of the Child Jesus. I decided that I would do a 24-day novena without telling anyone. Marriage is so important that I wanted some reassurance that I was on the right track for one of the most important decisions of my life. I continued to go to Adoration and every time I left, I felt a great peace about Gonzalo.

On the last day of the novena, I was coming home from a long day at work. As I made my way up the stairs, I saw not just twelve but 24 roses that Gonzalo had sent to me! I was shocked! I knew that St. Therese was showering me with her roses. I felt that my dreams were about to come true and that I was on the path to fulfilling my vocation of marriage and motherhood.

After Christmas that year, after finding a teaching job and some nice roommates up in Delaware, I moved so that we could have a "normal" relationship. We had our ups and downs but God always brought us peace that we were meant to be. Nothing good in life is easy!

That May, we traveled back south so that I could walk in my graduation. The evening of my graduation, with the stars in the sky and the ocean as our backdrop, Gonzalo had asked me to be his wife and partner in this beautiful thing called life.

We were married on December 8, 2001, in Palm Beach, Florida by a cousin of the family with all the traditions of a Hispanic wedding. We are coming up on our seventeenth wedding anniversary. We have five children at home and five saints in Heaven. We live in South Mississippi now and I still have a great devotion to St. Therese!

Travelin' East to Find a Wife

Liz Cunningham (E20/M21)
www.thiswesternlife.com
www.cunninghampasturedmeats.com

Love does not always come when you expect it or where you expect it.

In the old days, it was fairly common for a cowboy to go east to find his bride-to-be. Back then there weren't as many people out west and the women that came west typically were coming with a man, so if a cowboy who was settled wanted a wife, he literally had to go get one. In fact, my husband's great-grandfather went from Eastern Oregon back to Pittsburgh, PA to find his love and brought her back to the ranch after his second visit. These days cities are closer together and women are easier to come by.

Our meeting, dating, and marriage is nothing short of God's work in our lives and it was quite the adventure! In the Fall of 2006, I went to visit Franciscan University of Steubenville in Ohio. I was a senior in high school at the time and was pretty determined that I would be attending another college of choice, but my mom insisted I look at Franciscan since it was a college I had always dreamed about going to. The whole visit went really well, but one person really stuck out in my mind and it was a guy I met while I was there. Now the reason why he stuck out was because he was out of the ordinary; he was a gentleman and had no problem striking up a conversation despite the fact he had never even seen me before and had no idea that I wasn't a student there at the time. This man was a cowboy.

I couldn't believe it. I traveled from St. Louis, Missouri to Steubenville, Ohio to visit a college and I meet a genuine cowboy from the west. That cowboy is now my husband. Now it would've saved a lot of time if we talked all day and got to know each other and had fallen in love at first sight, but I believe God chuckled at us saying, "Wait to see what I have in store for you."

After visiting the college and having a great experience, I applied and started in the Fall of 2007. However, that cowboy didn't take too long to show up in the picture again. Within the first couple days of being on campus I ran into him again. There wasn't anything particularly special about us meeting again, but it still sticks out in my mind very vividly. It dawned on me that I had met him before when I had visited the school.

I said to him, "You're the cowboy from Oregon!" He was a little confused, but I further explained. "I met you when I was visiting the school, you told me that you were a cowboy from Oregon and since I've never met a real cowboy before, I remembered you." Now he didn't quite remember our meeting, but he does remember talking to a girl at some point in the student center. Obviously, I didn't really stick out to him, but that didn't matter, because I was just meeting new people.

Sean is one of those people if you meet him once, he would always remember to say hi to you on campus if he sees you, so, whenever I ran into him he would say hi to me. The first couple weeks of school went by and I started to run into Sean more often. Friends that I was making started overlapping with Sean's friends and more and more we would see each other and talk to each other. Sean would always sit at the same table for breakfast, lunch, and dinner and occasionally I would poke fun at him for never sitting with anyone else.

One day he sat down for lunch with me and a couple mutual friends, we ate lunch together and then he walked with me back to our dorms. He asked me what I was doing that weekend and I told him that I was going on a camping trip with a couple friends. I didn't want to be rude so I invited him to come join us. He thought it was a great idea and asked for my number so he could call me when he decided if he wanted to come or not. I really wasn't interested in him. In fact, there were other guys I had in mind but I just thought it would be nice to have another person coming along that I knew.

The camping trip was a lot of fun. It was my first real big college experience of being able to do whatever I wanted. I was meeting new people left and right! Sean wasn't on my mind at all, but apparently, I was making an impression on Sean.

Several days after the camping trip we all started talking about the crummy late-autumn rain and decided that it would be fun to go out and play football in the mud after classes were over that day. I kind of forgot about those plans and started working on homework when I got a phone call. It was Sean. In an excited voice he said, "You ready to go?!" I was not in the mood to play football anymore so I told him everyone canceled and that I was just going to work on homework. That answer didn't deter him.

Before I knew it, he had convinced me to go out and slide down the hills and get extremely muddy. It was just the two of us and it was a pretty weird event but even I will admit, I had fun! This was when Sean really started to like me and decided he wanted to get to know me better.

Things evolved slowly following all those events, but Sean and I got to know each other better over the next couple months. Sean would help me out with some schoolwork every now and then but I wouldn't have called it anything special, just friends really.

Then came Fall Formal. I wanted to go but I didn't want to go without a date. I kind of assumed that Sean would ask me but I wasn't quite sure if I really wanted to go with him because I didn't want to give him the wrong impression that I liked him. Within due time Sean asked me to formal, but he asked me a month in advance which is apparently not normal for someone who is "just a friend." The night of the formal came... it was the most awkward night of my life.

Sean had the whole formal night planned out with a friend of his. However, I didn't really know anyone in the group, making it even more uncomfortable for me. Thankfully there was one girl in the group that I was friends with who helped me make it through the night. Sean came and picked me up and wouldn't stop complimenting me on how nice I looked, which was nice of him, but a little overwhelming for me.

We all gathered into the car and started off to a "secret location" which ended up being a golf course that had a Christmas light display. The only problem was that it took about an hour longer than expected and when it was all said and done it was the worst light display I had ever seen. Sean, always keeping high hopes, didn't let that setback ruin his night. We then went to dinner at Applebee's with this group of people I didn't know. My friend and I tried to make light conversation, but it seemed pretty pointless. After a long agonizing dinner, we finally headed to the dance.

The location of the dance was at an old brewery in West Virginia. It had several levels so the main dance floor was on the bottom floor and the drinks and socializing were on the second and third floors. I took the opportunity to get lost with my friend so I didn't have to spend the whole evening being with a guy who really liked me but who...I wasn't so sure about.

After an hour of playing "hide-n-seek" with Sean, he finally tracked me down and asked me to dance. The first dance wasn't so bad since it was more of "group dancing" music, but then the next song was a slow song. Sean, naturally, asked me to dance and I couldn't say no. The song was a country song that Sean knew and so he started to sing it to me. At this point, I was so uncomfortable that I decided to not look at him by putting my head on his chest, so I didn't have to look him in the eye. I know I was a wimp. Apparently, that was the wrong sign for Sean because he took that as a sign that I was really starting to like him.

Following the dance, some friends invited Sean over to ride the mechanical bull that was in another part of the brewery. Why it was there we had no idea but Sean wouldn't back down from the challenge. He gladly saddled up and took the bull for a ride. After a good ride, the guy running the bull was so impressed that he offered Sean a second ride. Once again, not backing down, Sean mounted again and took his second ride. However, during that ride, his hand got caught and he ripped the skin off his knuckles. Not noticing the damage he went to adjust his tie, which resulted in him getting blood on his white dress shirt. Not only was I embarrassed by the whole bull riding thing, I now was with a guy who had blood on his shirt.

I just wanted the night to be over.

Finally, the dance came to an end and we all got in the car to head back to campus. I pretended to fall asleep in the back seat so I didn't have to try to initiate a conversation. When we got back to campus, the guys asked if we wanted to go out to a restaurant for a midnight snack. I pretended to groggily wake up and confessed that I should go to bed because I was exhausted. I was more than happy to be dropped off at the curb but Sean, being the gentleman that he is, escorted me back to my dorm.

When we got in the dorm, I quickly headed up the stairs and was ready to say goodnight and goodbye, but Sean insisted on complimenting me again. He then asked me what I was planning on doing tomorrow and said he wanted to take me out to breakfast. This was not something I wanted to do because I didn't want this little date to go any further. I told him maybe and that I would let him know the next day after Sunday Mass. I hugged him and said goodnight.

Most awkward night ever for me... Best night ever for Sean.

That night I talked to my roommate about the whole experience and she just thought it was so sweet everything Sean did for me. At this point I had never really dated any "men," so I didn't really see all the thoughtfulness that went into it. I told her that I didn't want to go out to breakfast with him the next morning, but she insisted that I must allow him to take me out because of all the thought and care he put into planning such a special night. I unwillingly agreed and decided I would go out with him in the morning.

The next day at Mass, I looked around the crowded church to see if he was there. I was pretty excited that I couldn't find him. Maybe it meant we wouldn't go on another awkward date. As I tried to quickly leave Mass following the procession, sure enough, Sean was waiting for me at the door. "Hi, Liz! I've got the car, so I'm ready to go when you are." I gave him a forced smile and said, "Okay, ready."

Sean drove us to a local breakfast shop not too far from school. This date was different, more down to earth, more Sean and more me. We had a nice conversation about his life and family and I finally felt comfortable with the fact that we were alone, together, on a date. The comfort didn't last long.

As we headed back to campus, Sean made it unbearably hard for me. "So, Liz, I've really enjoyed getting to know you and the dates we've been on... So I was thinking that I would really like to go on more dates with you next semester." Here I am... in the car, nowhere to go, nowhere to hide... and then came the biggest excuse I've ever made. "Um, well, you know I'm taking 18 credits and working, so I'm going to be really busy next semester. I don't think I'll have time to go on dates..." It was really quiet the rest of the ride home.

Sean left discouraged and I left... not so sure what to do next. I decided the best thing I could do was go to God. I was frustrated. I always dreamed of meeting a guy like Sean, polite, kind, and a gentleman. I had even dreamed of marrying a cowboy when I was younger! Here I had all that I had ever dreamed and for some reason, it just wasn't clicking for me. It came to the point that I had to look myself in the mirror and ask what was wrong with me?

Sean was doing all he could and I didn't want to accept any of it. There wasn't a huge revelation in my talk with God that night, but what I did hear was to stop worrying about the things on the outside and see myself and Sean for what is on the inside... and that made all the difference.

The next day I called Sean up and asked him if he could help me with some homework. The following day I had lunch with him and following that day we hung out with friends and watched a movie. Within two weeks, it was like things had changed completely and I was seeing Sean for who he was, and I couldn't have been happier. It was like the whole formal dance and date never existed and I was just hanging out with my really good friend, whom I was getting to know better every day.

The end of the semester was coming fast so Sean took another chance and asked me out on one more date before Christmas break. He took me down to Pittsburgh, PA to go ice skating and to see downtown. We had such a fun time ice skating together. At one point, I fell down and Sean picked me up and we held hands for the rest of the night. I was really starting to like Sean and could feel the first "butterflies" of having a crush on this cowboy.

After all the awkward moments, I finally let go of my pride and let God show me where I needed to go, and I'm so glad I did. During Christmas break, we talked on the phone and continued to get to know each other. When we came back from break, we started dating. It's all history from there.

Sean and I dated all through college and got engaged our senior year. I finally took the big leap after much deliberation and moved out to Sean's family's ranch the summer before we got married. On October 9, 2010, Sean and I were wed and we still live happily on the ranch with our four little children.

I knew God would have to put a man in my life that pursued me tirelessly and that I didn't like at first. Why might you ask? Well, I was very pushy and if I liked a guy I wanted him to know and have him start pursuing me right away. That didn't quite work out very well and it was a huge turn off for most guys, so when I met Sean and I wasn't very interested in him, it was the biggest blessing I could've asked for. Just goes to show that God knew way better than I did, and I'm sure glad His will worked out.

In the end, Sean went back to Steubenville, Ohio, pretty close to Pittsburgh, PA, found his wife-to-be and took me back to the ranch... just like his great-grandfather did before him.

SEND OFF

Are You Ready to Write Your Love Story?

On the previous pages, you have discovered nearly forty love stories from real Catholic women. Some of these stories are hilarious, some are heart-wrenching, some have inspired you with tales of holiness, and some have warned you with tales of caution. All of these stories have one thing in common: the truth.

These love stories are raw and genuine. They are meant to inspire hope that you can meet your husband in extraordinary and simply ordinary situations. There are no airbrushed actors or sappy soundtracks to shine up the very real moments that make up these true love stories.

I am so proud of all these women who have bravely written down their stories for you. I am in awe of the Lord and how His wisdom plays out in both quiet moments and in grand gestures. The sacrament of marriage continues to be a great and wonderful mystery to me. Like the thumbprints of spouses, no two marriages are the same. From beginning to end, each relationship has a unique journey to take and if we follow it faithfully, it leads us to the ultimate destination - an eternity in Heaven with God.

As always, be open to God's will for your life. He may be calling you to a religious vocation and He may be calling you to single adulthood. Often the Lord's plans seem confusing to us until we abandon ourselves to them. This isn't something that changes if you do get married. There are many twists and turns along the journey of life as we strive for sainthood and eternity with Christ in heaven.

No matter what vocation God calls you to, you will experience challenges discerning His will, suffering, and sometimes a lack of hope. It's good to cultivate the skills in dealing with these three feelings because they will be useful to you no matter what the future holds in store.

I would also highly recommend forming some relationships with saints. This was a huge game-changer in my own life and only one I discovered after I was married. Do some digging. Find someone you can relate to and simply begin by being their friend. Chat with them about your life. Bare your soul. Ask them to pray for you. Read the things they have written and try to understand how they were able to live a holy life in the midst of trials... and trust me, they all had trials!

I hope you have enjoyed these beautiful stories and that they lead you to a closer relationship with Christ!

"Lord, I am Yours, and I must belong to no one but You. My soul is Yours, and must live only by You. My will is Yours, and must love only for You. I must love You as my first cause, since I am from You. I must love You as my end and rest, since I am for You. I must love You more than my own being, since my being subsists by You. I must love You more than myself, since I am all Yours and all in You. Amen."

- St. Francis de Sales

SMITTEN JOURNAL

Want to dive deeper? Check out the 40-Day Smitten Journal, *Into The Wilderness*, designed to help single women form a deeper relationship with Christ while trying to discern His will for their lives.

Each day features commentary related to the stories in this book as well as saint quotes and Bible verses. Journal your way through this devotional that will bring you peace and lead you to Christ.

Journals are available at
www.sterlingjaquith.com and www.thelionofdesign.com.

ABOUT THE AUTHOR

Sterling Jaquith converted to Catholicism in 2010 before getting married. She and her husband live in Boise, Idaho with their five children Rose, Poppy, Violet, Forest and Blaise. She hosts the Coffee & Pearls podcast on Tuesdays and is the author of Catholic Mom Challenge, Not Of This World, and Be Merry.

She enjoys reading personal development books, drinking tea, taking bubble baths, and is constantly trying to learn how to be a proper homemaker! Sterling loves speaking at conferences and retreats, sharing her conversion story and the message that we should all be striving for sainthood!

You can read more of her writings at
www.sterlingjaquith.com,
www.Catholic365.com and
www.catholicmom.com.

ACKNOWLEDGEMENTS

Lord, only you know the plans you have for this book! It was not part of my plans to write it but the Holy Spirit kept poking me about it until I finally gave in! I'm not sure why you had an adult convert who is married and speaks to Catholic moms write this book, but I trust you and I hope it helps single women! Thank you for using me as your pencil even when I don't understand!

Thank you to my husband. We have had a rough three years with back-to-back pregnancies, financial uncertainty, and a marriage that was more challenging than either of us ever imagined. I love that you support my work even when it creates more work for you. I love that you choose to live out this crazy sacrament of marriage with me even when it seems far outside our comfort zone!

Thank you to my mother who has spent hours watching my kids and lifting my giant baby when I physically cannot do it at the end of the day!

Thank you to all the brave women who contributed to this book. This is your book. Be proud of your work and of the life you lead. Catholic marriage isn't for wussies and in a world that makes it easy to cut and run, bless you for staying!

Thank you to Meg Hunter-Kilmer for her excellent feedback. This book was greatly improved by her candid commentary!

And lastly, thank you to all the Coffee & Pearls supporters. Your stories continue to inspire me. Your hard work makes me want to work harder. I feel blessed to be part of such a great community of Catholics.

Not Of This World
A CATHOLIC GUIDE TO MINIMALISM

Check out Sterling's other book Not Of This World available at Amazon in both Kindle and paperback formats!

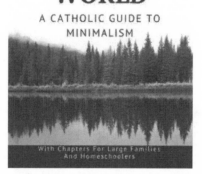

All Catholics are called to practice minimalism. Few of us are called to take a vow of poverty so we must learn to navigate our modern society without giving into consumerism and materialism. We know we should store up treasure in the Kingdom of God, not here on Earth but what does that look like day-to-day?

Follow Sterling on a journey as she explains how minimalism will bring you more peace and freedom. She will guide you step-by-step through your home with suggestions for how to embrace this lifestyle all at once or in baby steps.

With explanations for unique living situations, you're sure to find tips for how to live minimalism in our modern society by choosing the Lord over the shiny things of this world.And yes, you can keep your smart phone!

Catholic Mom Challenge

Check out Sterling's other book Catholic Mom Challenge available at Amazon in both Kindle and paperback formats!

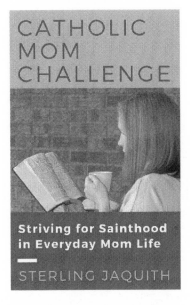

Filled with practical exercises and worksheets, this book is about helping moms figure out how to strive for sainthood among the piles of laundry, the mounting to-do list, and the stress of getting dinner ready!

The Catholic Mom Challenge system blends the power of Catholicism with discrete steps that busy moms can take to manage their lives while still striving for sainthood. This system works for everyone because it will teach you to always be refining what works for you.

Be Merry

HOW TO ADVENT WITHOUT LOSING YOUR MIND

Check out Sterling's other book Be Merry available at Amazon in both Kindle and paperback formats!

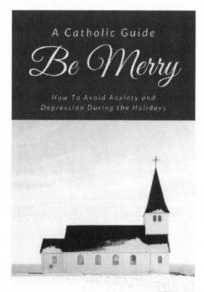

Do you feel anxious thinking about November and December? Are you worried about decorations, presents, and trying to survive your crazy family? This is not what Jesus intended for the season.

Be Merry is a practical book about how we can avoid the common anxious and depressed feelings that wash over us during the holidays. Find out how to squish your envy bug, how to give your family to Mary, and more! It's possible to have a joyful holiday season! Discover what can help you to set yourself up for success this year to draw closer to Christ and to find more peace in your life.

End Notes

1   Sterling Jaquith (2017) "Not of this World", Ever Catholic Publishing
2   "Romantics" by Taylor Swift, Songwriters: Johan Schuster / Max Martin / Taylor Swift, Kobalt Music Publishing Ltd.
3   "Some Enchanted Evening" by Frank Sinatra, Songwriters: Richard Rodgers, EMI Music Publishing
4   AZ Quotes (May 201*) http://www.azquotes.com/quote/1315964
5   Matthew Kelly (2005). "The Seven Levels of Intimacy: The Art of Loving and the Joy of Being Loved", Simon and Schuster
6   Gary Chapman (2015) The Five Love Languages, Northfield Publishing
7   "When You Say Nothing At All" by Allison Kraus, Songwriters: Paul Overstreet, Don Schlitz, Producer: Randy Scruggs
8   Greg Smalley (2008) Before You Plan You Wedding...Plan Your Marriage, Howard Books
9   Katherine Becker (2012) The Dating Fast: 40 Days to Reclaim Your Heart, Body and Sou, The Crossroad Publishing Companyl
10   Katherine Becker (2012) The Dating Fast: 40 Days to Reclaim Your Heart, Body and Sou, The Crossroad Publishing Company
11   "Dona Nobis Pacem" W.A. Mozart/arr. Patrick M. Liebergen - Alfred Music Publishing
12   Edward Sri (2015) Men, Women and the Mystery of Love, Servant
13   "Bless THe Broken Road: by Rascal Flatts, Songwriters: Jeff Hanna / Marcus Hummon / Robert E. Boyd, Universal Music Publishing Group.
14   Michele McCarty (1993) "Relating: A Christian Approach to Friendship and Love", Houpghton Mifflin Harcourt Religion
15   Paul VI, and Marc Caligari. Humanae Vitae: Encyclical Letter of His Holiness Pope Paul VI, on the Regulation of Births. San Francisco: Ignatius Press, 1983. Print.
16   John and Sheila Kippley (1996) The Art of Natural Family Planning, Couple to Couple League
17   John Paul II (2006) Man and Woman He Created Them: A Theology of the Body, Pauline Books and Media
18   John Paul II (2006) Man and Woman He Created Them: A Theology of the Body, Pauline Books and Media
19   Christopher West (2010) "Theology of the Bddy for Beginners" Ascension Press
20   "Be Satisfied With Me" by Anthony of Padua
21   Dante Alighieri (1935) "The Divine Comedy of Dante Alighieri : Inferno, Purgatory, Paradise" The Union Library Association
22   John Green (2014) "The Fault in Our Stars" Penguin Books
23   Stardust (2007) Dir. Matthew Vaughn. Perf. Charlie COx, Claire Danes, Sienna Miller, Michelle Pfeiffer
24   Gladiator (2000) Dir. Ridley Scott. Perf. Russell Crowe, Joaquin Phoenix, Connie Nielsen

Made in the USA
Middletown, DE
05 June 2018